Fragmented Families, Poverty, and Women's Reproductive Narratives in South Africa

By

Kammila Naidoo

Published by
Adonis & Abbey Publishers Ltd
P.O. Box 43418
London
SE11 4XZ
http://www.adonis-abbey.com
Email: editor@adonis-abbey.com

First Edition, August 2009

Copyright 2009 © Kammila Naidoo

British Library Cataloguing-in-Publication Data

A catalogue record for this book is available from the British Library.

ISBN: 9781906704469

Fragmented Families, Poverty, and Women's Reproductive Narratives in South Africa

By

Kammila Naidoo

TABLE OF CONTENTS

List of tables

List of maps

List of figures

PREFACE

In what ways do women's recurrent encounters and experiences with poverty serve to shape their sexual unions, social relationships and reproductive practices? The study examines the lives of a group of mothers and daughters from fifteen families in Merafeng[1], a demarcated part of the Winterveld area in South Africa, and draws attention to historical, socio-cultural, political and economic dimensions in order to place in context or *make sense* of reproductive dynamics and family life at the micro-level. The narrative thus integrates vignettes drawn from long-term fieldwork that highlight the particularities of the area: the persistence of historical tensions, diverse livelihoods and complex gender relationships. Life histories, group interview sessions and in-depth interviews with key informants are used to offer an understanding of the various struggles women face, given the few opportunities for formal employment, weakening kin support structures, violence, abandonment and the continuing necessity for much resourcefulness to survive daily adversity. The intergenerational stories of the women suggest that they live with immense and increasing difficulties and that strategies to contend with these sometimes include attempts to assert control over sexual encounters and reproductive outcomes.

In general, the study contributes to a continuing debate on how changing socio-economic conditions might influence prospects for and the nature of fertility transition in African countries. The findings of the case study concur with Lesthaeghe's argument that shifts toward lower levels of fertility might be due, in certain contexts, to experiences of hardship rather than economic improvement. It is argued that other areas in which people are experiencing deteriorating economic circumstances could also be witnessing similar transitions in fertility and fluidity of households and familial relationships. Rather than seeking security and risk-aversion through bearing many children the response of women in Merafeng has been largely to resist reproduction, at particular stages of their lives, whilst using sexual relationships and child-bearing as strategies to manipulate and secure resources. At the same time, fluctuating socio-economic circumstances, involvement in serial and multiple relationships, changes in health status and support networks introduce constant reappraisals of reproductive opportunities and decisions. Relatively easy access to contraception has been a key factor facilitating women's abilities to empower themselves in personal relationships, and to attempt to influence the context and timing of future child-bearing.

The study criticises demography's lack of temporal perspective and heavy reliance on the demographic survey. It draws attention to some of the difficulties faced by survey research in attempting to elicit 'accurate' representations of unions, reproductive behaviour and fertility preferences. Greater care in the construction of questionnaires and in the conducting of fieldwork can play an important role in withstanding some of the myriad problems posed by a complex South African terrain. Methodological experiments, in which qualitative methods are central, can enhance the value of demographic analyses and lead to multi-faceted understandings of the contexts and social forces shaping reproduction, family life and women's lives in South Africa.

Notes

1 This is a fictitious name offered in place of the actual site name within Winterveld to shield the identities of the women and men who wish to remain anonymous. I asked some of the women in the area to 'rename' their site and they suggested that Merafeng (meaning 'the place of many nations') would be highly appropriate. Thus, reference is made throughout to both Merafeng - as a smaller demarcated space within Winterveld – and to the broader Winterveld as a peri-urban area within the Northwest Province, South Africa.

ACKNOWLEDGEMENTS

There are numerous people who offered me much support and encouragement during the course of this study. I am immensely grateful to the many women and men who spent time telling me stories about their lives, about historical, political and social events and about day-to-day struggles. I have made them anonymous in the study and cannot list all their names. I am indebted to Pumla Maila, my friend, interpreter and colleague, who maintained regular contact with me throughout the period of fieldwork. Special thanks go to my PhD supervisors at the University of Manchester, Professors Colin Murray, Angela Dale and Mark Brown, for their guidance, criticisms and regular feedback meetings during the early fieldwork and the writing-up period (1998-2000). Colin Murray visited Merafeng and engaged my study participants in some important discussions.

Peter Mathebula of Medicos and Lerato Khunou of the Planned Parenthood Association (Winterveld branch) offered me an organisational base and shared their experiences of Winterveld with me. Nokuthula Mabuza, Lizzy Mokolo and Patricia Khumalo helped with the conducting of a survey in very hot, and trying circumstances. At the Human Sciences Research Council (HSRC) I would like to express my appreciation to Johan van Zyl for sending me the 1987-1989 SADHS dataset, S'bo Zama for producing my GIS maps and Logan Govender for facilitating contacts and rendering assistance. Ken Finlayson of the Development Bank of South Africa (DBSA) provided me with invaluable documentation on development initiatives in Winterveld in the 1980s.

At the University of South Africa (Unisa), Sanmarie Hugo entered and processed the Winterveld micro-survey data. Many thanks for that. I acknowledge the doctoral grant that I received from Unisa in September 1997 and the Association of Commonwealth Universities (ACU) for being my sponsor between 1998-2000. A modest Research and Development Programme (RDP) grant from the University of Pretoria (2004-2006) and a further one from the National Research Foundation (NRF) (2007) enabled on-going ethnographic work.

Chapter 1

BACKGROUND AND PURPOSE OF THE STUDY

Specific Focus and Key Objectives

This book offers a narrative of the social and reproductive dynamics of women's lives in Merafeng in the Winterveld area of South Africa. It conveys, simultaneously, a *particular* story about the multifaceted existences of a group of mothers and daughters who endure much insecurity and daily hardship. This is a story constructed in the course of my own changing perspectives and numerous encounters over a ten-year period in getting to know people and learning more about their diverse and difficult experiences. It is thus one of many narratives that can be built. My fieldwork strove to capture local history, collective sentiments, agency and intimate details of people's personal lives as part of an attempt to develop a more textured understanding of childbearing decisions and experiences. This chapter presents an overview of what the study entails and offers insights into findings developed in the process of conducting fieldwork.

The study set out to examine the social conditions and constraints shaping women's reproductive and family lives in South African localities, but adopted a case study approach. Case studies are used regularly in research efforts that attempt to delve into the details of a single case or single issue (Marshall, 1994:41- 42). They are used differently in different disciplines and by various authors. Some authors choose not to use case studies to develop generalisations but prefer to use the findings derived from case studies to criticise, challenge or draw attention to some of the limitations of existing claims (Reinharz, 1992). Other authors might use case studies to construct, at least, "fuzzy generalisations" (Bassey, 1999). As Bassey (1999:12) suggests: "The fuzzy generalisation arises from studies of singularities and typically claims that (it is possible, or likely, or unlikely that) what was found in the singularity will be found in similar situations elsewhere: it is a qualitative measure."

Sociologists and anthropologists have made ample use of case studies in explorations of kinship, family structure and households in southern Africa (e.g. Murray, 1981; Kotze & Van der Waal, 1992; Spiegel et al., 1996). Although the method has also been used in comparatively recent studies of teenage pregnancy and sexual behaviour (e.g. Preston-Whyte, 1990; Campbell et al., 1998) it has not been commonly used as a central tool in studies of reproduction. The study of fertility has involved mainly the use of macro-surveys to establish fertility trends and to develop estimations of unmet needs for contraception and family planning. A case study approach suggests a shift away from the greater reliance on macro-level analyses toward a more nuanced understanding of the 'patterns' and diverse forms of practices existing within a relatively small setting. It was with this intention that the case study of women's lives in Winterveld was undertaken. On the whole, investigating the personal domain and constructing the trajectories of women's life histories proved to be a challenging task. Over the years Winterveld has been the subject of numerous research endeavours, most of which have sought to uncover and describe obstacles facing the transformation and development of the area (e.g. Yawitch, 1981; DBSA, 1987; Simone, 1998). None of these projects however has had as its central aim the contextualisation of fertility and family life. The primary research concern of the Merafeng project however has been to consider how experiences of poverty shape, over time, the stability of unions and the 'reproductive decisions' of women. Thus, this study adopted three broad objectives.

The first objective was to study the context in which child-bearing occurs in Winterveld. The contextualisation required that close attention be paid to the changing nature of family relationships, unions and kinship bonds. The contextualisation was also partly an attempt to apply Susan Greenhalgh's (1990;1995) case study approach which strives to make sense of reproductive dynamics in a particular social environment by examining the historical, socio-cultural, political and economic dimensions. Her approach is a multi-levelled one which takes account of the interplay between micro- and macro-linkages, processes and institutions involved in the shaping of women's lives, their relationships and their fertility experiences. This project has not attempted to adopt the full implications of Greenhalgh's approach which makes comprehensive links between global and local contexts but, instead, to offer mainly a micro-demographic exploration of the nature of family life and reproductive experiences. (Greenhalgh's points are discussed in Chapter 2.)

The second objective was to draw on the nuances produced by this micro-level study to address a theoretical question concerning the forces driving fertility transition. A central demographic concern has been to seek explanations for shifts in fertility, particularly in African contexts. At

14

the micro-demographic level explanations for changing fertility must be sought by probing a variety of mechanisms and factors that might play a part in shaping differential fertility outcomes. A key challenge for the study, consequently, was to consider the circumstances in which women have children and to assess the ways in which motivations for child-bearing are shaped by changing structures and socio-economic realities. Related to this was the need to develop an understanding of how questions of women's agency and attempts at empowerment play a role in determining fertility outcomes amidst Winterveld's poverty. Lesthaeghe raised the question of whether sustained fertility transitions could occur in environments where living conditions did not appear to be improving, "that is, in contrast to the conventional wisdom of demographic transition theory which connects a fertility transition to increased prosperity and advancing structural transformation" (Lesthaeghe, 1989:476). The objective of this project was to consider an answer, based on the Merafeng experience, to Lesthaeghe's question.

The third objective arose from the use of the case study approach. Whilst there are no standard sets of methods and techniques that form part of the research design of case studies, it is generally assumed that the methods will be primarily qualitative (Marshall, 1994:41- 42). The research design of this study was adapted in the course of fieldwork. The reliance on macro- and micro-survey data lessened as I developed a much greater appreciation of the ways in which the insecurities and vicissitudes of life experiences created difficulties for quantitative, one-off data-gathering methods. The objective here is thus to offer a general assessment of the relative strengths of qualitative methodology in fertility research, the contribution it could make toward furthering understanding of reproductive and family life, and the extent to which it complements or offers an alternative to survey methods and quantitative data.

Addressing the primary research concern necessitated an exploration of the meanings that women attach to childbearing, 'marriage', and perceptions of their health, personal relationships and economic circumstances. This study therefore contributes to the debate on how the experience of poverty influences sexual and reproductive behaviour in some South African localities. A more grass-roots, long-term qualitative depiction of experiences should offer insights of value to policy-makers and researchers in the development and demography fields (see also Du Plessis, 2002).

Related questions on the research

During the early stages of my fieldwork, I was often asked why I chose Winterveld as a site for research. The question arose more out of concern that Winterveld was perhaps exceptional in many respects and that the experiences and lessons derived there could not be readily applied to other South African areas. Most often I responded by emphasising that I chose the area because of its close proximity to where I live and because I believed that the area, like any other area, was interesting in itself. Although the socio-historical origins of the area and its legacy of private land-ownership appear to set Winterveld apart from other areas, the routine of daily life, the living conditions and the survival strategies do not appear to differ fundamentally from those found in other South African peri-urban areas. I therefore suggest that whereas the stories that will be told in the following chapters might appear to show Winterveld to be somewhat different, in certain respects, it has also much in common with other areas with respect to experiences and responses to poverty. Consequently, the lessons here will be important in the offering of 'fuzzy generalisations' and in the questioning of theories and methods. Diverse ethnic identities and social origins and the fragmentary nature of 'community' in Winterveld make attempts to address the current concerns of demography with 'culture' a daunting task. At different stages of the study I have been asked about the role of local culture in shaping patterns of sexual and reproductive behaviour. There is much current interest in demography with regard to the extent to which the culture of African societies determines fertility and holds consequences for the ways in which fertility transition is seen to be occurring (Caldwell, 1982; Fricke, 1997; Bernardi & Hutter, 2007). There has always been a controversy about notions of culture by the different social science disciplines. At its most basic level, a sociological dictionary defines culture as "the symbolic and learned aspects of human society..." (Marshall, 1994:104). The symbolic, learned and selectively interpreted aspects are closely aligned to constructions of ethnic identities and perceptions of shared background. For those embracing more reified notions of culture, (e.g. culture as pre-given attributes of homogeneous ethnic groups), the selection of Winterveld, an area with diverse practices and identities, could be seen as having little potential to contribute to an understanding of how culture influences fertility. I have taken my understanding of culture from the women whom I have interviewed. The local people are active in making reference to "cultural practices" and to identifying "other nations" living in the same locality with whom they share many, though not all, common customs and ways of life. This book focuses on women's interpretations of how particular sets of life experiences, issues and customs play a part in shaping sexual and reproductive decisions. The book also emphasises culture in terms of the diverse practices and the transitory nature of relationships of a group of people sharing common space but held together in tenuous and changing ways.

The most common question that I have been asked when telling people about my focus on women's life histories is whether I am pursuing feminist research. Just as there is no uniform understanding of feminism, there is little agreement on what feminist research is and what a feminist methodology entails. In her book, *Feminist Methods in Social Research*, Reinharz (1992) suggests that researchers (who study women) ought to take a position at the outset and declare whether their research is feminist or not. Although my research did not involve the women (who participated in my study) in the formulation of the research questions or incorporate, within its research strategy, goals to conscientise and emancipate women (goals which are essential ingredients for feminist research according to Mies, 1993) it has sought to draw on the voices of women and make many parts of their various experiences visible. In this sense, this research does adopt a feminist agenda. The related question asked has been whether, in drawing on the voices of women, I have made men invisible. The more recent emphasis in reviewing gender in studies of reproduction and sexual behaviour has been to look at women's experiences in relation to men's. An understanding of masculine behaviour has become crucial in the current era of seeking interventions to curb the spread of HIV/AIDS. In methodological terms it would have required a study of men's life histories as well as those of women. I did not think that as an outside researcher and as a woman I would have been able to question men comprehensively on taboo issues associated with their sexual and marital lives. For this reason I chose, instead, to study women's lives in detail and learn about men's behaviour, and their roles within unions and families, through women's perspectives.

Perhaps a final question to raise, although it is one which I have not been asked frequently, is why I focus on issues around child-bearing and women's fertility when the research concerns in southern Africa have shifted toward questions of HIV/AIDS and rising mortality in the region. Clearly, many unanswered questions about the nature and direction of fertility change have become more urgent in the era of HIV/AIDS. My approach, however, to answering this question has been to emphasise that women's child-bearing decisions are inextricably connected with their perceptions of the state of their health, their sexual relationships and their exposure to and fears of contracting illnesses including HIV/AIDS infections. Any contextualisation of reproductive dynamics requires that insight into the way in which HIV/AIDS is affecting the lives of people be developed. However, at the time of my initial fieldwork, between July 1998 and July 1999, I did not find considerable awareness or concern about HIV infection. Thus, experiences of AIDS in the earlier period are fairly vague. The circumstances, though, in 2008 were quite changed and I include additional references to HIV/AIDS and rising mortality in Winterveld in Chapter 6. It remains, however, a sub-narrative of a larger story on reproduction.

Chapter outlines and findings of the study

An indication of what the individual chapters offer appears below.

Chapter 2 outlines the dominant theories and contemporary arguments relating to fertility transition and, in particular, to the way in which African fertility trends are being analysed. The chapter also discusses key elements of the debate on the transformation of family life in southern Africa. The purpose of the chapter is to present both literature review of relevant issues to be explored at different points in the book, and more specifically to introduce the usefulness of a micro-demographic, multi-levelled approach in exploring sexual, reproductive and family life in small-scale, local settings. Attention is paid to Greenhalgh's approach to the study of fertility and to her argument that case studies drawing on "whole demographies" offer opportunities for theoretical analysis.

Chapters 3, 4 and 5 address the first objective of the study.

Chapter 3 presents an overview of the history, politics and socio-economic circumstances of Winterveld's people. The intention is to offer some background to the origins of the area, the political tensions that have emerged over the years and the difficulties currently prevailing in transforming the area. The historical overview is selective and attempts to integrate the voices of the people whom I have interviewed. This chapter refers to the methods used in the study and offers some account of the value, problematics and ethical dilemmas associated with the use of qualitative methods in the course of fieldwork in Merafeng. It also introduces the use of macro- and micro-surveys as supplementing and comparative tools.

Chapter 4 examines early pregnancies and sexual experiences within Merafeng. Increasing the length of time girls spend in school is generally accepted as a key factor delaying their entry into unions and in empowering women in the long term. This chapter focuses on the dual role of schools in poor environments such as the Winterveld area: that is, it presents a context within which early childbearing is both facilitated and inhibited. A further aim is to examine the constraints, pressures and difficulties of the domestic environment and their consequences with regard to early and unwanted fertility. The chapter shows that early use of contraception is often encouraged by mothers who attempt to protect daughters from unplanned pregnancies. Often these pregnancies result from sexual activities that have transactional motives or from sexual abuse occurring mainly within the family.

Chapter 5 examines how changes in marriage, gender and kinship relations are shaping child-bearing patterns in Merafeng and broader Winterveld. The chapter offers a more detailed overview of how what are commonly referred to as the "distinguishing characteristics" of African family life are changing there on account of insecurities in the labour market, desertion and widespread poverty. The chapter draws attention to the fluidity of unions shaped by violence, infidelities and discord which make the sustaining of long-term relationships and stable households immensely difficult. The chapter also examines kin and family networks that are often seen to serve both as a buffer against hardships and as a support structure within which children are raised. The study found limited involvement of kin and support networks with respect to influencing childbearing decisions as well as a deterioration of kin relations particularly when reciprocal monetary benefits were not forthcoming.

Chapter 6 addresses the second objective of the study.

Chapter 6 offers more detailed insights into the contrasting life experiences, beliefs and perceptions of the small group of women (mainly mothers and daughters). Detailed vignettes are included which reflect women's experiences of poverty and unemployment and the ways in which these experiences shape reproductive intentions and outcomes. Comparisons between macro-survey, micro-survey and qualitative results are offered. This chapter examines a wide range of issues that intervene in the timing of births and decisions associated with the question whether or not to bear children. These issues include assessments of affordability, perceptions of ill-health and insecure, serial and multiple relationships. The chapter also explores the meanings attached to these issues by women, and then draws parallels with theoretical arguments on reproductive behaviour and fertility decline. Owing to a wide range of circumstances and hardships, women have, in some cases, fewer children than desired. Motivations expressed by women for wanting more children, in the event that their economic and familial situations improve, are also explored. More evidence for Lesthaeghe's notion of hardship-driven fertility decline appears to emerge in the life histories than in the survey statistics. Finally, the key arguments are elucidated and research question answered.

Chapter 7 addresses the third objective of the study.

Chapter 7 offers a conclusion to the question raised at the outset on the kind of contribution which qualitative methodology can make towards deepening understanding of the issues shaping reproduction and family life. The chapter considers the advantages that might be derived by using a qualitative research design and also addresses some of the difficulties faced in the use of a primarily quantitative methodology and of reliance on surveys in South African environments. These difficulties include attempts to categorise and measure socio-economic influences on fertility behaviour, and those associated with the snap-shot and thus limited way in which interviewers have to conduct interviews on deeply personal matters in the field. The chapter presents a brief review of the debate and literature on the use of qualitative methods in fertility research and suggests different ways in which qualitative work can be pursued: (1) as linked to survey research in a micro-demographic study, (2) as investigative work arising out of prior survey work or (3) as a critical and engaged attempt to explore familial and reproductive issues over an extended period of time.

Conventions adopted in the book

- The fieldwork site has been referred to as Merafeng. Although this is a fictitious name it has historical relevance as will be shown in Chapter 4.

- I have attempted to protect the identities of the women whom I interviewed by substituting pseudonyms for original names in the text.

- Chapters 3, 4, 5 and 6 offer vignettes from interviews that have been conducted in different local languages. Indication of the languages used in the different interviews will be offered in brackets at the end of the extract. The following languages were used in the field: Sesotho (s), Setswana (t), Zulu (z), Xhosa (x), English (e) and Afrikaans (a).

- Fifteen detailed 'family stories' have been constructed. Different interviews conducted at different points with mothers and daughters (a total of 33 women) in the course of the fieldwork, together with my own observations of family relationships and activities, have been the basis of these different mother-daughter life histories. The life histories have been numbered. When initial reference to the women who were the subject of life history interviews is made, a relevant life history number is indicated in square brackets e.g. [#1]. When detailed extracts of women's voices and experiences are included in the chapters they will be presented under the sub-heading of the relevant mother-daughter family life history. Summarised versions of these individual life histories are offered in **Appendix 1.**

- Discussions in nine group interview sessions were also recorded. Six groups, named as "Youth group I", "Ikageng group", "Ndlovu's group", "Mama's group", "Office group" and "Mozambican group" came together at different points during my fieldwork in the period 1998-2000. In 2002 and 2005, I interviewed a seventh group, of men ("Dube group") and between 2005 and 2007 I met intermittently with an eighth group of women who were dependent on state child grants ("Grant group"). An additional Youth group (Youth group II) was set up in 2007. When references to comments made in the groups are included in the chapters, the name of the group is indicated within brackets, e.g. (*Youth* group I).

- A point on the use of terminology needs to be made. Although, strictly speaking, demographers do not view 'reproduction' and 'fertility' as identical, the involvement of different disciplines in the population studies field has led to the interchangeable use of these concepts. This study, which does not make the precise measures of fertility or reproduction its central focus, but which is primarily qualitative, treats "child-bearing", "reproduction" and "fertility" as having the same meanings.

- A glossary is not provided. Attempts are made to clarify concepts when they are first mentioned in the text.

Chapter 2

DEMOGRAPHIC TRANSITION, REPRODUCTION AND EXPERIENCES OF POVERTY

The demographic transition theory

For decades Frank Notestein's formulation of the demographic transition theory remained the dominant paradigm in demography. In a paper written in 1945, *Population: the long view*, Notestein described the stages of fertility transition which nineteenth-century European countries were observed to have undergone. The argument he put forward can be summarised as follows: improved socio-economic and environmental conditions accompanying the processes of modernisation (industrial-isation, urbanisation etc.) shifted populations from a stage in which mortality and fertility rates were high and uncontrolled toward a second stage in which mortality and fertility declined, although at different rates. The agricultural and industrial revolutions in Europe were seen to have more immediate and positive effects on reducing the mortality than the fertility rate. Consequently the "lag" resulting from reduced mortality but relatively resistant or unchanging fertility meant that this second stage represented a phase of potentially high population growth. It was, however, a transitional stage within which a shift towards lower fertility would be witnessed. The decline in the birth rate resulted in a third stage of incipient mortality *and* fertility decline. The timing of this decline, however, was dependent upon a steady erosion of the "props" which maintained high fertility (such as community codes and customs), which, Notestein suggested, would be an inevitable process in an industrialising society. The decline was also dependent upon people no longer requiring large numbers of children as sources of labour, and on the emergence of more individualistic attitudes that would lead to the desire for smaller families and greater contraceptive use (Cleland, 1985:225-226; Caldwell, 1982:117-118; Findlay & Findlay, 1987:31). Notestein (Van de Kaa, 1996: 399), who saw his theory as universally applicable, regarded the key turning point to fertility decline in all countries as the gradual "shift in social goals from those directed towards the survival of the group to those directed toward the welfare and development of the individual". According to this view large extended families gave way to progressively smaller nucleated ones in which the status of women was improving, and dependence on large numbers of children was decreasing.

The trend towards smaller family size, according to Notestein, signified increasing "rationality", a feature of modern industrial society. A fertility transition, thus, was a necessary and reasonable response to the processes of modernisation occurring at the time. Just as modernisation theory predicted the unilinear routes of social change, which all societies would follow, namely, from 'traditional' to 'modern' forms, so too did demographic transition theory suggest that European countries had followed the stages of fertility decline and that the rest of the developing world would, similarly, "take off" as the modernising processes unfolded. In the 1960s and 1970s demographers found it convenient to categorise developing countries and continents as reflecting characteristics of different transition stages. In time, with the fall of fertility in Asia and Latin America, Africa was seen to be the last continent stuck in the stage of rapid transitional growth (with mortality declining but fertility remaining high) and with little sign of moving towards lowered levels of fertility (Findlay & Findlay, 1987).

In 1963 Notestein's transition theory was eventually put to the test by Ansley Coale and his collaborators at the Princeton European Fertility Project. Coale and his team set out to examine in detail the causes of fertility transition in Europe and, consequently, to test the validity of the demographic transition stages. They expected to find a clear correlation between modernisation variables and the onset of fertility decline (Kertzer, 1995:31). On the contrary, about 20 years of investigation led them to conclude that historical evidence did not support the claim that the forces associated with modernisation were the propellents of fertility decline. As Johannson (1997:628-629) maintains:

> it only became more and more clear that the rate of industrialisation and urbanisation was not inversely correlated with the decline of provincial fertility levels, even if fertility was measured in more refined ways than by the annual crude birth rates used by transition historians. Instead, "cultural" variables, like language, religion, and the education of women, were shown to have had a stronger impact on the timing and rate of fertility decline, even among otherwise socially and economically similar provinces.

With some loss of confidence in the demographic transition theory, scholars such as Lesthaeghe (who was associated with the Princeton project) became instrumental in analysing the part played by "culture" in demographic change, and its role in shaping fertility outcomes (Kertzer, 1995:32). In criticising demographic transition theory, McNicoll (1994:211) concludes: "[t]he theory was overdetermined, it neglected the subtleties and variability of the transition process, and it abstracted from historical specifics". Findlay and Findlay (1987:31) also suggest that, "even if demographic changes do reflect trends in "modernisation", Third World countries would differ from those of Europe not only in timing and speed of development, but also in character, since their economic histories have followed a very different course". Although it has been repeatedly challenged and marginalised by demographers seeking a general theory of fertility decline, elements of the theory often resonate in discussions of the ways in which socio-economic factors determine the pace of fertility decline. Van de Walle (1992:487) maintains:

> Demographic transition (without theory) persists today as a convenient shorthand for the change from high to low birth rates, an obvious and non-controversial empirical description ... Today it would be difficult to agree on more than very general links: that fertility and mortality often, but not always, tend to decline at the same time, and that highly developed countries are characterised by low levels of vital rates.

With the undermining of the demographic transition theory decades ago, alternative explanations that take account of the "subtleties" and "variability" of the transition processes have been pursued. Amongst the array of alternative explanations which gained prominence in the late 1970s to the 1980s dominant explanations for the persistence of high fertility in African countries rested either on a "cultural difference" and "cultural persistence" theme (Caldwell, 1982, Lesthaeghe, 1989) or on analysis of economic constraints and "forms of development" (Mburugu, 1994:75). Suggestions of cultural difference can be found through references to the

> universal entry of girls into sexual unions at an early age [as opposed to factors which facilitated the European fertility decline, viz. later marriage and non-marriage]...the generally permissive sexual mores and high coital frequency [which] all make high fertility and large families "natural" to Africa (Robinson, 1992:452).

Lesthaeghe's (1989: 1-2;50-55) more significant contribution to an understanding of African fertility dynamics has been to "connect ethnicity to selected characteristics of social organisation" - such as the land tenure system, the structure of gender relations, or the nature of lineage and kinship groupings. He suggests that Sub-Saharan Africa has emerged with forms of social organisation and technology not comparable with those of other developing societies, and that an examination of these will highlight possible routes for fertility transition.

Explanations for high fertility in Africa: 1970s - 1980s

Africa's population growth has seen both ebbs and flows over the centuries. About five hundred years ago (between the years 1500 and 1600) Africa's population was said to be about 19% of the world's population. In the 1990s it was predicted that by 2025 Africa's population would most probably rise to about 20% of the world's population (Himmelstrand et al., 1994:62). In between these two estimates there have been considerable changes caused by an African history of devastation due to the effects of the slave trade, colonialism and neo-colonialism. Having shown many fluctuations in the past, the African population was believed to be steadily increasing at a rate of 3% per annum. This increase represented the fastest growth rate in the world. Moreover, the potential for a much higher growth rate in the years beyond 2000 was said to exist, since the African population is comparatively young and therefore contains a "built-in momentum" (Segal, 1993:25). Rising mortality due to the spread of HIV/AIDS, however, has required a serious re-assessment of these earlier estimates.

Although sceptical, Isiugo-Abanihe (Himmelstrand, 1994:64) suggests that demographers, including African demographers, have tended to look to the demographic transition theory as offering an indication of the way in which African populations are likely to change. Alongside the recognition that economic growth and a wider set of socio-economic changes would be the instigators of mortality and fertility decline is the acknowledgement that many African countries are burdened with economic and political crises, and the constraints of structural adjustment programmes. These difficulties limit possibilities to invest sufficient resources to improve the social welfare of citizens. Nonetheless, steady improvements in women's education, increases in imported health technologies and facilities, and better nutrition, have contributed to a decline in mortality rates since the 1940s. The crude death rate in the mid-1980s was 15 per 1000 population, the infant mortality rate was 101 deaths per 1000 live births, and life expectancy stood at 51 years (Himmelstrand, 1994: 62-64). In demographic transition terms the infant mortality rate has been far too high. Caldwell et al. (1992:212) suggest that an infant mortality rate below 70 per 1000 live births might be the necessary impetus or threshold for African fertility decline.

In the 1970s the problems of economic underdevelopment and poverty in individual African countries were being blamed on their rising population levels. African governments, generally, did not accept the position that increasing population represented a constraint to economic growth, nor was it regarded as the cause of poverty. At the 1974 Bucharest World Population Conference, African governments reacted with contempt to Neo-Malthusian fears of a population increase that would usurp resources, and at the suggestion that they take action to curb population growth. In the debate that followed an alternative argument was raised: that is, that Africa was underpopulated and that large populations offered particular benefits rather than acted as barriers to development (Ayida & Chikelu, 1975:55-61). Amin and Okediji (1971: 410-411) maintained that population density served to boost agricultural and food production and that Africa's dependency and its subordinate position in the world capitalist system were the real cause of its underdevelopment, and not population growth *per se*. Thus "progress in agriculture is not handicapped by demographic pressure. The opposite is true." They argued, also, that the experience of marginalisation, under-employment and poverty meant that there was little motivation at the micro-level for families to reduce family size and use contraception. Large families served in these contexts as forms of social security. Thus, African development initiatives until about 1984 did not treat "population control" or "population planning" as a matter for urgent intervention. Rather, it was believed that with changing socio-economic conditions the population numbers would sort themselves out since (as it was contended at the 1974 Bucharest conference) "development is the best contraceptive" (Caldwell, 1982).

With much opposition from African governments to the use of contraception in the 1970s, international agencies considered investment in African family planning initiatives as having limited potential (see UNFPA, 1994:95). They chose instead to offer a larger share of financial support to Asian and Latin American projects (Bertrand et al., 1993:6-7). However, with the gradual spreading of the "family planning message" since 1974, and with the establishment of population planning bodies and population planning units within African countries, political resistance to family planning eventually lessened. Since the Mexico World Population Conference and the Arusha African Population Conference (both held in 1984) African governments have responded to the neo-Malthusian agenda, which viewed high growth rates as a threat to socio-economic development and have taken steps to provide and promote contraception. From an early stage of antagonism, a growing acceptance and shift in position emerged within the policy-making institutions of African countries. Population planning and the availability of contraception became integral elements of socio-economic planning, health and development policy. The shift in position did not imply that a narrow pro-population control approach had been accepted. Many African governments saw family planning as a component of a broad developmentalist approach (Lesthaeghe, 1989: 476; Cohen, 1997:5).

In the 1970s and 1980s John Caldwell played an important role in promoting an alternative theoretical understanding of fertility change in Africa. Caldwell's restatement of the demographic transition theory was written in the aftermath of the 1974 Bucharest conference. He was critical of the ethnocentrism of the original paradigm and its implicit assumption that high fertility was an irrational feature of pre-modern societies, which would be remedied, in modern industrial society (1982:119).

> The view that the fertility behaviour of the Third World arises largely from ignorance and should be combatted with education and guidance is held strongly by many family-planning movements and leads to friction and even confrontation; the same reaction arising out of much the same origins was witnessed writ a little larger at the Bucharest Conference (Caldwell,1982 :121).

For Caldwell, the main issue when considering demographic transition in Africa is the direction and magnitude of intergenerational "wealth flows" from children to parents (or from the younger to older generations). It is rational in this view to maintain high levels of fertility if children make necessary and productive contributions to the household economy. When the role of the household is transformed as a result of broader structural change, mass schooling, the erosion of male decision-making power, and families become nucleated and child-centred, we can anticipate a reversal in the flow of goods and services from parents to children. The shift toward investment in children reduces the necessity for large numbers of children and results in fertility decline. In contrast to the assumptions of demographic transition theory, Caldwell (1982:156) emphasises,

> [t]he major implication of this analysis is that fertility decline in the Third World is not dependent on the spread of industrialization or even

on the rate of economic development ... fertility decline is more likely to precede industrialization and to help bring it about than to follow it.

Caldwell derived the alternative theory after drawing on the experience of much fieldwork in Nigeria. There has been a number of criticisms of the theory; there have also been problems in operationalising the theory and there have been few attempts to test the theory (Greenhalgh, 1995:7). Nonetheless, Caldwell's wealth flows theory remains to some demographers a plausible explanation for the high levels of fertility that are generally sustained in Africa despite declining mortality.

Caldwell's work is often contrasted with Mead Cain's work on children as potential sources of social security. Cain's 1982 article, *Perspectives on family and fertility in developing countries*, is a detailed response to Caldwell's wealth flows thesis at the same time as presenting Mead's own research arguments on fertility transition and the transformation of family in developing countries. He praises Caldwell for giving family dynamics and processes prominence in his analysis of fertility decline. This, he maintains, was unlike most other analyses at the time, which depicted the family as simply "acted upon in the course of development" (Cain, 1982:159). He took issue, however, with two of Caldwell's central arguments. He claims firstly that Caldwell overemphasises the extent to which males benefit from high fertility. He suggests that women's dependence on men, and their awareness of their own vulnerability in situations of divorce, widowhood and other circumstances, which expose them to the risk of poverty, lead them to desire large numbers of children themselves. Since women's dependence on men varies in different societies the incentives for high fertility will also vary. Secondly, Cain does not regard the nucleation of family structure as synonymous with fertility decline. He maintains that strong and extended kin networks may in certain circumstances serve as more important and alternative sources of support and insurance (e.g. against natural or economic disasters) than do large numbers of children. When children are deemed to be less significant in shielding people against risk and hardship, the more likely will women be to have fewer children and the less resistant will society be to fertility decline (Cain, 1982). Caldwell's and Mead's contributions are of particular interest because they draw attention to issues of gender and power in micro-level settings.

Signs of fertility decline and transition in Africa: 1990s – 2010

As investment in African family planning intiatives increased in the 1980s, the question whether this would lead to a sustained decline in fertility was regularly asked. A contraceptive revolution was seen to have shaped a qualitatively different fertility transition in Asia and Latin America (from the spontaneous European one), but it has been uncertain whether similar interventions were beginning to have the same effect in African populations. Increased contraceptive use accompanied by a demand for smaller numbers of children is an indication that "natural" fertility regimes are being transformed into deliberately "controlled" regimes (Henry in Bongaarts & Potter, 1983:21). In their examination of fertility surveys conducted between 1975 and 1990, Bertrand et al. (1993) found the general use of contraception in Sub-Saharan Africa fairly low, and significant only in a few (largely Southern African) countries. Contraception, although becoming more available to the wider population, has intially been more accessible to upwardly mobile and middle class sectors of the population. Hill (1991:66-67) suggests that "there are some signs from Southern Africa and from some elite groups that contraceptive use is becoming more widespread, but for the moment, fertility regimes are still quite close to the patterns of 'natural' fertility described by non-contracepting populations in the past".

Fertility-depressing determinants in natural fertility populations can be seen in terms of long periods of breast-feeding (the effect being to inhibit ovulation), periods of post-partum sexual abstinence, the prevalence of sterility (largely due to exposure to various, including sexual, diseases), spontaneous intra-uterine mortality, and patterns associated with timing of, and entry into marriage (Bongaarts & Potter, 1983:21- 47). In terms of the natural fertility pattern early (and near universal) marriage, without the use of contraception and abortion, means that African women would find themselves exposed to high risk rates of child-bearing. Of course, this simple distinction between "natural" and "controlled" fertility regimes does not take account of anthropological evidence which shows cases in which intentional use is made of traditional methods to space and prevent births in natural fertility regimes (Greenhalgh, 1995:15).

Considerable attention continues to be paid to the indirect effects of modernisation variables on fertility change in Africa. *The World's Women* (1970-1990), a source book of the United Nations (1991), suggests that the social position of women has slowly but certainly improved throughout the world (including Africa). Of particular interest has been the effect of women's access to education and employment on the erosion of cultural practices such as extended breast-feeding durations and post-partum sexual abstinence. Shorter periods of post-partum amenorrhoea (as a result of changes in breast-feeding durations) and delayed entries into marriage could have significant effects on fertility in populations in which contraception is not readily used. In their studies on changes in natural fertility determinants, Bongaarts and Potter (1983:47) found that:

> a change in postpartum amenorrhoea from 2 years to 3 months causes fertility to double. This implies that, at least theoretically, differences in postpartum amenorrhoea could explain most of the observed differences in marital fertility of populations with natural fertility. In contrast ... variations in spontaneous intrauterine mortality and permanent natural sterility [have] only little effect on fertility.

Hill (1991:67-68) draws attention to the potential for fertility increase that could arise if the traditional birth-spacing mechanisms are eroded. He suggests that:

> if fertility is to fall by 30% of current levels by the year 2000 and if post-partum amenorrhoea remains at 16 months, contraceptive prevalence must rise to include 36% of currently married couples. If amenorrhoea drops to 8.5 months, however, 53% of all married couples will need to be [using contraception] to achieve the same proportional drop in fertility.

In the 1970s to 1980s the predominance of natural fertility regimes (as evidenced by high fertility and low contraceptive use) and the special features of African social organisation seemed to make the possibility of widespread fertility decline fairly unlikely.

In the mid- to late 1990s, however, there was growing but cautious recognition of the signs of fertility decline in some African countries such as Kenya, Zimbabwe, Botswana, Nigeria and South Africa (Robinson, 1992; Caldwell et al., 1992; Caldwell, 1993; Gaisie, 1998). With respect to the case of Kenya, Robinson (1992:457) states: "it now does appear that couples in Kenya *are* conceptualising an ideal family size, and that a rational weighing of costs and benefits now does frequently occur." He suggests that the modernisation of Kenyan society finds itself "in collision" with customs promoting pro-natalism. Health, immunisation and development programmes are improving child survival rates and the cost of having children is increasing. At the same time, contraception is becoming cheaper and more easily obtainable. With the continuation of these interventions alongside the modernisation of Kenya, fertility will continue to decline. Gaisie (1998: 292) says of the Botswana fertility decline: "Botswana's experience shows that a firm economic base providing a sustainably adequate standard of living for the people and a well organized family planning programme can, to a large extent, narrow the gap between fertility and mortality..." Optimism about the possibilities of a more general decline has been raised.

Other accounts express the apparent move towards a declining fertility in African countries with more uncertainty. In the mid-1990s the countries displaying signs of fertility decline were regarded as different in important ways from most other African countries. For example, fertility decline in Zimbabwe, Botswana and Kenya was associated with the lowest infant mortality rates (70 per 1000 live births) that other African states did not exhibit at the time. The fertility decline was also associated with relatively stable economies (although the Zimbabwean economy has since virtually collapsed), the mass education of girls and high levels of contraceptive use by women in all age groups (Caldwell et al., 1992). Caldwell et al. (1992: 237) emphasise the economic crises, which other African countries face as a major constraint and factor affecting mortality and fertility change. At the same time, it is also not clear whether the fertility decline in countries such as Botswana, Kenya and Zimbabwe is likely to be a sustained one because there is some speculation about whether the decline is reflecting more women willing to space births rather than reduce the number of children they eventually give birth to (Caldwell et al., 1992:237; Gould & Brown, 1996:8). Gould and Brown (1996:19) suggest that: "[t]he extent to which Africa can be considered as the lagging case in a universal transition, or whether it has Africa-specific features that make it stand as a fundamentally different case requiring fundamentally different explanations, cannot yet be resolved with certainty." There are a number of questions in the literature, which probe whether there are general lessons regarding fertility transition that have been derived, and whether these would be applicable across the length and breadth of sub-Saharan Africa. The history, politics, post-colonial legacies, socio-economic developments and familial structures of individual sub-Saharan African countries have been both diverse and complex. To what extent can Africa, as a whole, be seen to follow worldwide trends toward lower fertility levels? What different combinations of factors can be seen as more instrumental in triggering this decline in individual countries and in different socio-economic contexts? Can the fertility declines witnessed in the 1990s in some countries be seen as irreversible in the long term? These are some of the questions that remained issues of debate in the 1990s.

Lesthaeghe (1989) poses another speculative question, that is, one about the possible initiation of a "crisis-led" fertility decline in African countries experiencing the effects of severe economic downturns, natural disasters and the "shaking of aspirations". He raises the argument that fertility transitions could occur in environments where living conditions do not appear to be improving, "that is, in contrast to the conventional wisdom of demographic transition theory which connects a fertility transition to increased prosperity and advancing structural transformation?" (Lesthaeghe, 1989:476). He suggests that whilst there are many cases of short-term declines in fertility in response to hardship, there are few indications of sustained crisis-led fertility transitions. Nonetheless, he surmises that economic conditions in Africa might place enormous pressure on families and individuals to reduce the number of children they bear. Relatively recent evidence from sub-Saharan Africa indicates that people are beginning to elect to "forego ... some children in order merely to sustain consumption for themselves and their existing children at *reduced* levels" (Potts & Marks, 2001: 199). Such renderings contrast with those of Caldwell and Cain who link fertility changes to progressive transitions in the structure of families, improvements in women's education, the greater independence of women and improved coping mechanisms of familial and social networks, and not to responses to adversity.

As HIV/AIDS takes its toll, and further disentangles and reconfigures existing familial and community networks, there is a fair amount of consensus amongst policy-makers that, despite rising mortality, general fertility levels have not been fundamentally altered (UN, 2005). The reproductive lives of those who have tested positive for HIV, however, have been quite affected; infected women have reduced fecundity and higher chances of sexually transmitted diseases and spontaneous abortions. Amongst the general population, fears of infection and beliefs concerning personal risk can act to reshape the meanings surrounding childbearing, leading to reassessments on questions of family limitation. Baylies (1999), for example, argued in reviewing qualitative empirical data on reproduction in Minga, Zambia, that women are likely to take deliberate steps to limit the number of children they could have for two main reasons: first, because of consequences for their own health, and second, because of the fear of leaving their children to be cared for by others. Alternatively, access to anti-retroviral therapies and advances in preventing perinatal transmission, and the possibility of being able to manage HIV as a chronic illness rather than as an immediate life threatening disease, is bound to have an effect on the reproductive desires and decisions of individuals, in favour of childbearing (Cooper et al., 2007). Similarly, Levin and Dubler (1990: 336) suggest in their earlier work that infected women might seek to replace 'lost children' and that this may be a tendency in environments affected by high levels of child mortality, abandonment or "simply the complexities of life in poverty". Such contrasting arguments have relevance for African communities struggling through the vicissitudes of poverty.

The preceding review of theories, arguments and political responses influencing the policy environment is intended to serve as background to the discussion of reproduction and family life in South Africa that follows. South Africa's fertility transition, and the country's changing kin structures, should be studied by taking into account its history, politics and social and economic inequalities.

South African demographic regimes

Prior to the early 1990s South Africa's fertility transition, although believed to be the earliest fertility transition in Sub-Saharan Africa, did not enjoy much attention in the international literature (Camlin et al., 2004). Caldwell and Caldwell (1993:225) maintained that "South Africa has remained a little known area on the demographic map of Africa". They suggested that this exclusion had been partly due to the academic boycott against South Africa, and partly because of the shortcomings of available population data. Much has changed since then with more comprehensive and reliable data becoming available, particularly on the (black) African sector of the population.

There were approximately 41 million people living in South Africa in 1999 - an increase from 30.7 million in 1980. The South African population was said to be growing at a rate of 2.59% per annum. This growth rate was seen as being at odds with its status as one of the upper-middle-income countries of the world (Calitz, 1996:3). Calitz (1996:3) suggests that: "although South Africa is classified as an upper middle income country, it is [in terms of its population rate] squarely in the league of low income countries. The latter registered an average annual population growth of 2.8% between 1980 and 1990 ... population growth in the upper middle-income group averaged only 1.8% per year". In January 2000, however, it was predicted that the South African population growth rate in 2016 - 2021 would decline to 0.44 % because of the anticipated effects of

AIDS-related deaths. The Human Sciences Research Council (HSRC), which had previously predicted that the population would be around 80 million in 2020, now projected that the population would be 50 million (Honey, 2000:32).

South Africa's status as an upper middle-income-country masks the wealth disparities and income differentials that exist within the country. South African demographers have conventionally discussed changes in fertility in terms of racially defined fertility regimes which are viewed as coinciding with socio-economic strata. As Chimere-Dan (1994:55) states: "[a] unique feature of South African demography is the coexistence of distinct regimes of demographic transition which roughly coincide with a hierarchy of socioeconomic status among whites, Indians, coloureds and blacks". The total fertility rates (TFRs) and infant mortality rates of these regimes were calculated respectively, in the mid-1990s, as 1.7 and 12 for whites (which is below replacement level), 2.3 and 17 for Indians, and 2.7 and 51 for coloureds (Calitz, 1996:10). In the early 1990s the African TFR stood at 4.6 and the infant mortality rate at 61 deaths per 1000 births (Calitz, 1996:10). Calitz (1996:9) suggested that "informed demographers are of the view that this rate will not decline markedly unless the material standard of living of this population is increased significantly." He stated further that research had shown that the African TFR had declined noticeably since the 1960s, but that this decline "ha[d] been arrested during the latter part of the 1980s." The 1998 South African Demographic and Health Survey (SADHS) revealed the TFR and infant mortality rate as 2.9 and 45 deaths per 1000 births respectively. By 2003, the TFR was judged to have dropped significantly to 2 children per women whilst the infant mortality rate only marginally so to 4 per 1000 live births (SADHS, 2003). Most explanations for the decline have rested on analyses of government attempts to make contraception widely available and on increasing levels of knowledge about pregnancy prevention.

Familial, gender and reproductive dynamics in South Africa

In the early 1940s the issue of population control and the implications of the growing population did not feature highly on the policy-making agenda of the South African government. But as the international community began to focus on the increasing population numbers in the developing world (and in particular, in Africa), the newly formed (post-1948) apartheid government received alarmist neo-Malthusian projections of an impending population explosion which fed into a fear that black population numbers were going to escalate at an uncontrollable rate. Caldwell and Caldwell (1993:235) maintain that the fear was related to a belief that black population numbers were going to threaten the capacity of South Africa to grow economically, by spilling over from the Bantustans in which they were restricted into more viable urban economic areas.

Until the 1950s family planning services remained the initiative of health workers and voluntary associations catering primarily for an urbanised, English-speaking sector of the white population. Having struggled for government support to strengthen and spread its services to black areas, the voluntary sector was suddenly overwhelmed by a massive injection of funding and aid in the period between the late 1950s to the early 1960s (Caldwell & Caldwell, 1993:22-24), and was eventually overtaken by the more organised government initiative. From the 1970s to the early 1990s, family-planning programmes were integrated into the provision of general health services. The Population Development Programme (PDP), established in 1984, mobilised a wide spectrum of actors into the national initiative: educators, social workers, medical practitioners, and media workers were all used to legitimise the idea that benefits were to be derived from a reduced family size. Most attention was paid to contraceptive provision in urban (or peri-urban) areas, although rural areas were also catered for, through mobile services (Caldwell & Caldwell, 1993). The PDP also set itself targets. For example, it aimed to influence a decline in the fertility rate to 2.1 children per woman by 2010 (Ndegwa, 1996: 54). The PDP's main difficulty was that of political legitimacy. As Ndegwa (1996: 54) suggests,

> The fact that it centred on a community with no vote and therefore had no say about its existence, coupled with its participation in the National Security Management System, which was set up to undermine community mobilisation against apartheid and specifically the UDF [United Democratic Front], made it look, in the eyes of the majority population, like an apartheid government tool to reduce the black population.

However, despite the climate of suspicion and condemnation of contraceptive use in the 1970s and 1980s, black women, including women in the Bantustans, began to seek out services and make use of contraception in increasing numbers (Kaufman, 1998:432). Caldwell and Caldwell's (1993) assessment of the South African Family Planning Programme was that it was an extremely significant and powerful initiative, which, if the political context was less constraining, could have influenced a speedier dip in fertility (Kaufman, 1998; Camlin et al., 2004). The 1998 SADHS results show that three-quarters of the women of reproductive age and half of all women in South Africa were using contraception at the time of the survey.

Caldwell and Caldwell (1993) raise an important question. They ask why the contraceptive revolution in South Africa did not encourage a very significant fertility decline in the period prior to 1990. Specifically, they ask whether a strong pro-natalist culture persisted, or whether men and women had been opposed to contraceptive use because of the widespread belief that the family planning programme was politically designed to keep black numbers low (see also Potts & Marks, 2001:194). They conclude that the reasons are varied but that the key explanation for the slower than expected fertility decline was the problem of low social and economic status held by African people living under apartheid. Where enormous social and economic insecurities in daily survival exist, children may remain valued as sources of wealth and insurance. They suggest that for a smaller family norm to prevail, there should be signs that upward mobility is possible. In other words, even if parents chose to reduce family sizes, what gains were to be made if there were barriers to social and economic advancement? They draw this argument from analysis put forward by Schoen (Caldwell & Caldwell, 1993:250), who contends that black fertility decline in apartheid South Africa was modest because it was a caste society, with black people restricted from climbing up occupational ladders. Although this analysis is simplistic, it does attempt to offer a broader contextualisation of fertility by linking the desire for and value of children to the effects of political constraints and socio-economic inequalities.

The related question raised is whether real and perceived efforts at political and socio-economic transformation in a democratic South Africa could significantly affect fertility outcomes. Caldwell and Caldwell (1993: 253-255) suggest that fertility patterns will change in South Africa when black people with low fertility can be seen to experience upward economic and social mobility, or expect to see their children make such advancements. In the late 1990s demographers offered mixed but largely negative accounts of the effects of future economic growth (Calitz, 1996). It was also not so evident, and still remains unclear, whether political change in the country (real and anticipated) has generated expectations of mobility, which could in turn be linked, to changing desires concerning fertility and family size.

Another special feature to consider is urbanisation and the way in which it has unfolded in South Africa. Urbanisation, in demographic transition terms, is an important factor undermining extended families and creating the environment for a transition to nuclear families. According to this view family limitation and widespread contraceptive use become reflective of westernisation and changing lifestyles, mind-sets and attitudes in modern urban society (Notestein in Caldwell, 1982). South African demographers are generally in agreement that urbanisation is a key determinant of fertility decline; there are regular contrasts between urban and rural environments and fertility data in the 1980s and 1990s show lower fertility for urban as opposed to rural areas (Mostert & Hofmeyr, 1988; Chimere-Dan, 1994:55). In the past, under apartheid, the processes of urbanisation were inhibited by the enforcement of labour controls such as influx control, and the pass laws and group areas legislation. African workers (male and female) moved between the cities, in which they found employment, and the rurally based Bantustans with which they were expected to identify (Smith, 1992:2). By the time attempts to control and constrain the processes of urbanisation broke down, there were in place "white cities", racially segregated peri-urban townships, growing informal and shack settlements on the fringes of towns and much movement and poverty spread between rural homesteads and urban places of temporary residence and employment. The simultaneously "rural" and "urban" existences and experiences of people as illuminated through the phenomenon of "displaced urbanisation" (Murray, 1987) undermine analyses, which attempt to offer unambiguous distinctions between rural and urban fertility. Circulatory migration, and movement between homesteads and workplaces, has also been significant in shaping fertility and household patterns in southern Africa because it has entrenched long periods in which spouses live and work apart from each other (Timaeus & Graham in Lesthaeghe, 1989). Since the late 1980s the expanding shack settlements have, arguably, facilitated the living together of family members because entire families, rather than individual migrants, are in a position to move closer to places of employment. However, the compounding effects of job insecurities and political and domestic violence have continued to fragment unions and subject families to much stress and discord. The instability of family life and marriage extends beyond South Africa and encompasses southern Africa as a whole. For example, Gaisie (1998) suggests that labour migration played a key role in changing nuptiality patterns in Botswana: the consequences of reduced exposure time in marriage, changes in sexual and reproductive behaviour, and disorganisation of the family have been principal causes of fertility decline.

The debate on the transformation of African family, kinship and household structure in South Africa reflects disagreement on a range of diverse matters. Three areas of controversy are most dominant in the literature as apparent in exchanges between Amoateng (1997), Russell (1998) and Koen (1998) in the *African Sociological Review*. The first controversy revolves around continuing efforts on the part of family researchers to offer empirical evidence showing that the structure of African families is changing from extended to nuclear forms. Amoateng (1997: 22 - 40) re-ignited the debate by presenting new survey evidence to show that the "nuclear family type" is becoming the norm amongst Africans and coloureds living in the Cape Flats of South Africa. He maintains that, due to economic constraints and cultural factors, extended family forms continue to have a presence amongst Africans. However, his evidence suggests that households are becoming smaller and converging towards the structure of households of white South Africans. Amoateng embraces demographic transition theory and the framework of modernisation theory to argue for a steady movement toward nucleation of families and smaller-sized households in which fewer unrelated persons were living.

In response Russell (1998) and Koen (1998) reiterate two additional controversies central to the debate on the changing nature of families and household structure in South Africa. These have to do with the fluidity of household structure, and the extent to which survey data adequately capture "family patterns". In criticising Amoateng, Russell suggests that his definition of households might be appropriate in western societies where household surveys can tell a lot about the sharing of resources and membership of fixed domestic units, that is, of people who share the same physical space. The debilitated processes of urbanisation, the history of migrant labour and oscillation between work-places in urban areas and homesteads in rural areas, and the instability of daily existence, have left the boundaries of households and household membership in constant flux. Russell (1998:175) states:

> In South Africa, with its diverse population groups (each with its distinctive social experience and cultural baggage), data based on such households is particularly treacherous, sometimes capturing the important, resource-sharing family of close kin, sometimes an incomplete segment of such a family, and sometimes a casual contingent

assemblage of temporarily co-resident kin whose individual dependents are scattered.

Russell's point is that "we cannot leap from a snapshot of who is sharing space with whom, to conclusions about the prevailing family system" (Russell, 1998:175). Conclusions regarding the prevailing family system can best be developed by going beyond a study of co-residence to incorporate an understanding of the "broader context of other binding social ties" (Russell, 1998:177). Koen (1998) also draws attention to the difficulties of survey data in capturing the complexity of forces shaping households. Koen argues that the study of household formation and family structure should adopt "a more flexible economic approach". This implies looking more closely at the "ensemble of economic forces" (Koen, 1998: 171) influencing the way in which household members respond to poverty, how they attempt to re-shape household structure and how they attempt to maximise gains through different kinds of household arrangements. The sociological and anthropological literature drawing attention to the fluid nature of households and domestic arrangements has, arguably, not had considerable impact on fertility research in South Africa (Naidoo, 2007).

Since the beginning of the twentieth century the migrant labour system has been a dominant force in shaping family life and intra-household dynamics in Southern Africa (Murray, 1981; Timaeus & Graham, 1989; Walker, 1990; Posel, 1991). The consequence of long-term separations, and in particular the absence of men, is commonly argued to be plausible explanation for the fragmentation of domestic units, high levels of marital dissolution and discord, as well as the weakening of bonds between kin (Brown, 1983; Datt, 1998; Posel, 2001). Younger women today are growing up in a situation where female headship is both more pronounced and less stigmatised. In a study utilising household survey data, Posel (2001:669) maintains that (predominantly older) women head about one-third of all African households in South Africa, and that increasing numbers of women indicate that their partners are absent. She suggests that female-headed households are generally poorer, with fewer working people but with more dependents that male-headed households. This vulnerability prompts migration, influencing changed nuptial and fertility patterns and household structure (Gaisie, 1998).

Apart from high levels of male migration, since the early decades of the twentieth century a substantial number of women have migrated from the rural areas to the urban centres to trade or seek out alternative livelihoods (Ulicki & Crush, 2000;Walker, 1990). Thus, although there is much to be said about how families were affected by the absence of men, a lot more needs to be understood about how families were affected or reconfigured by temporary and more long-term departures of women. Whilst some writing attests to women's agency, there is also evidence of women's dependence, vulnerability and marginality (Elder, 2003). There is little doubt that relations within domestic units and among kin generally have been severely challenged in the course of South Africa's difficult history. Some authors consequently argue that the notion of 'family' is no longer sensible and that alternative conceptualisations should be sought (Sharp & Spiegel, 1984). Nonetheless, as others suggest, notions of 'family' can still be usefully engaged when "social relationships are defined, social networks are weaved, resources mobilized and claims are legitimatised" (Ramphele, 1996: 44). This is particularly relevant in the current global, neo-liberal context in which male retrenchment is occurring alongside the increase in low-wage working opportunities for women (Ulicki & Crush, 2000; Cross et al., 2006:262).

Whilst a small sector of the black population has become rapidly upwardly mobile, about half of the population continues to endure deep economic insecurity and hardship (Naidoo, 2005). The associations between poverty and vulnerability to disease are well established (Wojcicki, 2005; Tladi, 2006) – but what of associations between poverty and inclinations towards low fertility? Low fertility, it has been argued, is associated with *improvements* in the social and economic positions of women. In a 1996 report summarising the findings of an international conference on *The status of women and demographic change: what do we know?*, Karen Mason (1996) emphasises that the strongest links to women desiring smaller family sizes seem to be increases in women's education and improvements in health. Unlike in the developed world, in developing countries the fertility-depressing role of employment outside the home appears to be ambiguous because, in some settings, employment does not increase the opportunity costs of having large numbers of children. Here women who work outside the home often return to assume major roles in household, domestic and child-rearing tasks and remain within sometimes constraining personal relationships and social contexts in which their ability to assert "reproductive choices" might be limited. This is generally the case where women endure poverty and powerlessness and where they are valued largely as wives and child-bearers (Mason, 1996). Mason (1996) suggests, however, that the popularisation of child health and family-planning programmes have served to empower women by offering them choices with respect to whether they should bear additional children and what methods they could employ to delay and space pregnancies. High fertility is thus associated with patriarchal societies in which women experience subordination and fewer personal freedoms and rights whereas lower levels of fertility are said to be most prevalent in contexts in which women enjoy greater autonomy and equality with men (Longwe in March et al., 1999).

Whilst the South African media and women's activist groups suggest that women are being subjected to increasing acts of violence, these estimates have been imprecise, given the problem of underreporting. The 1998 SADHS found that 4% of women had experienced rape at some point during their life-time; the HSRC and Statistics South Africa argue that about 30% to 70% of rapes are not reported each year (Forgey, 2001). A National Victimisation Survey (SAPS, 2001) which was carried out in 1998 found that most assaults (54%) and sexual offences (68%) occur within the victim's home and that most perpetrators (33,8%) are closely related to the victim. Against this background, Candice Bradley's (1995:157-178) discussion of women's empowerment, domestic violence and fertility decline offers an alternative focus for seeking out the routes of fertility transition which might be applicable in South Africa. She argues that in the case of Kenya women have made much progress in increasing their participation in the areas of education and employment. These signs of women's empowerment correlate highly with the increased intention to plan births and use contraception. In the South African context as well, an increase in education and employment have correlated significantly with increased contraceptive use and lowered demand for children (Du Plessis, 1996:43-44). Bradley (1995:176) suggests, though, that paradoxically fertility decline may be a result of women making gains on the one hand, but acquiring losses on the other. With reference to Kenya, she suggests that violence against women has increased tremendously over the years partly as a consequence of increasing competition between men and women. In conditions of slow economic growth, levels of scarcity mean that women find themselves in constant competition with men. "More equitable education and broader career choices do not occur in a vacuum. In an atmosphere of growing scarcity, both men and women feel the pinch. It may be scarcity rather than empowerment which is fuelling a turn toward lower fertility" (Bradley, 1995:176-177). This analysis might also hold true for South

Africa. The changing state of the South African economy, the effects of the global recession, much expectation of social and economic transformation, and attempts to remedy past inequalities mean that women often find themselves in constant competition with men for employment, resources and opportunities. Excessively high levels of violence against women are perhaps indications of competition and bargaining that undermine the stability of households and relationships.

There is, in short, a multiplicity of factors to consider when attempting to explain the processes of reproductive change and dynamics in South Africa. Analysis of fertility transition has to take into account how structures inherited from the past are shaping reproductive motivations and outcomes. It has to also take account of the complexities surrounding union and household formation, and gender relations, under changing and contrasting social and economic conditions. The two critical themes that persist in South African demography, although they have been treated as subjects for largely macro-level analyses, are (1) the influence of the prevailing socio-economic realities on proximate determinants such as union formation and contraceptive use, and (2) the contexts in which, and purposes for which, women have (over time) taken measures to deliberately control their reproductive outcomes. This study focuses on these themes in the course of analysing the varied life experiences of a small group of women.

Embracing an alternative "making sense" approach

Apart from the demographic transition theory and wealth flows thesis other approaches commonly cited when studying reproduction in African contexts have been (1) the cultural or diffusion approach, (2) the approaches which focus on women's roles and changing status, and the (3) micro-economic approaches to fertility decision-making. These have been consistently criticised for their narrowness of focus, and the generally unsatisfactory way in which explanations of fertility change are offered (Greenhalgh, 1995:5-8). The popular cultural diffusion approach sees the widespread use of contraception, "a technological issue" (Greenhalgh, 1995:9), as more crucial than socio-economic forces in the shaping of fertility outcomes. Demographers also continue to use the concepts of "women's roles" and "women's status" as indicators of social and economic change and empowerment despite these being sidelined by feminist critique (Greenhalgh, 1995:5). Implicit in the use of these concepts is the assumption that the position of women improves with the passing of time and improvements in the economy, factors essential in fertility decline. The implications of the contradictory gains made by women who might live either in improving or deteriorating socio-economic circumstances are often not explored. Micro-economic theories see fertility decisions as analogous to economic household decisions made by consumers in their day-to-day existences (Simmons, 1985:34). Consumer choice models and examinations of the economic dimensions of fertility decision-making (such as quantity-quality tradeoffs) are criticised for not taking into account contextual and historical factors intervening in these micro-level deliberations (Greenhalgh, 1995:8).

Susan Greenhalgh (1995) maintains that, in comparison with these approaches, the "institutional approach" is more credible in the way it brings together combinations of context and history. Institutions, in this sense, do not refer to public bodies such as schools or hospitals but rather to "clusters of habits" underpinning the way social life is organised and perpetuated. McNicoll (1994) suggests that institutions (e.g. the sexual division of labour) are perpetuated unconsciously until they are consciously and deliberately engaged. Institutions thus evolve from past and present behaviour and are "endowments" which undergo continuing engagement, negotiation and renegotiation (McNicoll, 1994:201). Institutions are also path-dependent. Although path-dependency and history place constraints on present and future circumstances and on social action, McNicoll (1994:201-211) maintains that "small perturbations" or "accidental shocks" along the way can lead to unanticipated paths or outcomes. McNicoll describes institutional patterns, which, in his view, have determined paths of fertility transition in different regions of the world. Fertility declines across the world might appear to look similar from afar. A closer look however would reveal that these declines were probably driven by quite different sets of forces. He identifies historical, economic and political factors in the different regions of the world, which could explain the differences in the timing, and speed of fertility decline. He offers labels for the dominant institutional patterns evolving in the different regions. He labels Africa's institutional pattern as "lineage dominance" and states that it is likely that Africa is following a different kind of demographic pattern, one dominated by the influence of lineage and distinctive kin-based family systems. He identifies the challenge posed by AIDS, increasing land scarcity and reduced demand for rural labour as having anti-natal effects, but contends that the influence of family still remains most powerful. McNicoll's institutional approach for fertility analysis is useful in that it directs attention to the historical routes of fertility transition. According to this approach fertility regimes must be studied and understood in terms of local, regional and global institutional dimensions. Fertility regimes must also be understood in terms of a continuing process of institutionalisation of individual behaviour and expectations. He emphasises that institutions are not "timeless structures" - although inclined to perpetuate past patterns, they adjust to new pressures, and may lead to unpredictable outcomes in the long run (McNicoll, 1994:211).

Greenhalgh (1995:12) states that as opposed to:

> the universalising and quantifying thrusts of most demographies, McNicoll's institutional demography recognizes historical contingency and societal specificity, and embraces narrative modes of explanation that can accommodate such forces as gender and power that are difficult to incorporate into standard empirical models of demographic behaviour.

However she offers as an alternative her own "culture and political economy approach". Although her culture and political economy approach bears a resemblance to McNicoll's approach in that both emphasise structure and institutions, McNicoll's approach "gives greater weight to structures, while [Greenhalgh's approach] pays more attention to agency".

Greenhalgh's (1990; 1995) contribution takes as its starting point the view that an understanding of the multiplicity of "reproductive institutions and outcomes" represents a more interesting area of study than the shift from high to low fertility. There may be just as many, if not more, variations between high fertility societies, and between low-fertility societies, than there may be between high- and low-fertility societies. Greenhalgh (1995:12) suggests that the aim of fertility research should be the creation of "whole demographies": a multi-levelled analysis that takes account of the interplay between micro- and macro-linkages, processes and institutions involved in the shaping of reproductive dynamics and outcomes. She argues that "a political economy of fertility must be an explicitly historical field of inquiry" in which close attention is paid to "the links between political and economic processes" and the "political-economic dimension of social and cultural organization" (Greenhalgh, 1990:94). Greenhalgh's analysis does not limit itself to an understanding of the complexities of macro-level or global institutions, but seeks explanations for fertility behaviour through analysing the interconnected workings of a variety of local processes and institutions. Given the inadequacy of existing theories of demography, particularly in their ability to explain diverse forms of reproductive behaviours, Greenhalgh's emphasis is on "situating fertility", that is "to show how it *makes sense* given the socio-cultural and political economic context in which it is embedded" (Greenhalgh, 1995:17). This approach is intended to encourage researchers to make use of case studies as a means towards enhancing fertility analysis. This is regarded as an important stage for theory-building because "[o]nce enough cases are collected and understood, they might serve as the building blocks of more general understandings of reproductive dynamics"(Greenhalgh, 1995:17). For anthropologists, Greenhalgh's approach is not a novel one. In the field of demography, arguably, an approach which offers greater weight to institutional patterns and contextual issues such as local politics, history and gender relations (factors conventionally regarded as having "indirect influences" on fertility) does represent a shift away from the norm.

Although anthropologically informed demographers have applied this culture and political-economy approach, different dimensions of the approach tend to be emphasised. Fricke, for instance, emphasises the kinship, familial dimension of the political-economic approach. Fricke (1995:205) states that:

> [w]hile sophisticated analysis of [relationships between the family, kinship and other groups] and their implications for particular forms of marriage dates from the work of Leach (1961), their incorporation into the political-economic framework argued for by Greenhalgh has lagged. I argue here that such a connection enlarges the scope of a political economy of fertility by drawing attention to the reproduction of relations in pre-transition settings.

Studying the family and marriage patterns within a culture and political-economy framework will also allow for a more meaningful contextualisation of the concept of "fertility" itself. A criticism of demography's use of the concept "fertility" is that the concept is used simplistically as a "biological one in which children are attributed unproblematically to the women who gave birth to them" (Townsend, 1997:96-98). A person's fertility, it is argued, should be explained in terms of a description of a place in a web of relationships with offspring, with other kin, and with a range of social groups and institutions. From this perspective different formulations of "parenthood" could be developed which could also incorporate foster and adopted children. It could also illuminate the importance of other people, particularly senior kin, in reproductive decisions, which are conventionally seen as decisions of couples alone. In the course of this study, I have attempted to make sense of the dynamics within a particular locality by integrating different levels of analysis. The emphasis, however, is on the micro-level. Since the methodological approach has involved gathering details of women's reproductive experiences, I have tended to pay greater attention to these rather than macro-level processes.

Conclusion

This chapter presents a review of salient issues, theories and background to the study of fertility and family life in South Africa. The review is deliberately eclectic and touches on a range of matters, rather than offering a comprehensive discussion of a few aspects. This is because the fields of demography (and family sociology), often criticised as fields lacking in theory (Kertzer & Fricke, 1997), have begun to draw on multi-disciplinary insights and multi-level analyses in attempting to develop new understandings of fertility behaviour (Johnson-Hanks, 2007). Perhaps, as Greenhalgh (1995:17) advocates, greater use of case study findings could serve as the "building blocks of more general understandings of reproductive dynamics". A shift towards multi-level studies or micro-level explorations could become meaningful exercises in demography especially if it places the various experiences of women, power relations structuring gender hierarchies, and the extent to which "choices" and "decisions" exist, at the centre of enquiry. Closer examination of contextual issues and the fluidity of unions and household structure, particularly in the southern African context, will become increasingly critical in analyses of how and in what direction(s) fertility is changing. An understanding of transforming, stable and contradictory "reproductive decisions" will become urgent as HIV/AIDS begins to affect mortality, adult and child survival more significantly than it has already. The way in which women, as the poorest stratum of South African society, experience poverty and power and their consequences for family life and fertility will be the focus of the chapters which follow.

Chapter 3

DOING FIELDWORK: LEARNING ABOUT HISTORY AND CONSTRUCTING LIFE HISTORIES

Introductory Comment

In this chapter I offer a selective overview of the history, politics, and socio-economic circumstances of Winterveld's men and women. Although the intention is to make use of secondary sources and some survey data, the greater emphasis here is to integrate vignettes that reflect memories and experiences of the lives of people within Merafeng. A secondary aim is to draw attention to the research methods used and the ethical dilemmas encountered in the course of fieldwork. Demography has only recently begun to embrace micro-level investigations of reproductive behaviour, and a low-key debate continues to raise questions about the respectability of qualitative data and the usefulness of qualitative approaches in this predominantly quantitative field. This chapter does not address the more comprehensive issues associated with how and in what combinations one uses qualitative methods in fertility research. These issues will be reflected on in the final chapter of this book. Rather than a separate and detailed discussion on the use of methods, Chapter 3 focuses on sharing the experience of doing fieldwork given the complexities and peculiarities of my fieldwork site. Thus this chapter offers a context through which we can begin to understand both the lives and struggles of women in Merafeng, Winterveld, and the difficulties presented by such a setting for the application of various methods in the course of fieldwork.

Fieldwork methods and site selection

Using qualitative methods

The adoption of a qualitative, interpretive methodology was prompted by a need to construct a meaningful and nuanced account of reproductive dynamics in a particular setting, or, rather, to situate fertility within a particular socio-cultural and historical context. An interpretive approach, epistemologically different from an objectivist/ positivist one which sees reality as 'out there' capable of being efficiently measured and captured, emphasises the precarious, complex and 'unfinished' nature of social reality. As Scheper-Hughes (1997:203) suggests, "interpretive research is less concerned with orderly explanations than with achieving a fuller, richer, deeper understanding of social life as the negotiation of meanings". In striving for this richer understanding of social life, this project draws on the voices of a select group of people through whom we can learn much about history and socio-cultural constraints.

As stated in Chapter 1, the focus of this research is on Merafeng as a case study. Four types of case studies have been described most often by different writers (Stenhouse, 1985, cited in Bassey, 1999: 27-30). These are the ethnographic, evaluative, educational and action research case studies. Of these, Stenhouse's account of the ethnographic and evaluative case studies bears some resemblance to my use of the case study method in this project. It can be categorised as an ethnographic case study in that it draws on the understandings and experiences of a group of research subjects and it uses methods of observation and interviews similar to those used in social anthropology. It is also evaluative in that the case is studied with the intention of making judgements regarding the appropriateness of theories and methods. As a unit the case could refer to an individual, group, or community. Here I use the term "case study" to refer to the study of a small group of people resident within a demarcated area of Winterveld. (See Map 1 in **Appendix 2** for Winterveld's location in relation to Pretoria.)

Engaging in qualitative research in an effort to "make sense" of the multiple realities of a particular case generally implies the use of more than one method. Triangulation in this sense involves attempts to deepen understanding of particular situations or phenomena and does not represent an attempt at validation (Denzin & Lincoln, 1998). Despite the suggestions of incompatibility between interpretive approaches (which rely on meanings) and positivist approaches (which rely on numbers), many qualitative researchers often attempt creative ways of integrating diverse statistical measures to locate a group of subjects within a larger population, and as a way of drawing comparisons between relationships within larger and smaller contexts. In this project there is some integration of survey data and secondary data analysis. This is not an attempt to advocate a mixed methodological approach. Rather, the use of some basic statistics is afforded a supplementary role to clarify and add content within a predominantly qualitative framework.

The three primary qualitative methods were:

Discussions with key informants. These were crucial as an initial and continuing activity to gain clarity on aspects of the history, social practices and services in the area. Both men and women were active informants and this pool widened substantially before the fieldwork ended.

Life histories of mothers and daughters. These offered a select set of intergenerational family histories important in revealing the lived experiences and histories of women in the area. This represented my main fieldwork tool; it was an immensely difficult research activity and illustrated the impossibility of researcher neutrality in qualitative research.

Focus groups. These were envisaged as important to add meaningful content to specific topics that required further in-depth exploring. As a qualitative instrument, a single focus-group session becomes a forum in which a group of individuals is brought together to participate in a discussion. These discussions, however, became less useful for learning about sexual or reproductive practices and more helpful in gaining general insights into commonly held beliefs, attitudes and experiences. Some thoughts about the appropriateness of using groups to learn about private matters will be offered later in this chapter.

A special note on life histories

A life history can be defined simply as an account of a person's life as it is told to another person (the researcher). If our purpose is to maximise the inclusion of details of a range of aspects and stages of the person's life, then a life history could include the use of a variety of records and archival material in its construction. In this sense the life history becomes a detailed (though necessarily incomplete) biographical account of an individual's life and experiences. For most authors the significance of the life history lies in the way the individual account illuminates broader historical processes, social practices and change. When numerous individual life histories are constructed it becomes the researcher's task to bind these stories together (often thematically) in an attempt to clarify in what ways the set of individual stories can be seen to typify or reflect the whole and offer an understanding of unfolding historical processes (Angrosino, 1989).

In demography and family sociology life histories could become more than a means to construct broader histories. As a reflection of individual women's experiences they touch on diverse and changing fertility practices, family and marital relations that often do not find much place in more generalised historical accounts. In constructing these accounts and delving into both the "public" and "private" domains of women's lives, the researcher asks a lot and perhaps witnesses just as much. Scheper-Hughes (1997: 218), an anthropological demographer, suggests that *witnessing* becomes a crucial way of sustaining an "open dialogue" with people. It means that in learning about individual histories and in experiencing history the researcher does not stand "above and outside the fray, coolly observing and recording facts and turning these into scientific models ..." (Scheper-Hughes, 1997: 218).

Life histories as individual accounts are shaped by (amongst other factors) the personality of the individual and the particular historical moment at which the interviewing (and witnessing) begins. In his portrayal of Kas Maine, a South African share-cropper, Van Onselen draws on Jean-Paul Sartre's "hierarchy of mediations" as a way of linking the individual to a class context whilst simultaneously "doing justice to the peculiarities of personality and the psychology of the individual ..." (1993:498). This implies that, in interviewing an individual and constructing her life history, close attention has also to be paid to the actions and roles of individuals surrounding her, that is, to "suitable primary groups", in order to avoid distortions which come from viewing individual behaviour as "moving society". These would include key informants from, for example, the person's family, cohort, area and class position. I attempted, in the course of interviewing individuals, to engage, to some extent, others surrounding the individual. Specifically, I found it useful to interview mothers and daughters from families representing different class interests, ethnic identities and cohorts, as well as key informants operating in the vicinity of the women being interviewed.

Researchers are beginning to make use of life histories in explorations of sexual and reproductive experiences in South Africa (see e.g. Harrison & Montgomery, 2001). Many of these accounts, however, do not go beyond two sets of interviews per woman. Criticisms of surveys as "snap-shot exercises" in map-making (Caldwell, 1985) should also be extended to snap-shot ventures in qualitative research. Scheper-Hughes's (1997) methodology illustrates the other extreme. Her exceptionally detailed study of child mortality in Brazilian shanty towns has been a result of (albeit intermittently) 25 years of fieldwork. My period of approximately ten years, therefore, is an attempt at more in-depth learning, but it does not pretend to be completely comprehensive.

Selecting Merafeng in Winterveld as a fieldwork site

Two practical considerations guided my initial selection of Merafeng in Winterveld as a fieldwork site. It was 55 km from the south of Pretoria where I live - and its close proximity to me meant that I did not need to live away from home. I thought it would be easy for me to travel to and from Winterveld on an almost daily basis. A further reason was that I had made contact with the Medical University of Southern Africa's Institute for Community Services (Medicos) and I was promised access to some of their community-based projects working amongst women in Winterveld. Thus, for reasons of access and convenience over and above other judgements of suitability of site, Winterveld became the preferred option.

Reading through newspapers, books and articles that focused on varying aspects of the history, life and turmoil in Winterveld filled me with immense trepidation. Reference to "throwaway people", to a predominantly destitute "squatter" settlement, to the prevalence of disease and high levels of crime filled me with much unease shortly before beginning fieldwork. This reinforced my initial thinking which was that, without assistance from Medicos in gaining access to women in the area, my fieldwork would not be possible.

Unfortunately, my arrival in South Africa to begin fieldwork coincided with one of Medicos's busy work periods, and it was some time before I was able to make arrangements through its director to work through one of its link projects - the Planned Parenthood Association (PPA), Winterveld branch. In retrospect, this setback became a useful experience because without any protective organisational base I was prompted to begin fieldwork independently. Under the auspices of a health organisation, I would have associated myself with its reputation and its function. As an independent researcher I presented myself as someone simply intent on understanding the area, its people and their experiences over the years. This initial entry into Winterveld initiated a pattern of following leads and engaging numerous stories simultaneously with key informants, mothers and daughters and groups of women. The history, social and economic circumstances of the men and women in Winterveld which I learnt about over the months (and consequently years) are presented in the sections that follow.

Using quantitative methods

Some months after beginning fieldwork I was contacted by the director of Medicos who introduced me to the personnel of the PPA

(Winterveld branch) with the expectation that I would work with the project at the same time as I would be entitled to draw on its resources. It was at this stage that the possibility of a survey of my fieldwork site arose. Prior to conducting a micro-survey I had intended to integrate quantitative insights drawn only from the 1987-1989 South African Demographic and Health Survey (SADHS). I thought that the micro-survey, as an additional survey, would offer data that could be compared with the SADHS macro-survey as well as with the qualitative insights derived from the individual and group interviews.

The plan to conduct the micro-survey did not begin with the construction of a sampling frame or complete list of households within my fieldwork site. Except for a formal list of plots and names of landowners, a list of tenants' households is unobtainable. An invisible set of boundaries demarcating what I referred to as 'Merafeng' became the site within which the survey was to be conducted. Approximately 10,000 people were estimated to live in this part of Winterveld. A total of 293 women were interviewed in this area. Although the attempt was to keep the selection as random as possible, it was initiated using a snowball sampling technique in that the initial group of women interviewed helped to identify other prospective interviewees. The specific findings of this micro-survey are thus not offered, on their own, as generalisations of the entire Winterveld area. They are included in this study because they offer important contextual insights into such matters as contraceptive use and on associations between socio-economic differentials and desires to have children.

The chapters that follow will, in certain places, compare results of the SADHS and the micro-survey conducted in Winterveld (WS). The 1987-1989 SADHS dataset was used because it was the only demographic and health survey dataset readily available for research use in 1998. The results of the internationally recognised 1998 and 2003 South African demographic surveys are now available and will be included, when considered relevant, in the different chapters. Although the 1987-1989 SADHS is regarded as offering the first reliable data on all racial groups in South Africa (Caldwell, 1993) the survey itself has not enjoyed much international recognition. It was conducted during the apartheid era and at a time when academic sanctions were in place. It is thus referred to as a DHS-type survey because it was modelled on the USAid-Macro-International Demographic and Health Survey though it received no financial assistance from international funding bodies (Kaufman, 1998). A total of 21,894 individual and 14,878 household interviews were conducted. Women aged 12-55 were included in the clustered and stratified, random probability sample. The women were questioned on such issues as current and previous marital/union status, on births of children, on economic activities, types of household and contraceptive use. The most serious criticism of the survey is that it has underestimated contraceptive use by excluding unmarried, childless women who might well have been using contraceptives (Kaufman, 1998:424-425). I have selected for analysis a subset of the dataset, viz. only the sample of African women. This sample is made up of 16,474 individual interviews.

A selective overview of the history and politics of Winterveld: 1930s-2000s

Winterveld has a fascinating history. It is not difficult for outsiders to begin to develop a sense of what has happened in the past because both men and women are quite forthcoming with stories about the "early days". As a South African from nearby (Pretoria) I was not treated as an absolute outsider. It was assumed that I knew many things such as how forced removals compounded suffering during apartheid. Being identified as an Indian, however, meant that my presence often elicited various kinds of responses from those whom I encountered for the first time. One response was enthusiasm to inform me about "cultural ways" and social problems of the area and to establish how different they were from those of where I came from, and another was curiosity about who I was and why I was interested in a place like Winterveld. I was constantly faced with people's attempts to compare things in Winterveld to what they believed I was more familiar with. Rather than shying away from such comparisons (often riddled with stereotypes), my approach throughout was to share stories that I thought would be of interest to the people I was talking to. For example, Elias Monyepao (64) of the Winterveld Plot-owners' Association (WPA) interrogated me at length about aspects of the history of KwaZulu-Natal (from where I originate) before making his assessment about whether or not I could be regarded as being serious about wanting to learn about Winterveld. He was then always available for my questions and queries. He also held a special meeting of the WPA to get plot-owners to "record some knowledge" so that my history-gathering task would be facilitated. The points they noted for me were rather interesting – it was clear that far from seeing themselves as being freed by the new South Africa they saw "the struggle" as continuing.

There are two crucial phases which emerge as embedded in the memories of the people interviewed and that are important to elaborate on, largely because they shape the tensions and social relations of present-day Winterveld. These are (1) the arrival of the land-owners, their early attempts at farming, and their shift to leasing land and (2) the transition from the days under the Bophuthatswana government to the days under a democratic government.

From farming to leasing land

Since the history of Winterveld as a freehold territory is a fairly recent history, many plot-owners remember arriving there as children or as young adults. The origins of Winterveld as a black (African), freehold, agricultural settlement can be found in the implementation of the 1936 Native Trust and Land Act. In 1913 the Natives Land Act had restricted African people to the reserves (which represented only 7% of all land in South Africa). Living outside these proclaimed boundaries was permissible only for the purpose of work as labour tenants or wage labourers. The 1936 Act increased the land potentially available for black occupation to 13% of all land. After the 1936 Act was passed, two adjacent farms - Winterveld and Klippan, which covered an area of 10,386 hectares, were bought by a group of land speculators who constituted the Winterveld Agricultural Holdings Syndicate. The syndicate subdivided the two farms into 1,658 plots ranging from 4 to 12 morgen in size [In South Africa 1 morgen is just over 2 acres of land. In other countries this measure may differ, e.g. in Norway 1 morgen is two-thirds of an acre]. (Most plots on Klippan were 5 morgen, whilst most in Winterveld were 10 morgen.) The syndicate began selling off the plots provisionally and cheaply to black purchasers at 75 pounds for a 5-morgen plot and 135 pounds for a 10-morgen plot before applying to the Native Affairs Department for permission to establish a black agricultural holdings settlement on the farms. Archival material (Central Archives Depot, NTS 3707: 1765/308) shows much correspondence about the problem of inadequate water supply in the area. Before the syndicate's plans were approved only three bore-holes were available for use. Between 1940 and 1941, and after the plans for a settlement were approved, the syndicate sank a few more boreholes in Winterveld. Winterveld became the generic name for the area covering both farms.

It is also apparent that, although people came in droves, presumably to begin farming on their own lands, the land was not suitable for all kinds of farming. The plots on the farms Klippan and Winterveld were sold as places suitable for cattle-grazing and cattle-holding only. In one-to-one correspondence, members of the syndicate were forthright about the difficulties of farming on this land, but adverts to the general public were quite misleading. In an internal memorandum, the Assistant Director of Native Agriculture said the following to the Director of Native Agriculture after a field inspection in 1939:

> The soil is composed of a loose quartzite fine gravel. These farms in the past have been used for ranching and the bush has been protected ... In this particular case the area is in a low rainfall belt and unsuited to cropping. One can depend on one or two light crops in 5 years. In any case the plot holders will not have sufficient stock to work their holdings ... Under the circumstances the plot holders will not be able to rely on supplementing their family budget by depending on crops grown on their plots. These holdings at best will give the head of the family a security of tenure where he can dump his family and be free from tribal customs and police molestation ... (Central Archives Depot, NTS 3707: 1765/308).

Despite suspecting that the land was quite "unsuited to cropping", it would seem that many land-owners arrived not just for the "security of tenure" and to be free of the stresses of life on the reserves and elsewhere in South Africa, but to explore all the possibilities of farming. This was for many not just a place for cattle-holding. Louis Dube is regarded as the pioneer of Winterveld not just because he was the first owner to move in but because he served as an agent of the syndicate. It was his task to canvas prospective buyers and tell them about the plots, the land and the purposes for which it could be used - but he too (it would seem) saw it as a place to begin farming. He grew crops for domestic subsistence use and for selling to markets outside Winterveld. Nozizwe Radebe (66) [#3] remembered the day in 1939 when her family arrived. They were one of the first families to arrive there and set up a makeshift home amidst the wild forests and animals. Her father's intention had been to begin farming. They grew beans, mealies and wheat and reared cattle, sheep, turkeys and chickens. She claimed that, until the early 1960s farming was quite successful, and then after that it seemed to deteriorate. Crops did not grow well and this was worsened by the fact that there had been little or no rainfall.

Oupa Leshabani (72), who also arrived there as a boy, claimed:

> Winterveld was very good. The only thing is that there was no water. There was no rainfall. Some people came. Then others followed. This

place was just a big bush. When we came we planted mealies and beans. Everything used to grow well, especially if it was raining. We were doing subsistence farming. We had fowls and pigs. We would eat some of them and give some of them away. We used to share them with our neighbours. Thieves did not give us problems in those days (s).

In the 1950s when communal boreholes were regarded as too few and thus a deterrent to farming, Sam Maropeng, an early plot-owner, became famous through his suggestion that plot-owners take steps to sink boreholes on their plots. Thabo Maduna (70) recalled:

People came here with a sole aim of practising agriculture. Each plot-owner built a borehole through Sam Maropeng's advice. This helped a lot, so when the Farmers Association was formed in about 1960 people were more encouraged to do farming. We had poultry and we were growing vegetables such as sweet potatoes (e).

Like Nozizwe Radebe, Thabo Maduna maintained that something went wrong with farming in the 1960s. He blamed it on the anti-farming attitudes of the younger generation. "Our children did not take up farming. They believed that you could earn more money by working. You could be better dressed. They did not want to be like the women and men who were farming before ... The soil is good here; this is one of the best places for farming" (e).

Kehla Nyamakazi (64), the current leader of the WPA, said:

I was 10 years old in 1946. I remember the plot-owners cutting down trees and cutting grass. The land was used mainly for grazing but also for growing crops. People came from different areas - Pedi, Shangaans, Zulus, Sothos. It didn't matter which group you came from. Men and women worked as farmers (e).

In conducting the micro-survey we found the backgrounds of the women interviewed to be quite diverse: 65% of the women were migrants from elsewhere, having lived in the area for varying periods of time, with 35% having been born there. About 88% of those interviewed were tenants and 12% were plot-owners. The predominant languages spoken (of this sample) were Northern Sotho (18.4%), Zulu (18.1%), Shangaan (11.9%), Setswana (10.9%) and Ndebele (10.6%), Southern Sotho (8.5%), Swazi (6.8%), Xhosa (6.5%) and other (8.5%).

It is important to point out that Winterveld's earliest inhabitants came here as a highly diverse group of people, not just in terms of different ethnic backgrounds, but also in terms of social positions. Ex-miners, ex-teachers, retired people from an assortment of trades, those paid off when moved from their land before the 1936 Land Act, all sought land in which they could invest their monies and possibly begin subsistence, semi-capitalist farming or trading (Simone, 1998:274). It would seem that some outsiders from southern Africa also gained access to land in Winterveld after the closure of the salt factory nearby in Tswaing. When the factory closed down due to diminishing profits, some part of the predominantly Zimbabwean workforce found a place in Winterveld's diversity. In general, people were not just looking for farming land as secure investments, but for freedom from the insecurity of life in the reserves, and on trust lands, and from labour tenancy on white farms. Some of the people I interviewed expressed different reasons for buying land and settling in Winterveld:

Mbulelo Molamu (83) said:

We came here because we were forced to move. We had a farm in Leeuwspruit but the area was declared white. We were told we had to exchange it for another farm elsewhere. My father did not move for many years until his land was forcibly "expropriated". He was paid off with a little money. He then bought a farm in Winterveld. We came mainly to begin farming(e).

Khanyi Mabetwa (78) [#4] said:

We [Khanyi's natal family] were staying in Zebediela - where the chiefs are - on tribal land. It did not belong to us. It was trust land. We moved from there to Eastwood but we were affected by forced removals. We [Khanyi's husband and herself] arrived here in Winterveld in the 1950s during the days of the Pass Campaigns. My husband came from a wealthy family. He came to open up shops and to start businesses (s).

George Mphahlele (62) said:

I came to Winterveld in 1945. I was seven years old then. My father bought the plot. He was working as a nightwatchman in town. We came to do farming here. We used to grow a lot of vegetables. Our main aim was to sell. We used to go to Lady Selborne to sell right until the time Lady Selborne was demolished(e).

Thandi Ramashala (37) [#8]lived in 1999 as a tenant. Her family, though, arrived as part of the early wave of land-owners in the 1940s. Thandi took me to visit her father (Baba Rametsi), who lived outside

Winterveld, to find out about their early history. He told me that the Rametsi family had originated in Mmabolo in Pietersburg.

> Mmamabolo was a rural place. It was owned by the chief. We were ploughing and doing cattle-farming there. My parents worked as labour tenants so we moved to Hartebeeshoek and then to Klipfontein doing farming for the whites. We used to work three months at a time. In 1940 we were in Engel de Bos doing farming. The owner at that time was in Heidelberg, but we heard from the foreman there - a Mr Maluleke - about land in Klipgat. We left with all our cattle. We stayed there on somebody else's plot. Then my father heard about the plots in Winterveld. He thought we'd be freer there. So he bought a plot and we moved to Winterveld (e).

By 1941 all of the 1,658 plots had been sold. Whilst some plot-owners opted out of Winterveld later, most of the title deeds are still held by relatives of the earliest owners even though many of them are absentee owners, particularly of the 10-morgen plots. In 1953 Winterveld was regarded as a sparsely populated area, with only 464 homes. At this time plot-owners looked forward to the arrival of more families in Winterveld. A population increase was expected to have beneficial effects particularly for the purposes of growing and selling crops, and for sustaining successful businesses. The population increase which was to follow, however, was most unanticipated. A large number of people - a non-land-owning class - descended upon Winterveld in steadily increasing numbers from the early 1960s to the late 1970s. This increase was prompted mainly by the movement of people off white farms due to evictions, forced removals and the search for employment in the Pretoria-Vereeniging-Witwatersrand (PWV) and Brits/ Rosslyn industrial centres (Yawitch, 1981: 201-202). (See Map 3 in **Appendix 2** for an indication of Winterveld's population density as revealed by the 1996 census.)

The initial wave of tenants was welcomed by plot-owners. Subsistence farming was on the decline and letting became a way of making money. As Nozizwe Radebe recalled: "The plot-owners wanted money. They thought they could earn money by renting"(e). Some even planned for the accommodation of growing numbers of tenants by building homes on their land, just as Khanyi Mabetwa's husband had done. She said:

> When we first arrived here in Winterveld, Winterveld was very poor. We were the first people to start building on this stretch of land in 1958. We also built some small houses and let them out to tenants who were at

that stage moving into Winterveld in large numbers. On our plot in
Winterveld we used to plant vegetables but mainly sweet potatoes. It
was hard to cultivate vegetables because there was no water, and no
rain. It was good to let the land out then (s).

Up until the late 1980s some plot-owners continued to build homes
for potential leasing as was the case with Patience Khutsoane's (48) [#9]
father-in-law. He had built a large house on the edge of his plot, leaving
sufficient space to build 98 smaller flat-topped houses for leasing to
tenants. By the time Patience became the sole owner in the mid-1990s,
relations with tenants on her plot had soured, and this large property had
become a burden to her. Most tenants, however, arrived in Winterveld,
negotiated access to a small piece of land and then built their own homes
from mud bricks and with zinc roofs. As a rule, the rent is much cheaper
for self-built homes.

For many plot-owners, the initial welcome to tenants unleashed a
considerably large and uncontrollable number of people on to their lands.
Thabo Maduna explained:

White farmers needed to pay farm workers. They got rid of their
labourers. They had nowhere to go. Farmers encouraged labourers to go
to Winterveld because there were black farmers here. The municipality
told us to keep the tenants for a while. Ever since we have been waiting
for the municipality. Now the municipality knows we have a problem ...
Being good samaritans got us into trouble (e).

Kehla Nyamakazi also suggested that:

In the 1960s people were forcibly removed from areas like Eastwood,
Wallmannsthal, and Lady Selborne and from white farming areas as far
off as Groblersdal. Those who had plots in Lady Selborne and
Wallmannsthal were given other plots in places such as Atteridgeville or
close by in Boekenhoutfontein. If you were a squatter in an area and you
were forcibly removed - you arrived here also as a squatter. We gave
many of these squatters temporary rights here in Winterveld. The
government promised that they would come and collect them. We are
still waiting (e).

Kehla Nyamakazi, like many plot-owners, continued to refer to
tenants as "squatters". By definition a squatter is someone who occupies
land illegally and without authority. This definition would exclude most
non-landowners in Winterveld. Most came to be there having gained

permission from land-owners and arranged to pay monthly rent (Yawitch, 1981).

A wide variety of tenant-plot-owner relationships has developed over the years. Some are fairly cordial, some are patronage relationships in which tenants are highly exploited, some are antagonistic relationships stemming largely from the tenants' refusal to pay rent, and some are those in which tenants (given absent landlords) subdivide and let out land to newer tenants (Simone, 1998). There is some distinction currently between new and old tenants. Older tenants, i.e. people who have been there for decades and who had earlier assumed docile and compliant positions, are now being regarded as troublemakers engaging in conspiracies to rob owners of their land. Newer tenants, who are predominantly Mozambican and Zimbabwean, most of whom live and work illegally, are despised because of their alleged associations with criminal activities, but at the same time often preferred as tenants because they are more vulnerable and easier to control.

It took me about three months after beginning fieldwork in Winterveld before I managed to begin seriously interviewing tenants. Language had not posed a problem in my interviewing of plot-owners since most men and women whom I encountered were fairly fluent in English (or Afrikaans). Except for some tenants, with whom I spoke predominantly in Afrikaans or English, interviews had to be conducted mainly in Sesotho, Ndebele or Zulu. For assistance here I had to rely on a multilingual interpreter, Pumla Maila, a 47-year-old unemployed plot-owner who had both the time and interest to accompany me for many months of interviewing. Later, when my interest in Mozambican women grew, I had to rely on Martina, a Shangaan-speaking woman, for assistance as an interpreter. Initially, Pumla's plot-owner status and my outsider status created obstacles to the quality of responses we were gaining from women tenants. We had to work much harder here in winning the confidence of very poor women and in building levels of trust. An unexpected bit of help came from Aubrey Ndlovu, a tenant with much credibility as the leader of the Community Policing Forum (CPF) within my fieldwork area. His intervention served to strengthen tremendously my relationship with a whole range of poorer women. After hearing about my intention to do fieldwork in Wards 10 and 11, Aubrey Ndlovu, afraid that as an outsider I might fall prey to criminal elements, set up a public meeting of both men and women in these wards. He introduced me as someone they should get to know, someone who could be used because I had "university knowledge" and someone who should be "protected from criminals". Such an introduction made me set aside my interviewing tasks to become involved in "helping activities" with income-generation possibilities, e.g. gardening, baking, embroidery and candle-making. Spending lengthy periods of time with tenants, however, had the unfortunate effect of complicating my earlier and well-developed relationships with some plot-owners, e.g. Nozizwe Radebe became upset with me and hinted that I had betrayed her trust through associating with tenants. She had also heard through the grapevine that I was involved in "project work" with tenants and could not understand why I did not start similar things with her group. I shall refer to this again in a later section.

The tenant population has become more mobile since 1994. It was common to see a bustling household become an empty mud shell as people simply picked up their belongings and left to move closer to the fringes of town. Many people referred to missing family members who had left fairly recently for shacks nearby in Soshanguve or in town. Some tenants talked about the earlier phases of migration into the area and their fears when they were initially dumped on Winterveld's doorstep, or were forced to seek shelter there having no other place to go to. Dora Mkize (40) [#13] said:

> Tenants came when Lady Selborne was destroyed. We came and stayed next to Boekenhoutfontein. Then we came to Winterveld. We were afraid that the white people would chase us away because we were crowding the place. Then we came here. The cost of living was low. Not like it is now. We used to pay R1 rent when we first came. Plot-owners carried us because the government said so (z).

Interestingly, many tenants whom I interviewed expressed very similar reasons to those of the plot-owners for having come to Winterveld: to be free of restrictions and to begin farming (even though on someone else's land). But they also suggested that relations with plot-owners were changing over time.

In the *Ikageng* group of tenant pensioners, one person said:

> We came in the 1950s. We came here because we thought Winterveld was a nice place. Here we are free. It is open. There were no thugs at first. It was not so hot. There were no problems with plot-owners. Now there are many problems. I am lucky. After the plot-owner, on whose stand we stayed, died, her children did not want to stay here. So they left. Now I live alone on the plot as though it is mine (s).

Two of the women, whom I spent time interviewing, did not find the situation as welcoming. Elsie Mashinini (81) [#7] said:

> I moved to Winterveld in 1974. We moved from the farm to come here. It was cheap here. When we came we were not welcomed. No, we struggled. The plot-owners were difficult. We came with no permits. We had to buy water from another plot. This plot has no water. The plot-owner had a bore-hole, but it was dry and the pump was broken (s).

Thoko Skosana (69) [#2] also said: "We came to Winterveld because we were tired of moving and moving. My husband's brother initiated the move. The whole family came. My husband also came later. I then started working in Pretoria"(s). Her daughter, Martha Sibiya (55) [#2], lived elsewhere but eventually arrived to join the family there. She said: "I followed my parents here. I came here after my husband died. I did not like it. I just came because my parents were here. It is hard to stay because of the hunger. If I did not earn money, I would not know how to survive"(s). For tenants, as in the case of plot-owners, Winterveld, although not offering much in terms of financial security, represented a safe haven - a place of refuge from the turmoil outside.

Living during different times: from Mangope to Mandela

In 1977 Winterveld was forcibly incorporated into a newly independent Bophuthatswana. Prior to this incorporation Winterveld had been officially administered by the South African government (DBSA, 1987:57; Simone, 1998:275; de Clercq, 1994:381). The people living in Winterveld had not been consulted about this shift in administration to the Tswana Bantustan. Most people (both plot-owners and tenants) resident in Winterveld at the time were non-Tswana. In terms of the Bophuthatswana Independence Agreement of 1977 South Africa was to assist in the resettlement of Winterveld's non-Tswana "squatter" population, as well as in the expropriation of land from those land-owners who were not citizens of Bophuthatswana (that is, those unable to gain Tswana classification) if they were unwilling to cooperate with the resettlement initiative (DBSA, 1987:57). In addition to resettlement the South African government undertook to provide Bophuthatswana with R200 million for development planning and projects in Winterveld (Simone, 1998:). In reality, though, resettlement was partially successful and not seriously attempted. Instead of resettlement, Chief Minister Mangope chose to attempt large-scale evictions of non-Tswana from Winterveld before alternative plans could be finalised. By November

1978, 500 people from the Winterveld area were arrested and found guilty of squatting, and thousands of people were evicted. Many then left for the trust farms surrounding Winterveld and the relocation camps in KwaNdebele (since many tenants were Ndebele) (SPP, 1983:317). It was only in the mid- to late 1980s that the areas known as Beirut, Lebanon and Slovoville were built on the outskirts of Winterveld in an attempt to accommodate large numbers of tenants. On the whole, attempts at resettlement were dismal failures. Willie Mogaladi, who was the Chief Executive Officer (CEO) of the Transitional Representative Council (TRC) in 1998, claimed that, having squatted for so long, people just could not live outside Winterveld. "The majority could not cope with township life. I once read that people have coping problems when they leave the informal settlement. Many of those we tried to resettle went back to Winterveld. Then others from elsewhere came and occupied the newly built homes" (e). An additional reason for tenants not clamouring for the newly built homes was the problem of the rent differentials. In 1998 a tenant living in Winterveld would pay from R10 to R50 per month for rent. In the surrounding "townships", the rent was between R120 and R150 a month. In 2008 these rental amounts had barely changed.

Living with the constant threat of arrest in the 1980s forced many tenants (particularly Ndebele) into clandestine and insecure living arrangements. Those times are remembered by most people, including children. A schoolboy in one of my group sessions (*Youth* group) recalled:

I remember in 1985 - 1986 Mangope's police roamed around asking for permits. It was late in the night and they were flashing torches. Both my parents were working in Johannesburg. They knocked at the door shouting "police, police". They were asking to see permits. When we opened the door and said our parents were away they did not believe us. They searched the house and the land outside. They did not arrest us. We were very small then. Our neighbour used to get into trouble every month. He did not have a permit. I think he had to keep bribing them (e).

Elizabeth Mabena (58), a tenant, expressed the irony of living in Winterveld under the Bophuthatswana government. She had come there to escape harassment elsewhere in South Africa and instead she was confronted by worse discrimination than she had ever encountered before. She said:

I came to Winterveld to be independent. I wanted to be in a place where I could live independently with my children. I loved Winterveld. It was good. I was feeling fine to stay with other people. I also found a new job in Pretoria. I could leave my previous sleep-in job and travel daily ... Then during Mangope's time we started to struggle - they used to hound us for our permits. If we did not have them, we went to jail. One day the police came ... They went to my son's room. My son ran away. They did not get him. He had no permit. They did not find me because I was sleeping in the other room (z).

Rosina Mabasa (42) and Bongi Msimang (43) [#5] depended, for their livelihoods, on selling vegetables on the pavement. The Land Control Amendment Act passed in 1983 made it illegal for non-Bophuthatswana citizens or those without permits to occupy land or engage in business activities in Bophuthatswana (de Clercq, 1994:382). Street- vendoring was an offence and vendors could have their goods confiscated and serve a term of imprisonment if found without a permit. Rosina said: "I came to Winterveld after forced removals drove me out of Lady Selborne. I even became a Tswana citizen to avoid police harassment. Still the police were always harassing and coming to check on my citizenship. Luckily, I always had one and didn't go to jail"(s). Bongi said: "I did have a permit. I came to Winterveld because it was close to town. I used to sell vegetables. The police caught me one day. They kicked the box down. They chased me away after checking my permit ... Things are much better now. We are living in peace now"(e). Sometimes when vendors were caught selling without a permit, police would confiscate goods and then accompany the person to her home to see whether more goods were kept there. This was the case with Mama (an elderly women in a group session) who was caught selling liquor. When taken home, she disclosed a refrigerator packed with beers. The Bophuthatswana police confiscated both beer and refrigerator.

Even though the Winterveld Community Authority (WCA) and WPA (comprising only plot-owners) were recognised and favoured by the Bophuthatswana government with which they collaborated, local people did not talk about relations between plot-owners and tenants as being particularly antagonistic during the late 1970s to mid-1980s. In fact, non-Tswana plot-owners had much empathy and much in common with their landless tenants. Khanyi Mabetwa (78) [#4] became a Bophuthatswana citizen after declaring herself to be Ndebele-Tswana. Her tenants, however, with whom she had built a good relationship, were not fortunate enough to gain citizenship and eventually left Winterveld. Khanyi said: "Mangope was very cruel. He chased the tenants away. He wanted them to become Tswanas and be forced into the Tswana population. Yet this was supposed to be private land. We did not want links with tribal land. We now had to live with a chief"(s). Khanyi also talked about an act of brutality that virtually everyone living in Winterveld in the early 1980s remembers: that is, the day the donkeys were killed. At some point around 1982 the Bophuthatswana government blamed the large number of donkeys (kept by many, but mainly by land-owners) for the inability of crops to grow successfully. I have heard some people say that it was believed that once the donkeys ate the grass, the grass did not grow again. This was because of the poison in the donkeys' teeth. Donkeys at this time were essential for transporting water-carriers and for getting around in Winterveld. Khanyi said:

> Mangope killed the donkeys. He called the people and told them to bring their donkeys. He said he was going to stamp them. But they were shot by Malope, the station commander of the police. At the Total Garage where people were selling vegetables and chickens they poured petrol on the chickens and burnt them alive (s).

Chickens were also believed to be affecting the growth of the grass, though to a lesser extent. Emily Mothoa (61), another sympathetic plot-owner, said:

> When Mangope took over this place he did nothing for Winterveld. He was full of discrimination concerning nationality. If you were Ndebele and you went to the offices they would ask: what nationality? If you were Ndebele you could not get an identity document. Only Tswanas could get what they wanted. Even the plot-owners got nothing unless they became Ndebele-Tswana. He expected everyone to become Tswana. Then the other thing which he did which was painful is that he had all the donkeys shot. The invitation came in such a way that people believed that they were to be helped. We were told that the donkeys were to be vaccinated. People went with carts and donkeys. The carts were left outside with the old people. The donkeys were then shot. Lots of children witnessed the killings next to the Community Hall (e).

In 1979 the Winterveld Action Committee (WAC) was initiated by outsiders: the active members were initially from the Pretoria Council of Churches and the Black Sash. In the early to mid-1980s, as local participation in the WAC grew, quite a bit of public attention became focused on Winterveld and the struggles of its people. A Winterveld Tenants' Committee was formed in 1980 but this committee became defunct as it was increasingly shown to be incapable of delivering much to its tenant supporters given the prevailing political climate. The WAC then became the main opposition force promoting the interests of tenants in Winterveld. Surprisingly, hardly anyone today remembers much about the Winterveld Action Committee. What seems to be better remembered is the political activity of the 'comrades' during a brief period of anti-Bophuthatswana campaigning during 1985-1987. Like the day the donkeys were killed, the 26th of March 1986 is a day many people still remember. It was a day when a public meeting was held to denounce Mangope and air the political views of the community. Kehla Nyamakazi explained:

> What happened was that while the meeting was going on Brigadier Malope ordered his police to open fire. Eleven people are known to have died and numerous others injured ... Some time later Malope was found dead. Malope was eliminated by people in the community. No one was arrested for his murder, and none of the injured have ever been compensated for their misfortune (e).

Experiences like these have (over the years) hardened attitudes toward the police in Winterveld. During the time in which I conducted fieldwork there appeared to be very little respect for the law and very little faith in the ability of the present police force to control what was perceived as escalating levels of petty crime. People continued to claim that police were accomplices in corruption and crime. Aubrey Ndlovu's Community Policing Forum (CPF) was an attempt at mobilising local people into becoming directly involved in taking charge of the security of their areas. The CPF, however, worked closely with the local police whose task it was to formally arrest those apprehended by the CPF and to follow up prosecution procedures. Outside of these CPF-police initiatives in my fieldwork area, two other crime-fighting forces were apparent: (1) vigilante-type action was common. If a rumour spread about a criminal deed committed by someone living close by, e.g in the case of child-rape or witchcraft, it was not uncommon for people to gang up and discipline the perpetrator; (2) the leadership of the taxi associations (the "Skoyeya") has assumed a mafia-like control over the area. They do collaborate with the police but local people are turning to them more readily because, I was once told, their disciplinary methods are more violent, and unconventional in the present circumstances.

In the past "Mangope's law" was the common enemy and it was this recognition of a common enemy that made it possible for plot-owners and tenants to engage in common campaigns. Kehla Nyamakazi said: "During the apartheid days we were living together as black people and in peace. Now with the new government we are divided"(e). Kehla Nyamakazi suggested that "the problems really began in 1993 and 1994 when people heard that the new government was coming. Tenants then started organising as tenants. They organised a boycott of rents. There was no need to pay for rents anymore because [the belief was that] all the land was Mandela's land ...". In the ensuing conflict, eight plot-owners' houses were burnt down and marches were now being organised against the WCA. Locals refer to the WCA offices (which as a vestige of the past remains controlled by a small group of plot-owners) simply as "the office". The office is located at the heart of my fieldwork site. It also represented a source of immense tension in the area.

When I first interviewed Kehla Nyamakazi (in August 1998) he said that he felt a sense of disappointment at the deterioration of relations in Winterveld, that he was not a conservative man and that he found himself in a difficult position. He claimed that he supported the new government, was an African National Congress (ANC) member, that he had been harassed and detained during Mangope's time, and that he took the opportunity to work around the system during the days of the old regime to enable tenants to gain their necessary work permits. Problems from his point of view intensified after the local government elections when predominantly young, tenant-councillors were elected to the Transitional Representative Council (TRC). "The TRC is made up only of tenants ... they are now the local government ... but the local government should represent all the people ... we are the land-owners but they have become the bosses". Most plot-owners, however, including Kehla Nyamakazi, did not participate in the elections, believing that it would be unwise to do so because they would be simply outnumbered. Having failed to enter into the democratic processes, plot-owners who were occupying the Winterveld Community Authority (WCA) offices then refused to leave the premises to make way for the implemention of the new local government in Winterveld. Instead, they attempted to fight their way through the Supreme Court. The judge ruled against the WCA, declaring that refusal to leave "the office" would result in a 90-day incarceration of those occupying the premises. Unsatisfied with the court's decision in 1995 the WCA appealed, and attempted to meet government ministers (including Thabo Mbeki); they also raised their case with the Human Rights Commission (HRC). In the interim, the TRC office was set up in nearby Beirut. In the first twelve months that I spent in Winterveld, I noted the growing disappointment of plot-owners as Thabo Mbeki, Darky Africa and other officials made brief appearances in

Winterveld, but excluded appointments with their organisations. This reinforced a closing of ranks amongst the innercircle of plot-owners, who saw themselves as facing an increasingly hostile outside world. In 1999 the fear that their lands would be forcibly taken away or that they will be done down remained fairly strong. Oupa Leshabani said: "We have heard that Winterveld is going to be divided and made into a township. Darky Africa said he is going to build houses here in Winterveld, whether we like it or not. When Africa comes he talks to the tenants. They like to talk to the tenants and not the plot-owners. When are they going to hear what we have to say?"(e).

In early 1999 I learnt that Kehla Nyamakazi had switched his political allegiances to the United Democratic Movement (UDM). Winterveld, which had for years been regarded as a predominantly ANC stronghold, began to see much campaigning in the pre-1999 election period for the UDM. Clearly, the support for the UDM was more of a symbolic gesture of an ardent group of plot-owners in the post-apartheid period to declare their independence and non-collaborative stance with respect to the government of the day. A few months before the election, Kehla Nyamakazi was arrested and spent 90 days in detention. Plot-owners were taken aback by the timing of the arrest, seeing it as politically motivated (because Nyamakazi had been campaiging for the UDM) and not as an attempt to break the plot-owner control of "the office". The period in which Kehla Nyamakazi was in detention was a difficult time for my fieldwork. I had during that stage been spending more time with councillors and with tenants. When I had casually remarked to Elias Monyepao and George Chilowane (who were based at the office) that "it would be nice to interview councillors" I was sharply reminded that "we are fighting with them. If you go there you will not be our friend." Prior to beginning fieldwork I had been keen to adopt an overt approach in order to avoid misunderstandings and to build positive relationships with people whom I was interviewing. In the midst of fieldwork, and in trying to build relationships with people "fighting with each other", my prior conception of fieldwork ethics had to be set aside, as a less public way of interviewing became the norm.

Willie Mogaladi, the TRC's CEO, spoke with frustration and a sense of helplessness about the situation in Winterveld. He said:

> The situation here, between owners and tenants, is one of "haves" and "have-nots". It is giving this government problems. There is no coordinated town planning scheme for Winterveld. We have to get permission from plot-owners to build infrastructure. Ninety per cent of

the land is owned by individuals. People like Kehla Nyamakazi are not committed to development. Some of these plot-owners are stalling the government's buying of plots so that they can sell them eventually at higher prices. Some, though, are willing to sell now (e).

One of the major sources of tension between plot-owners and tenants had been the fact that rents (for many) were no longer being paid. It was well known that many campaigners had been elected as councillors because of the support received from tenants largely because tenants were told that, if voted in, they would no longer have to pay rents. To this Willie, the CEO, said: "In life, those who suffer become the weapons of those in power. People use these poor, illiterate people to get themselves voted in. This is a poor point of democracy." Unlike the plot-owners, tenants do not operate through organisational structures nor do we find leadership with whom tenants can readily identify. In saying this, I have seen growing numbers of tenants come together through the coordinating efforts of the ANC Youth League or on an ad-hoc basis to march or engage in protest activity. Few tenants appear to be clear about the TRC and what it is supposed to do for them. During the time that I was in Winterveld I saw no councillors either set up meetings, or report to the people who had elected them.

The news about Kehla Nyamakazi's arrest spread rapidly throughout my fieldwork area. Since I was preoccupied with interviewing tenant women at the time, I witnessed much jubilation. Mama declared: "It's good that he's now locked up. He was "blocking traffic". Now we are going to see great things happen in Winterveld. We are going to see development"(s). Since the new government came in, the only changes that people claimed to have experienced were the freedom to move around without harassment, an increase in crime and public taps in the streets. In 1999 there were a few demonstrations outside the Rand Water Board (RWB) as tenants demanded water on the plots. As with everything else in Winterveld, permission for water on the plots has to be sought from land-owners. According to an official at the RWB, which is the implementing arm of the Department of Water Affairs and Forestry (DWAF), their new strategy was to appeal to plot-owners on an individual basis rather than work through the resistant leadership of the Winterveld Plot-owners' Association. The RWB official said: "Quite a number of plot-owners are now signing up for water on their plots. Some are resistant on the grounds of rental disputes with tenants. But these are the last kicks of a dying horse. We are telling plot-owners that the connection fee is going to increase. If they want it later it is going to be a lot more expensive"(e). Apart from indications of slow progress with respect to water in streets and yards, there appeared to be no plans for an electricity supply to homes, for basic municipal services and for infrastructural development. If these developments were dependent on the government buying the underdeveloped and under-utilised land from plot-owners, there had by July 1999 been no negotiations in this regard. Ninety days later when Kehla Nyamakazi was released from jail, Winterveld had not seen any attempt by the local government to take over "the office" nor as some had hoped were any "developments" on their way. In 2007, when I again spoke to the same plot-owners about progress with regard to negotiations and township planning, they shrugged their heads in despair. In November 2008 large numbers of tenants and plot-owners joined forces to demonstrate outside the municipal offices to demand the installation of electricity. "We are tired of waiting," many of them cried. "Keep your promises or we will not vote in 2009".

Simone (1998:274) suggests that in 1977 Winterveld was relegated to the status of a "twilight zone" because it was unwanted by both the South African and Bophuthatswana governments. This description, perhaps, is also fairly apt to Winterveld thirty years later. It would seem that it has become convenient to treat Winterveld as a 'problem area' and consequently invest few state funds in building its infrastructure and little time to intervene in its long and difficult dispute. It is against this background of class antagonisms, increasing insecurity and disregard for the law that the social and economic activities of the people living in Winterveld should be understood.

Surviving through multiple sources and dependent relations in Winterveld

Each morning I travelled via Mabopane on the tarred road (the R80 from Pretoria) and entered Winterveld from its southern side (Klippan South and North). My daily routine involved passing through its most densely populated area, locally referred to as Stakaneng (Shanty). It was in Stakaneng that the largest concentration of tenants were either dumped or settled because of its closer proximity to the Pretoria-Witwatersrand-Vereeniging business districts and easier access to public transport. If I arrived at peak hours in the morning I would have to negotiate my way through the buses and taxis that competed for passengers, people pushing wheelbarrows loaded with water containers, and unattended goats that would often rush across the road at inappropriate times. On either side of the road were signs of a declining makeshift "central business district" - mud and tin shops with signs indicating a range of services: car repairs, tyre repairs, dressmaking, hairdressing, taverns, traditional medicine, fresh vegetables and farm chickens. Some competition emerged for these service providers in 1998. A brick-faced, modern-looking (but small) shopping centre was built further down in Klippan. I believe, though, that this centre has not reaped many profits. Not only are the people in Stakaneng particularly poor, but depopulation which has been occurring steadily since the 1994 elections has hit new business ventures in this area particularly hard. A large tenant population lived a crowded existence there since the 1960s and 1970s. It was also there that the rent boycott had been most effective and plot-owner-tenant relations most challenged. (See **Appendix 4** for photographs taken whilst doing fieldwork).

Merafeng, my fieldwork site, however, bypassed most of Klippan and began with an invisible line drawn from Aubrey Ndlovu's "district" on the extreme right-hand side of the tarred road (the area representing the border between Klippan and the 5-morgen plots) and Patience Khutsoane's [#9] house on the extreme left-hand side of the same road. It was through contact with the many poor tenant women in Aubrey Ndlovu's district that I learned of the immense difficulties women faced when living through long periods of unemployment, when food was scarce, and when children were sometimes in jail. It was through Patience's experiences that I also learned of the difficulties which land-owners face when relying on rent-collecting as a source of regular income. Of the 98 houses from which she could collect rent (between R30 to R55 a month) only a small proportion paid her. She failed to evict defaulters for fear of reprisals. Tenants, she claimed, threatened to burn her house down on numerous occasions, and some did not recognise her as the rightful owner since they had originally paid rent to her (now deceased) father-in-law. Patience charged higher prices for rent, because the houses were built by her family, unlike most land-owners who charged R10 a month. For land-owners, who sometimes had as many as three or more families living in separate homes on their plots, the earnings from tenants amounted to (as Elias Monyepao once remarked) "mere donations". The donation served simply to remind all parties who was the boss on the plot. Since these remittances hardly ever enriched the land-owner, most land-owners have had to look to other sources of income for survival.

Further north, toward the 10-morgen plots, the bustle of the urban fringe transforms progressively into more sparsely populated spaces where larger families live, and where the sight of farming activities appeared to be more common. Although farming activities predominated in the northern part of Winterveld, particularly with the growing of mealies, beans, cabbage and spinach, small-scale subsistence farming was also evident in the south. Where people lived close to a source of water, i.e. to a plot-owner's borehole or to a street tap, then producing a good crop was often possible. The Mpilas, a wealthy family in the area, probably had the best farm within my fieldwork site. Manto Mosele [#14] and Sarah Gamede [#14], two life-history participants, are part of this family. The Mpilas invested vast amounts of money into treating the soil, developing an irrigation system and employing labour to get an assortment of different crops growing on their land. They sold both to internal and external markets. Most plot-owners, however, were not actively involved in farming in 1999. For some tenants the lack of water and the resistance of plot-owners to agree to allowing them access to running water on the plots was hindering possible attempts to experiment with cultivating gardens. On the grounds of St. Michael's Church hundreds of poor women, local and Mozambican tenants, had been given gardening plots as part of an experimental self-help gardening scheme. Josina Dlamini [#15], one of the women whose life histories I have attempted to construct, came daily to the church grounds to tend a small patch of garden. The beetroot, beans and spinach on this patch offered her something to consume as a daily meal, but it was often not enough. Water was plentiful on the church property and health services were also available for the women. Gardening for the purpose of individual consumption (on this small scale) still existed, but large-scale farming that was profitable for the owner was very rare in Winterveld.

People in Winterveld earned income mainly through working in formal or informal jobs in the PWV area, rather than through farming activities or through leasing land. For women in Winterveld, most of this income was derived from domestic labour. Not only tenants, but many of the wives and daughters of plot-owners have worked as domestic labourers. In the short survey (WS) conducted on the fieldwork site it was found that about 53% of women were unemployed and 47% were earning money. A qualitative examination of the open-ended question asking women who earned incomes about how they earned incomes showed the overwhelming majority to be involved in domestic work for individual households or companies. Others were involved in selling and hawking activities (e.g. selling vegetables, fruit, clothes and cooldrinks). State pensions also featured as an important source of income for women. Most of this income appeared to be supplementary and was regarded as insufficient in itself as a source for a reasonably good life or as a means to prevent starvation. About 83% of all women interviewed claimed that they survived through support from others (in particular partners, or pensioners) and about 50% had total monthly family incomes in 1999 of less than R800. In June 1999 I interviewed Joanna Chauke and Christina Mathebula, two tenants in Aubrey Ndlovu's district, in an attempt to get them to assist me with a crude estimate of a minimum survival rate ("poverty level") for Winterveld. By then I had already developed a subjective assessment but needed some confirmation of when women see themselves as destitute or in need. Joanna and Christina calculated that they needed R800 a month to pay for rent, food (including mealie-meal), paraffin, candles, school lunch (for children) and taxi fares. In June 1999 I also asked Lucy Dlali (61) [#11], a plot-owner who started receiving a pension fairly recently, about her monthly costs. The monthly survival amount that she estimated was similar, between R700 - R800. In fact, since she started getting a pension, her daughter, whose child she looked after, stopped giving her any money. Lucy said that, if she had to, she could survive on just her pension which amounted to about R520 a month in 1999. Surviving on this amount would imply that she was catering for basic feeding and nothing more.

In 1999 with the movement of predominantly working people to the shacklands of Soshanguve and Mabopane, the Winterveld population was beginning to reflect increasing proportions of aged people, children, and those marginalised by years of unemployment, discrimination and a lack of job skills. In interviews with elderly people it was quite apparent that those who earned pensions could assert much control over what their children and grandchildren did through nurturing a system of monetary rewards and penalties. However, given the meagre amount involved and the harshness of life here, it was not surprising that there were numerous stories about elderly people being abused, kept in captivity, and killed for their pensions. On the whole, those who earned money and remained resident in Winterveld have had to endure much preying upon by neighbours, family and friends who often came to borrow money or a cup of mealie-meal or who arrived without warning to share a meal. Dependence on neighbours was thought to be a source of much bad blood in most parts of the area, resulting in working people shrugging off friendships, and remaining suspicious and on guard when meeting people for the first time. Aside from contact with immediate family members, many women there lived socially isolated existences. Through her fieldwork experience in Winterveld approximately twenty-five years ago, Yawitch (1981:220) suggested:

> It would seem that in Winterveld the fear and insecurity that characterise life, especially in view of the threats of eviction, has in many cases led to the creation of a 'cut-throat' mentality. Women do not trust, speak to or help neighbours - "friends destroy marriages" is a typical response to questions related to the nature of social interaction.

Whilst these responses prevailed in the 1998-2008 period, they were being counteracted, in part, by many efforts of individuals, churches and welfare organisations to instil a community spirit through the formation of a series of groups aimed at income-generation. These groups in Merafeng tended to cut across the divides of age, ethnic identity, plot-owner and tenant, earner and non-earner.

Dudu Mabunda's [#10] home, north of the Dube Centre and past the Winterveld Secondary School, represented the northernmost invisible line of my fieldwork site. Dudu believed that she was simply doing God's work in being part of initiating fourteen clubs largely for elderly people in Winterveld. She worked closely with Elsie Mmola, a social worker, who was fondly remembered for her acts of charity, particularly in being able to bring food parcels on a large scale into the area. This traditional social work approach, whilst providing short-term relief for small numbers of women, created immense long-term difficulties both for Dudu and outsiders like myself. For Dudu the eventual collapsing of the food parcel scheme (which had lasted many years) led to her becoming a lot less popular in the area. As an outsider, I had to constantly deal with expectations by explaining to people at the outset that I was a mere researcher and did not come with donations. Groups such as *Ikageng,* through which I met Thoko Skosana [#2] and Elsie Mashinini [#7], were important instruments through which poorer women could come together to make goods (mats, hats, blankets etc.) for selling. However, they were not able to gain access to outside markets to sell their goods and were becoming over-reliant on relatives and friends to buy things. Such groups, therefore, served mainly as social clubs designed to beat the social isolation of life in Winterveld. The women's group based at "the office" (*Office* group), in which Nozizwe Radebe [#3] was a central member, also set itself tasks to make things to sell, but a lot of these efforts were undermined by leadership fights, and in schemes to gain access to sources of money from government departments specialising in promoting women's small business projects and initiatives. In June 1999 the group was awarded R30 000 for project work from the government. Interestingly, this is one of the most privileged groups in Winterveld, comprising mainly plot-owners.

At the Sisters of Mercy (attached to the Roman Catholic Church) hundreds of women come for help on a regular basis. In addition to providing food and water, the sisters facilitated many projects that required particular and skilled training, e.g. embroidery, knitting, dressmaking, woodwork, paper and glass-making. I met Thandi Ramashala [#8] and Bongi Msimang [#5] when I visited the embroidery group at the Sisters of Mercy. Embroidering cushion covers and outfits involved time-consuming work and the market was not a steady one. Selling was managed by the Soroptimists (a group of women with access to international markets) who marketed their embroidery as far afield as Europe and the United States. Selling also occurred regularly at a few selected local venues. For Thandi the embroidery project had been tremendously helpful in teaching her skills and offering her a source of income - but there had been good seasons and bad seasons and the money was rarely enough for her to support her family. She remained dependent on her husband for financial support. The point here is that groups can play a role in offering women some training and some piecemeal income, in addition to some sense of worth, but are rarely sufficient to decrease their dependence on others who earn regular incomes. One of the spin-offs in becoming part of groups is stokvels (rotating credit associations) that are usually initiated to cushion the effect of hardships should nothing get sold or should goods get sold infrequently. Each month Thandi's group collected twenty rands from thirty-three earners; this meant that about R660 per month found itself in a common pool. Each woman who contributed enjoyed a month in which she could reap some substantial reward: a large cooking pot and other much needed items. Loans for women in dire need were sometimes permitted as long as the group was reasonably convinced that the money would be paid back.

The struggle for survival through piece-jobs and piecemeal, low-reward informal activities opened Winterveld up to organised crime and to acting as a conduit for the storing and distribution of illegal and stolen goods. To some extent the centrality of these unconventional activities to Winterveld's economy can be found by examining years of suffering that people have experienced in evading and being punished by the law.

Aubrey Ndlovu has been central to attempts to restore law and order in Winterveld. In 1999 his CPF was mobilising local men, in particular, into daily patrols of the area and into following up incidents of crime in Merafeng. Having experienced acts of vandalism, housebreaking and theft on a large scale in the recent past, people within my fieldwork site suggest that things improved since the CPF began its activities. At the same time, however, there was not much criticism of engaging in illegal acts that did not appear to harm the local inhabitants much. For example it had been common to hear of people who electrified their homes by tapping into illegal sources of power and who therefore paid no electricity bill to Eskom. Local people also talk of 'most wanted' criminals who had been safely hidden in Winterveld before being eventually caught when they left the area to go elsewhere. Similarly, I often heard numerous justifications for the selling and buying of stolen goods. Clara Molefe [#8], Nozizwe Radebe [#3], Elias Monyepao and Nani Nkomo [#12] all experienced children or relatives being sent to jail during the period of my fieldwork for (some or other) illegal activities. In addition, I watched with great interest as a group of five well-off plot-owners, who were duped by a social worker into giving away thousands of rands to buy second-hand (probably stolen) goods, chose not to go to the police, but to deal with the misappropriation in their own way. These comments are made here only to suggest tolerance of, and particular attitudes towards, contending with issues of petty crime.

In 1998 Simone (1998) suggested that criminal, illicit activities in Winterveld were becoming bigger and more sustained than many other legitimate businesses. Syndicates and gangs had, arguably, become part of the social fabric. My own observation in the course of fieldwork was that, whilst there appeared to be a reliance on theft and illegal activities, this was not altogether replacing efforts at gaining an income through informal sector activities and piece-work. What is apparent is that, as old inhabitants move away, more desperate locals and foreigners from the surrounding states trickle in. Whilst many of them are active in informal sector trading, some are believed to be promoting organised crime. In interviewing a group of Mozambican women who could always be found during the day, I learnt that their husbands who had been previously employed by the Rustenberg mines were now doing 'odd' jobs since becoming unemployed. At first I was told that some of the men were hawking items such as facecloths and radio cassettes. Later I heard it being claimed that some of them had become a lot more resourceful in linking up with smuggling networks.

Locals, together with mine-workers and ex-mine-workers still living in the country, have allegedly established illicit networks to and through Winterveld to local and outside markets. These networks are not new creations and had existed during the apartheid days as well. The thriving status of this field of work was partly due to the freedom of movement which people had begun to enjoy and through the apparent relaxing of border controls. Titus Mphahlele, a key informant, was initiated into illegal diamond-selling in the early 1980s when he was "naive and didn't know what it was all about". He was caught and made wiser through nine years of imprisonment. In 1999 it was speculated that these networks had become a lot more established and embedded.

Irrespective of the scale of smuggling and illicit forms of trading, what seemed clear was that these activities were a predominantly male-controlled and managed set of activities. Women in Winterveld played supplementary and marginal roles in this highly skilled and dangerous work. They benefited as wives and girlfriends. At the same time, the dependence on men often meant that they bore the brunt of aggressive and abusive behaviour at the hands of men who lived on the edge, and who endured high risks in the course of their varied activities. Many women have learnt to endure abuse, rape and subordination and consequently live with the stress of keeping many secrets.

With depopulation affecting the business of shops in Winterveld, many of these small-time entrepreneurs have succumbed to buying stolen goods, and using their premises as operating bases for illicit activities. These activities are often pursued under the watchful eyes of the local police, who, for their part, sometimes extract levies. Zimbabweans, in particular, are familiar with police efforts to extract levies over the years. In one of my earliest introductions to how people who wished to find work have had to contend with corrupt and unconventional practices, I was told by Mary Mafete, a Zimbabwean living illegally in South Africa, about how some businesses employed mainly Zimbabweans and made them work "on the fields" as a large contingent, offering to pay them when the job was done at the end of the month. She had once worked as part of such a labour force. When the end of the month had come "the businessman" packed them off into a van and drove somewhere, saying that they were going to get their wages. Somehow, they were intercepted by the police and all arrested because they were illegals and their documents were not in order. The "businessman" then had to "bail them out". Eventually they found themselves released from jail but were neither instructed to leave South

Africa nor dumped at the border post. Although it was obvious that they had been duped by a collaborative scheme in which the police were involved, they were grateful to be released and not sent back home. The fact that they were not paid was therefore not a big issue. The significance of this is that the newer residents who today make up a noticeable proportion of Winterveld, and who are often ostracised for taking jobs of established inhabitants at less pay, are sometimes led, through poor treatment and exploitation, into a wide variety of illegal activities.

On 8 February 1999 I heard on the (morning) radio news that 500 troops (the combined forces of the Gauteng and North West Province crime-fighting units) had been deployed in the areas surrounding Soshanguve including Winterveld, Mabopane and Hammanskraal. I decided not to go to Winterveld that day. In the evening of 9 February the *Pretoria News* reported that over R1.5 million worth of stolen goods had been recovered and a large number of possibly stolen vehicles confiscated. When I drove into Winterveld the following day (on 10 February), it resembled a ghost-town. Instead of the usual bustling of taxis, there were very few on the road. Except for some people waiting for buses, others seemed to keep away from the main road. Clearly, many of the taxis on the road had been stolen or were taxis without legitimate licences. People had many stories to tell, and were highly excited about what had happened during the previous days. Drivers had attempted to hide taxis in the bushes, under the trees and some even abandoned them on vacant plots, but these were detected by the spotter helicopters which were used in this highly sophisticated raid. However, since buying vehicles and stolen goods was not an uncommon way of furthering business there, partly because it was much cheaper, it is not unreasonable to assume that the taxis which reappeared a week or so later were replacements, again stolen from other areas or bought through illicit and increasingly profitable markets.

I became aware of just how powerful a hold the taxi association had over the activities in Winterveld when a young woman whom I had interviewed in a group session was placed under "house arrest" by the Skoyeya after two of her previous boyfriends (both taxi-drivers) had been shot dead. The taxi association wanted to establish whether she was part of a conspiracy to have them killed. She remained under guard at her home for about a month until they were satisfied that she was not involved in the two deaths. During this time the police did not interfere in the taxi association's investigations. Rivalry between different taxi associations, often resulting in shoot-outs, around Soshanguve, in particular, was a common occurrence in the late 1990s to early 2000s. Winterveld taxis use the Mabopane station as a depot. It is also a place from which owners and drivers operate secondary trades. The most profitable of these trades are liquor trading and prostitution (Simone, 1998). In this environment, where men determine the terms and nature of trading, young girls who are recruited as sex workers have little control over clientele and rates of pay. The fact that women engage in a wide range of survival activities simultaneously, that some of these are obvious and some are hidden, and that the struggle for resources leads them into a range of unstable and dependent relationships, serves to hint at the complexities involved in studying and learning about all the facets of their lives.

In the aftermath of completing my PhD in 2001, I have continued visiting the area, engaging in and recording conversations and investigating in greater detail specific and changing phenomena. Since 2002, I have found opportunities to interview men and to draw out more detail on their practices and dilemmas. Six women from the fifteen families originally studied have died of AIDS-related illnesses in the space of the last six years. Since 2003 child grants have become noticeably a feature of the larger scheme of survival strategies of young women and their families. Chapter 6 will address this in greater detail.

Difficulties of the qualitative approach in studying women's experiences

Learning about the social and historical experiences of women, through hearing their stories and witnessing the drudgery and turmoil of everyday life, has been an absorbing fieldwork task. It has been, however, not as intense as attempting to learn about issues surrounding sexual and reproductive behaviours which for most people are intrinsically private matters, for example, whether a woman continues to have a sexual relationship with her husband, whether they have other sexual partners, and what variety of methods she might use to prevent a pregnancy or conceive a child. Normally, it was only after engaging someone about the general context, the things that had happened in the past, and about her present circumstances, that I would develop the confidence to probe the other more personal matters. Most often, younger women were freer in conversation with me whilst older women tended to be more cautious, revealing matters little by little in different interviews. On the whole, though, I found my outsider and university status very helpful in my relationships with women. I believe that it made them happier about telling me things because they regarded me as no threat to them. A lot of detail was also often offered in the hope that I would be able to offer advice on family and marital dilemmas. Sometimes, when personal issues were being discussed, a woman would suggest that Pumla (my interpreter, and an "insider") should excuse herself so that she did not hear what was being said.

Talking about their lives was not an easy experience for most women. Living with much secrecy, abuse and poverty usually meant that the process of "unpacking" became an increasingly emotional one from which we had to take many breaks. On one occasion, Louisa Makgoba [#4], with whom I had built a fairly good relationship, overwhelmed me with a calm disclosure of intimate details of her life and relationships. When I went to see her again, though, she was in a highly emotional state. The enormity of what she had done had sunk in, and depressed her. She said, "you have made me open up things in my head that I had blacked out for many years. You have made me remember what a pathetic, terrible state I am in"(e). It was months after that before Louisa could speak to me again. Similarly, Kebone (Dudu Mabunda's daughter) [#10], a woman who has never had children and who now considers herself to be infertile, talked openly about herself, her marriage and her fears. Given the necessarily "open" nature of life history interviewing, Kebone offered details of her marriage which I had not deliberately probed. Days later, I was prevented from seeing Kebone again because she had become very ill. Kebone's husband insinuated that I had "done something to her" because she was suffering from enormous stress. He added that if I wanted to see her again I should first visit the police and make a statement. Instead, I explained myself to Dudu Mabunda, who had harsh words for her son-in-law's suggestions of "bewitchment", and who helped me rebuild my relationship with Kebone. The point here (which I do not believe is a simple one) is that recording women's histories, in an effort to learn about the many issues and events that affect their lives, requires much determination through numerous visits. It requires anticipating different reactions and spending more time with the women interviewed, especially after they have revealed something painful. When fieldworkers "extract" a (sensitive) story and then leave a fieldwork area (as most qualitative researchers eventually have to do) they often, I am sure, leave the women they have probed with feelings of having been violated. Before leaving my fieldwork site I had to spend extra time with women whom I had interviewed, assuring them of confidentiality, informing them about how I would use their stories and telling them that I would visit them again. With respect to Nozizwe Radebe, I had to take special care to address her distress as well as her fears that I could tell others (especially the tenants) her many stories. In addition, I had to explain the necessity of interviewing "all kinds of women" for my research. In the end, I feel convinced that she was certain that I would not be part of intentionally engaging in actions to make her "lose face in the community." In saying this, I must emphasise that not all women displayed anxieties (during or after the interviews) in relating their life histories. I was told by some, particularly the poorest of women (in Aubrey Ndlovu's area), that they felt good and important to think that what they had to say could teach other people about women's experiences in Winterveld. Nonetheless, I have become more aware now of the different ways in which fieldwork can be conducted, and the problems which invariably arise as misunderstandings and sensitivities come to the fore.

For me, the recognition that women tend not to discuss matters of a (remotely) personal nature with friends and neighbours offered a partial explanation why focus groups became immensely difficult. A focus group designed to give further content to community practices like breast-feeding or contraceptive use faces two main difficulties: (1) the "community" here is a formation reflecting disparate groups and interests and, whilst groups could be useful in drawing out contrasting practices, in practice they often do not. This is because (2) there is an unwillingness on the part of women to discuss individual or "group" practices that have to do with sex or child-bearing in front of others who could use this information against them at some later stage. A focus group intended to pick out aspects of fertility behaviour would never have worked if wealthier and poorer, and old and young were all drawn together in discussion. Even attempts to keep interest groups separate, e.g. a small group of tenants, a small group of pensioners etc., proved to be difficult exercises in learning about child-bearing and reproductive practices. Attempts to divert questions away from themselves to what they know "about the general" were equally difficult, e.g. "do women in this part of Winterveld make use of contraception?" Questions aimed at understanding the "community" were often met with answers such as "we don't know what other women do." In some of the groups, however, women were forthcoming about circumstances around giving birth, about how many children they had had, about whether they had used contraception and about marriage problems. Parts of this were offered in attempts to entertain and humour me, with many meaningful facets of experiences remaining carefully hidden. To add to the difficulties, I was often confronted by women (when the group-interview was over) who would explain that they could not say much because they feared someone in the group would relate their comments to their families or their husbands. They would ask, instead, to talk to me privately. However, if questions such as "what are some of the problems faced by the community?" or "what happened during the days under the Mangope government?" were asked, conversation was very forthcoming. People could talk openly about the lack of water, the poverty, unemployment and all kinds of struggles experienced in the area. They could also reflect on common experiences in the past. "Focus" groups then became more useful as exploratory group sessions, and of value in learning about the history and broader social experiences of people within my fieldwork site.

I have learnt, in the course of fieldwork in Winterveld, that as valuable as a qualitative methodology is for South African fertility research, it becomes considerably more complicated the longer one remains in the field. Some authors might remind researchers about not becoming "overfamiliar" with research subjects - but it is difficult to invite discussions on deeply private matters for months and even years and still maintain a "critical distance" (Mies, 1993). It is also difficult to remain outside area disputes and family fights if the people you are interviewing are caught up in such difficulties. Yet a long period of involvement with women and their families is what is required if we are to make sense of the many factors shaping social and reproductive behaviour in these small settings. Thus, in an "unsettled" area like Winterveld, where people have for years devised ways of evading, misleading and manipulating outsiders (and insiders), shorter-term attempts at doing fieldwork, or using ethnographic methods simply to enhance the data quality of surveys, can produce little more than that of a one-off survey. To obtain a fuller picture of life and reproduction in Winterveld requires persistence and patience in getting to know people, sensitivity in working through their stories and an understanding that the interviews will never be completely over, nor the "complete stories" ever known.

Conclusion

Winterveld's identity has shifted over the years: it has been described historically as prosperous freehold territory, a settlement of mixed fortunes, and later an area exhibiting pervasive poverty, class tensions and high levels of unemployment. Increasing marginalisation and various struggles endured under different regimes have led the people living in Winterveld to adopt many different survival strategies and modes of life. Poverty has structured a socio-cultural context in which a sense of "community" is lacking and where social co-operation is most often dependent on reciprocal gains and compensation. Women in this social environment are the most vulnerable to the stresses of economic hardship and thus often live insecure and relatively secretive existences. Part of the purpose of this chapter has been to reflect on the methods used to study life experiences in this area, and to suggest that the process of constructing the stories of the many sides of women's lives is a difficult and challenging process. A more detailed discussion of the appropriateness of qualitative methods for fertility research in South Africa will be the subject of Chapter 7.

Chapter 4

EARLY PREGNANCIES: EFFECT OF SCHOOL, POVERTY AND THE DOMESTIC ENVIRONMENT

Introductory Comment

In this chapter, I examine the occurrence of early pregnancy in Merafeng. I refer to 'early' pregnancies rather than 'premarital' pregnancies largely because 'marriage' has become increasingly difficult to define both in the Winterveld and broader South African context. Apart from the fact that a variety of definitions of 'marriage' and 'union' co-exist, many women, of all ages, continue to bear and rear children outside the confines of a stable partnership. The continued use of the concept 'premarital' is misleading in that it presumes that never-married women will eventually marry. Thus, the term early pregnancy instead of premarital pregnancy is preferred because it is an all-encompassing one (that includes premarital, planned and unplanned pregnancies). My intention in this chapter is to offer some insight into the early experiences of young women, most of whom are teenage schoolgirls, who face possibilities of unplanned, unanticipated births. Some schoolgirls who will be referred to are in their twenties, and not all the teenagers are unmarried or attend school.

The first aim of this chapter is to consider the dual role of schooling: that is, as a context which both facilitates and delays early pregnancies. The second aim is to examine the constraints of the domestic environment and their consequences for early fertility. In other words, this chapter illustrates some of the difficulties and pressures which schoolgirls and young women have to contend with in their daily lives, and the way in which these may relate to immediate and longer-term child-bearing decisions.

The 'premarital' pregnancy pattern

Any review of contemporary literature on young women's fertility will reveal much concern about exposure to sexual and reproductive health risks and infections (see e.g. Mfono, 1998, Creel & Perry, 2003, Burgard, 2004). In my group sessions (*Youth* group) there was often much uninhibited talk about sexual relationships, romantic liaisons and about young women's encounters with many different partners. At the same time, concerns about the consequences of unprotected sexual experiences for the spread of STDs and HIV/AIDS were also expressed. Rather than HIV/AIDS, the more talked-about concern during my fieldwork in Winterveld, however, was the fact that much of this early experimentation results in an unwanted pregnancy which interrupts a girl's schooling and adds to the family's burden. In her study of teenage fertility, Preston-Whyte (1990) suggested that, although unplanned, the early pregnancy is often accepted albeit with some resignation by the family, and the child is integrated into and supported by the girl's household and/or network of relatives. This is often the case in Winterveld as well.

Recent reports argue that in many African societies the process of getting married is being delayed by (amongst other factors) the need to complete more years of schooling, and increasingly urban lifestyles (Meekers, 1994:47). This delay in marriage, however, has not inhibited early initiation into sexual activity. Engagement in sexual relations at youthful ages has given rise to high levels of 'premarital' fertility particularly in southern Africa. Garenne and Halifax (1999) suggest that one-third of total fertility in southern Africa is made up of premarital births. They also suggest that high levels of early premarital births have created two peaks (modes) in age-specific fertility rate (ASFR) values. One peak is centred on ages 18-20 years (predominantly premarital fertility) and the other on 28-30 years (predominantly marital fertility). High levels of premarital child-bearing appear to be followed by a period in which fertility declines significantly. Garenne and Halifax have referred to the prevalence of these two peaks as unusual and difficult to explain (see as well Dickson, 2002).

Caldwell (1992:216-217) suggests that, if much of this premarital fertility is unwanted, then an increasing demand for fertility control by young, unmarried women could serve as an important engine of fertility transition. If, on the other hand, it can be shown that teenage girls desire early pregnancies, and have little regard for marriage or contraceptive use, then we can expect to see these high levels of premarital fertility sustained over time. Although these rates are now declining, statistics show that teenage and 'premarital' pregnancies in South Africa remain fairly substantial. The 1987-1989 SADHS shows that about 50% of women aged 25-34 years reported having first given birth when they were teenagers (Du Plessis et al., 1996). The 1998 South African Demographic and Health Survey reveals that 35% of all teenagers interviewed had been pregnant or had given birth to a child by the age of 19 years. By 2003, the proportion of teenagers 'ever pregnant' had dropped to 27%. An indication of the percentage of teenagers or adolescents in the different provinces who were mothers or who had been pregnant is presented in Table 8. Adolescents in both the 1998 and 2003 reports are defined as girls between the ages of 15 and 19 years.

At the time of my research Winterveld was regarded as a part of the North-West Province, which seems to have a slightly lower teenage pregnancy rate than that of most other provinces. Although these provincial estimates are comparatively low, within Merafeng strong concerns about the rate of teenage pregnancy were often expressed.

Explanations for the incidence of early fertility

In Merafeng there were frequent references to the problem of young girls becoming pregnant, as the following comment from a group session (*Ndlovu's* group) illustrated:

> Today, girls fall pregnant early. Mostly in standard 8 [10th year of schooling]. Some can be pregnant in standard 5. Middle School is the dangerous time. Many fall pregnant at 16, 15, 14 years. Girls sometimes even fall pregnant at 12 years. Guidance counsellors come to school. They come to talk to teenagers mainly at the time they start menstruating or when there are changes in the body. They speak to both boys and girls. But it does not seem that these teenagers take this advice seriously. Maybe they are serious in those few minutes when spoken to. After 2 to 3 months some of them are already pregnant (e).

The survey that I conducted was not stratified to allow for a sizeable representation of all age groups. Most often the more senior and most available female member of the household was interviewed. *Only nineteen* women from 15 to 20 years were included in the sample. Although this number is far too small for the purpose of generalising it may be of interest to note that ten of these young women were already mothers. Eight had one child each, whilst one had two children and another woman of 19 years had three children already. Seven of the women were "in unions", and sixteen were using modern contraception. Of the total sample of 293 women 55% had had their first child as a teenager.

What explanations are there for high levels of early pregnancies? Meekers (1994:48) states that two hypotheses are usually offered in explaining high rates of premarital sexual activity and reproduction. The *first* and more common hypothesis is that premarital fertility is due to an erosion of traditional controls and norms. In other words, sexual activity of teenagers is no longer under the scrutiny and guidance of families and kin. Family and community life have become unsettled by the effects of wider societal disorganisation and teenage sexuality and rates of premarital pregnancy reflect this state of affairs. There appears to be evidence to support this hypothesis. In Preston-Whyte's (1990) qualitative examination of teenage fertility in South Africa she cites cases of peer pressure, an increasing tendency for engaging in full intercourse, rather than external intercourse which was previously the norm, and ultimately the diminution of controls over teenage sexuality in the urban areas. She suggests that "parents and even teenagers themselves often comment that there is little to control young people 'these days' and that particularly in the town 'they do what they like'"(Preston-Whyte, 1990:81). To this we could add much dissatisfaction commonly expressed about the ability of schools to sustain "controls" and influence changes in the sexual behaviour of schoolchildren. Unhappy comments were frequently heard in Winterveld. An elderly person in a group session (*Ikageng* group) suggested the following:

> Relations between young and old are not the same as before. They don't listen anymore. Not like elder ones before. Teenage pregnancy is high because of the looseness of the younger ones. They tell you it's now their time. There used to be a distance between older people and younger ones before. When elder people used to meet children used to play a distance away. Now they hang around their parents. They want to be like adults. They tell you about sex education because they're learning it at school (s).

The social disorganisation hypothesis raises opposing and gendered questions on adolescent sexuality and pregnancy. In its original formulation, this hypothesis raises the question of 'lack of control' over early sexual activity or the "looseness of the younger ones" (both boys and girls) as the cause of unwanted early births. Social disorganisation arguments can also be used, however, to focus on a growing occurrence in South Africa and in Winterveld - that of the risk of early pregnancy for girls arising out of coercive sex and sexual abuse (Wood & Jewkes, 1997). Meekers does not look at this aspect. A qualitative attempt to address the relevance of social disorganisation arguments will have to look at the prevalence and consequences of these experiences for schoolgirls.

The *second* and alternative hypothesis offered by Meekers (1994:48) is that teenage sexual relations and pregnancy can be seen in terms of attempts by teenagers to attain particular objectives. Specifically, if teenage girls are engaging in sex with men for money or because they believe it would lead to marriage, then it cannot be argued that this behaviour is confined to an irrational or careless stage of adolescence. Further, if young women do not anticipate marriage but desire children because of the social status afforded to motherhood, then an early pregnancy cannot be categorised as unplanned or unwanted. According to this view early sexual experiences that result in high levels of pregnancy are a consequence of deliberate and rational decision-making. Meekers' (1994) view is that there is possibly greater support for the social disorganisation hypothesis than there is for an argument that early pregnancies result from "rational" behaviour. The fact that schoolgirls have sex with men for money and gifts has emerged as a constant theme in my Merafeng interviews (akin to the findings of Hunter, 2002, 2007). This aspect will be elaborated on when reference to the narratives that reflect on the sexual behaviour and motivations of teenagers will be made.

The role of education in shaping early fertility

The curious fact that school attendance is argued to be one of the strongest factors contributing to the delay of marriage, but at the same time provides a context in which sexual activity is common and the risk of pregnancy is high, implies that it is important to take special note of the socialising functions of the school and its role in facilitating and preventing early, and often unplanned births.

Demographers regularly examine the relationship between education and fertility with the aid of the analytical framework popularised by Easterlin and Crimmins. In Easterlin and Crimmins's (1985:13) attempt to seek out what causes the shift from a natural fertility regime to one characterised by deliberate control, they link core variables, that is, demand, supply and regulation, to proximate determinants of fertility and fertility behaviour. The framework presented on the following page is an adaptation of the Easterlin and Crimmins (1985) model, teased out to take account of Greenhalgh's cultural and political economy thesis to produce "whole demographies".

Figure 1: How proximate determinants shape fertility behaviour

Factors -----	Supply of births -----	Fertility in...
Economic	Entry into marriage	Particular social context
	Breast-feeding	(Peri-urban area)
Political	Post-partum amenorrhoea	
	Post-partum abstinence	
<u>**Educational**</u>	Child mortality	
Cultural	Demand for children --------	
Historical	Preference for sons or daughters	
	Support by sons in childhood	
Health	Support by daughters in childhood	
	Expected support by children in future	
Gender relationships	Costs of children	
	Economic self-reliance	
Communal relationships	Desired family size	
Kin relationships	Costs of regulation -----	
	Contraceptive prevalence	
	Duration of use	
	Attitudes of others, self	
	Interspousal communication	

Source: Adapted Easterlin and Crimmins, 1985

The following generalisations are made with respect to how education works through supply, demand and regulation factors. Higher levels of education could firstly increase the *supply* of births through the weakening of cultural practices that serve to reduce fertility (such as prolonged breast-feeding and post-partum sexual abstinence). Women's education could also increase knowledge about nutrition and health care, resulting in increased fecundity, fewer spontaneous foetal deaths and lower levels of child mortality. In the long run, however, more years of schooling are more strongly associated with smaller numbers of children ever-born through delays in marriage and consequently (in theory) the shortening of the period of exposure to pregnancy (UN, 1995:24-25).

Higher levels of education could also affect the *demand* for children. Woman with more education tend to desire smaller family sizes. The desire for a smaller family size is argued as linked to a re-orientation in the thinking and values of women which higher levels of education are supposed to influence. Education thus makes qualitative changes in the mind-sets of women. Child-bearing is no longer required to improve a woman's social position in the society. Other factors such as access to better employment and entry into power-holding institutions are of greater importance in enhancing a woman's status than are larger numbers of children. Thus, educated women might prefer to have fewer children and invest more resources in child-care and children's education (UN, 1995:15). Educated women are assumed to be more economically independent and will therefore not rely on large numbers of children as security in later life.

With respect to *regulation*, educated women are regarded as being more aware of and more willing to use contraception to actively control fertility (UN, 1995:25). Thus, although educated women are less likely to breast-feed for long periods or practise post-partum sexual abstinence, the erosion of these natural protective measures is usually more than compensated for by an increase in the use of contraception.

This analytical framework, with its emphasis on examining the interplay between supply and demand factors, has been fairly standard in establishing macro-level, comparative education-fertility trends in various social contexts. In South Africa explorations of the education-fertility relationship show that education plays an important part in depressing levels of fertility. In the 1970s, Lotter (1975:23) used the 1974 (South African DHS-type) survey to show that differences in fertility existed among women who had attained different levels of schooling. He maintained that these differences existed at every age in urban areas (where among 40-44-year-old women those with 9+ years of schooling had 1.1 fewer children than the less educated), and at younger ages in rural areas. In the 1987-1989 SADHS it was found that higher levels of education were leading to gradual reductions in women's fertility. The somewhat unchanged category was the continuing high rate of teenage pregnancies, irrespective of level of schooling. Although relatively recent survey results continue to show that increasing levels of education act to reduce fertility, contradictory results have been found in some provinces. Parts of the eastern Free State, Mpumalanga, KwaZulu-Natal and the Northern Province have been shown to be high fertility areas which also have higher than average levels of education (Mostert & Hofmeyer, 1997).

Since 1979 when Susan Cochrane drew attention to the complexities surrounding the link between educational levels and fertility outcomes, there has been greater emphasis on attempting to understand better the nature of the education-fertility relationship through an examination of surrounding socio-economic and cultural factors (UN, 1995). Micro-level studies which illuminate the variety of factors moulding the education-fertility relationship have grown in significance. In addition the emphasis on levels of education and quantity of schooling has also invited questions on the quality of schooling and the usefulness of cross-national comparisons which do not take account of this factor. Schools may differ considerably in terms of where they are, and what and how they teach. On the more technical side, the quality of education within schooling systems is dependent on facilities available for study, the training and application of teachers to their teaching tasks, and the quality of the study material. Here, too, we need to distinguish between the more explicit elements of the formal curriculum and "the informal curriculum" of schools. The informal curriculum refers to the indirect learning that takes place within schools, e.g. about gender expectations and forms of interaction, about power differentials and hierarchies within the classroom, and about sexual behaviour etc., all of which are integral to formative experiences shaping the values and personal development of adolescent schoolchildren.

Increasing levels and amounts of education have been consistently linked to higher status, empowerment and improved abilities of women to make independent reproductive decisions (Caldwell, 1982). Whilst Caldwell linked women's education to egalitarian family structures and low fertility, others such as Handwerker (1991) have drawn closer attention to the rather insignificant role of education in environments where employment opportunities are minimal. Conversely, Handwerker's research (on West Indian fertility) shows that, where employment opportunities exist, women are able to free themselves from dependence on men, have fewer children and experience less domestic violence.

The effects of schooling in Merafeng, Winterveld

The historical and social context

When I first started fieldwork in July 1998 I was warmly incorporated into the women's circles in which the elite of the area, predominantly plot-owners, participated. At the helm of these groups were retired school principals, school teachers and - as I was constantly reminded - "the more learned". My attempts to make contact with tenants, poorer and "less learned" women were constantly thwarted by comments such as "what can they tell you about Winterveld?" When opportunities to interview poorer women arose I would be reminded by them as well that they "did not know all the answers" and that I would benefit more from speaking to those "who had been to school". Being recognised as having completed high school is an important component in building one's esteem in the area. Although there is some coincidence between property ownership and educational achievements, the fact that schools today are open to all suggests (for some of the people that I've spoken to) that opportunities exist to improve one's lot in life. For the very poor a high-school education is usually welcomed as a possible route towards obtaining employment and having a better life away from the squalor and misery. Although unemployment amongst school-leavers has remained very high in the 1998-2008 period, there is still much faith placed in the value of schooling by both young and old. The life histories reveal many regrets of those women who dropped out of school prematurely and who consequently blame themselves for their impoverished circumstances. There are also increasing expectations expressed by schoolchildren who believe that job opportunities will have become available by the time they complete their schooling.

When older people in Winterveld who are familiar with its very early history talk about changes over the years, they almost always refer to the way in which the plot-owners invested their time and effort to build the schools. When the first landowners arrived between the 1930s and 1950s they were faced with having to build their homes, community centres, churches, shops and schools. Winterveld had previously been a cattle-grazing territory and thus was a place without any infrastructure. Much collaboration was needed amongst plot-owners, as well as discussions with government departments, in order to begin to co-ordinate the construction of community buildings and centres on communal land.

Locals refer to the important role of Paulina Dube, who took the initiative in establishing the first school under a tree. In 1951-1952, when the number of schoolchildren attending classes grew larger, Paulina and others gained permission to use the premises of the Dutch Reformed Church (DRC). Schooling took place on these premises until the first formal primary school was built in 1953. Merafeng Primary School[1] was built by Winterveld's landlords, who undertook the building and construction work themselves, and who raised funds for operating the schools from government and private sources. Teachers were also drawn initially from the local community. There is much pride expressed in the resilience of the early teachers, especially in the way they soldiered on despite not being paid, and in their commitment to teaching standards.

95

When Merafeng Primary School was built in 1953 Winterveld was a sparsely populated rural-like area. For the reasons outlined in Chapter 3, within 10-15 years of Merafeng being built, an unprecedented and massive population increase followed. A few more community schools were built offering multilingual language instruction. The difficulties for multi-lingual language instruction arose during Bophuthatswana's administration of Winterveld. Before being incorporated into Bophuthatswana the schools in Winterveld taught Zulu, Northern and Southern Sotho, and Tsonga. Under the administrative control of the Bophuthatswana Department of Education only Tswana, English and Afrikaans were permitted in the schools. Non-Tswana-speaking residents responded to this exclusion in the following ways: either they sent their children to schools outside Winterveld, or they removed their children from the schools altogether, or sent them to one of the 14 'private' unregistered schools (which catered for Zulu and Tsonga- speakers) that emerged over the period from 1977 to 1992 (Fleish et al., 1993:3-6). Just as the plot-owners had set up schools in the 1950s, in the 1970s to early 1990s a predominantly tenant initiative saw the establishment of private schools in response to a hostile political environment.

In 1983 the National Building Research Institute (NBRI) undertook a study of Winterveld's educational facilities. They found that 33.5% of Winterveld's population or 41,334 people were of school-going age. Of this figure, some 24,180 (58,5%) were at school, implying that a substantial proportion of the youth, viz. 41.5%, had dropped out at varying levels, or had received no formal education at all. Of the 24,180 children in schools, 15,674 attended formal state schools whilst 4,027 attended private schools. In the survey (WS) I did not distinguish between state and private schools. Clearly, though, this raises the difficulty of comparing level and quality of education. Although offering schoolchildren the chance to learn in their mother tongues, private schools have never been seen as a suitable alternative to state schools. Enormous problems arose in the post-1992 period when these schools were closed down and children were re-integrated into the state schools. Many of these children were required to repeat years of schooling in order to match the standard of the state schools. As Peter Mashaba, the principal of Manamelong School, said, "Private schools have let us down. They did not have qualified teachers. These were unrecognised schools. They did not teach as the syllabus demanded. Re-integration is a problem because some of these children just can't cope"(e).

Schooling today, as in the past, remains staggered in that it is not a smooth continuous upgrading from one level to the next. Besides the difficulties associated with setbacks due to changing schools, a fair section of pupils continue to begin schooling late, often drop out due to financial reasons or failure, and re-enter schools a year or so later. In 2007, focus group discussions reaffirmed the continuing problem of high drop-out rates and about the disorderly state of schools (*Youth Group* 2). Pregnancy is an added reason for girls dropping out and returning even three or more years later. The reference, thus, to school-going youth as teenagers or adolescents is problematic. Classrooms incorporate different age groups particularly at high-school level where a senior class could range from pupils as young as 16 years to as old as 25 years. It is therefore useful to discuss the experiences of schoolchildren with this range in mind.

Garenne and Halifax (1999) suggest that the risk of pregnancy is highest when girls are in high school. What is it about the high-school social environment that can be seen to be conducive to increasing risks to pregnancy? *Four themes* emerge from the responses of schoolgirls interviewed within my fieldwork site.

Theme 1: The first and most obvious cause appears to be peer pressure. Schoolgirls talk about being taunted by friends to have a boyfriend. As one commented: "They say that guy loves you. Then I go out with him. Then I get pregnant. Then they laugh at me"(e). The problem of sexually mature pupils interacting in the classroom with younger adolescents also means that there are ample opportunities for schoolgirls to be "proposed" and initiated into sexual activity at much younger ages. It would, however, be a misrepresentation to reduce the sexual activity of girls to peer pressure only. Given the absence of, for example, social clubs and recreational events, schools are the primary meeting places where boys and girls from the area get to know each other over extended periods of time. The risk of pregnancy through relationships started at school is understandably high. As an example, Nompumelelo Nkomo (22) was breast-feeding an 8-month-old child when I first met her. She had dropped out of school at 21 years. Her boyfriend (23) was in the same class. They had been dating for 4 years. She had used contraception all along but stopped when she developed an allergic reaction to the injection. It was then that the "accident" occurred. Two observations are important here: (1) Nompumelelo and her boyfriend, although still at school, were fairly mature at the time of the pregnancy, and (2) despite an appearance of carelessness she had been taking precautions to prevent conception.

Theme 2: A related cause identified by both teenagers and health officials in the early period of fieldwork was the lack of adequate sex education and guidance. It was also suggested that initiation schools, that is, informal schools run by elders or community members, which played some part in the past in teaching adolescents about expected sexual behaviour, had been marginalised. By 2008, both these 'causes' had changed somewhat: there was more confidence in life skills training offered by the schools and initiation schools were making their presence felt, albeit in notorious ways. However, it was lamented that very little about sex is learnt in the home (see Whitaker et al., 1999, Indongo, 2007). Instead, the school represents the context for learning about sex (both through the formal and informal curricula). Having a boyfriend means (I have been told) having sexual relations. Refusal to have sex with your boyfriend is interpreted as meaning that you are having sex with someone else. The expectations that go with this often blur the lines between coercive and non-coercive sex. In a group session (*Youth* group 1) schoolgirls suggested the following as the most important answers to teenage pregnancy: it is about "better advice and self-knowledge".

Theme 3: Ironically, a further cause of teenage pregnancy is the way in which the school has responded to reduce these pregnancies. Since it is generally held that teenage romance entails sexual intercourse, sex education in the schools has become synonymous with "prevention" or contraceptive advice. The guidance counsellor makes available condoms for boys and a mobile of the Planned Parenthood Assocation used to make its rounds to the schools offering condoms, advising girls to go to the clinics, and examining and treating STDs. The mobile does not do its rounds in 2008 and most girls go to public clinics. The clinics however vary in the way they offer contraceptives, in the form of either the injection or the pill. Whilst there is little hesitation in offering contraception even to under-age girls, some clinics advise girls to have a baby first, and then consider contraception to prevent a further pregnancy. However, the fact that there are many girls who fall pregnant while "on contraception" suggests ineffective and inconsistent use of contraception. Being advised to be "safe" on contraception does not take into account problems in use. Some of the girls interviewed also talk about, what they consider to be, the "trickery" of boys who seem to mislead them into believing that they will be using a condom, when in fact they do not.

Theme 4: A further recurring difficulty talked about by schoolgirls has been the role of teachers and taxi-drivers, that is, men regarded as having status and money. As a school pupil in a group session (*Youth group 1*) claimed,

> Male teachers are not too strict because some are going with schoolgirls - even 14 and 15-year-olds ... [T]here was this teacher who taught Afrikaans - he promised a girl a number one pass - in exchange for sex. At the end of the year that girl fainted when she saw her results because she had failed. That teacher got into serious trouble (e).

Another pupil remarked,"Sometimes teachers do give students a child and promise to look after them. But they have their own wives and children to look after." Not only was it claimed that teachers often abuse their authority in initiating relationships with schoolgirls, but it was also suggested that money is sometimes exchanged in these encounters. Money is also the main reason offered for schoolgirls pursuing relationships with taxi-drivers. Having a taxi-driver's baby is also a way of ensuring some measure of financial support over the years. Taxi-drivers (I observed) are often parked outside the school grounds with little other purpose than to pick up schoolgirls. Sometimes schoolgirls compete with each other for the attention of these taxi-drivers. One of the ways in which the authorities in one of the schools I have visited have chosen to prevent scholars leaving the school during school hours is to lock and guard the gates from the morning until 3 pm.

Thus, as a result of the long duration of schooling, Winterveld's schoolgirls are likely to run the risk of pregnancy sooner or later. Schools play an important role in offering advice on preventive measures, but the social environment and the often poor use of contraception can potentially negate the efforts of schools to limit schoolgirl pregnancy.

Some reflection on the way in which the Winterveld micro-survey revealed the effects of levels of schooling on the proximate determinants of fertility will be offered now. The number of women 15-25 years of age constituted a small sub-set of the general sample (N=79). In the following tables women with primary school education (5 to 7 years of schooling) are compared with women who have had some years of or a completed secondary school education (8 to 12 years of schooling). Only three women in this age group had had no education. Since the number was small, women without any education were excluded from the tables. In most of the tables the results of the 1987-1989 SADHS are compared with those of the WS. These comparisons are offered merely to facilitate the qualitative discussion. The mean ages of the groups of women with primary and secondary school education in the SADHS are 21 years. In the WS, the mean age of women with primary school education is 22 years whilst the mean age of those with secondary school education is 21 years.

Education and supply factors in fieldwork site

Table 1: Proportion of women in unions, aged 15-25 years, by education: WS and SADHS

	Education level	Currently in a union: SADHS	Never in a union: SADHS	Previously in a union: SADHS	Currently in a union: WS	Never in a union: WS	Previously in a union: WS
	Primary school	52.1% (1111)	42.2% (900)	5.7% (121)	85% (11)	15% (2)	0 (0)
15-25 years old	Secondary school	42.3% (1911)	50% (2261)	7.7% (349)	44% (28)	49% (31)	7% (4)

Sources: South African Demographic and Health Survey, 1987-1989, recode file; Winterveld Survey, 1998, recode file.

The SADHS shows the generally expected pattern, viz. that education, in particular secondary school education, plays an important role (at the macro-level) in delaying the entry of women into unions. Fewer women with secondary school education are in a union and more are separated than those with lower levels of education. In the WS a larger proportion of women with a primary school education were in partnerships than those with a secondary education. Even though we are dealing with too few numbers to draw adequate comparisons it would seem that high school education in Merafeng shows similar effects to high school education in the SADHS. All 11 of the women with primary school education, who claimed to be "in a union", were involved in "living-together" and not formally sanctioned marriages. Many of these unions were probably entered into after an early, unplanned pregnancy. Given the wide variety of definitions of marriage here, it is possible that these unions included visiting partners and men with whom some of the women had unstable relationships. Of those with high school education, 5 were legally married and 23 were in cohabiting unions of various descriptions. In any event, the delay in marriage as influenced possibly by the effects of a secondary school education does not often coincide with the delay in the first birth. Women often interrupt their schooling, give birth to a child, and then return to complete more years of schooling. Levels of schooling are thus only partly helpful in offering indications of delays in union formation and child-bearing.

Table 2: Mean duration breast-feeding of women aged 15-25 years, by education: WS and SADHS

	Education level	Mean months breastfed: SADHS	Mean months breastfed: WS
15-25 years	Primary school	14.4 (1451)	19 (11)
	Secondary school	13.2 (2822)	15 (33)

Sources: South African Demographic and Health Survey, 1987-1989, recode file; Winterveld Survey, 1998, recode file.

Throughout the world women with a high-school education have been found to breast-feed their children for shorter periods of time than women with lower levels of education (UN, 1995). The shortening of the breast-feeding period in the absence of deliberate attempts to limit fertility is seen to have a potentially fecundity-enhancing effect which is problematic if a further birth is undesired in the very near future. In Winterveld 91.9% of women claimed to have breast-fed their last child. The 8.1% who did not breast-feed at all were largely teenagers whose child-rearing responsibilities were taken over by other family members. The fact that very young women with primary school education are usually homebound (having not returned to school) and unemployed could account for their longer period of breast-feeding. Women who wish to return to school might often not cut their breast-feeding time too short since returning to school about 18 months or so after giving birth is not uncommon. In the field a fair number of much shorter breast-feeding periods amongst teenagers was observed, especially where mothers took over the responsibility of childcare and when girls were considered too young to breast-feed. Rather than educational effects, the period of time young women would spend breast-feeding tended to depend on their ability to gather support, largely from mothers or sisters, for child-care responsibilities. Where support was available a woman would be free to look for work or go back to school.

Statistics on breast-feeding duration do not usually reveal much about whether the breast-feeding was continuous or not, or whether other kinds of feeding were adopted simultaneously. Amongst younger women I found almost no awareness of the potential use of continuous breastfeeding for delaying the return of menstruation. Although the durations seem to be fairly long this is not a proper indication of lengthy periods of "natural protection" since menstruation was most often resumed after about 2 to 4 months.

Periods of sexual abstinence are also of importance in considering what determines the timing of the next birth (if contraception is not used). The SADHS did not ask questions about the duration of post-partum sexual abstinence. Duration of abstinence was investigated in the WS, and the durations of 3 age categories are included for purposes of comparison.

Table 3: Mean duration (in months) post-partum sexual abstinence, by education and age: WS

	Between 15 and 25 years	Between 26 and 34 years	35 years and over
Primary school	12 (6)	10 (11)	10 (36)
Secondary school	14 (12)	7 (40)	9 (25)

Source: Winterveld Survey, 1998, recode file.

A majority of all women (64.1%) claimed to practise some period of *customary* abstention from engaging in sex immediately after childbirth. The duration of abstention increases however amongst the youngest cohort (15-25 years) with an increase in education. In the field it was evident that many young girls do subscribe to the belief that sex while breast-feeding is harmful to the health of the child. This is an area in which a fair number of women (including the young) seem to fear bewitchment, "bad lucks" and acts of retribution. It is not surprising then to find large numbers of young women "following the custom". The fourteen month abstinence, however, of secondary-educated women probably has less to do with these beliefs about the child being adversely affected and more to do with the fact that secondary schoolgirls who fall pregnant are usually abandoned by their boyfriends and, therefore, are likely to delay future post-partum sexual relations. Hence, these reported periods of customary abstinence appear to include periods of sexual inactivity. Periods of inactivity decrease as education increases in the 26-34 year group, suggesting the higher exposure to risk that these women probably face given that these births probably occurred within a formal or informal union.

Education and the demand for children

Table 4: Mean number of children desired by women aged 15-25 years, by education: WS and SADHS

	Education level	Mean number of children desired: SADHS	Mean number of children desired: WS
15-25 years	Primary school	3.3 (1428)	2.4 (13)
	Secondary school	3.0 (3195)	2.5 (63)

Sources: South African Demographic and Health Survey, 1987-1989, recode file; Winterveld Survey, 1998, recode file.

The mean number of children desired by women in the Winterveld sample is similar (though it appears to be a bit lower) than that revealed in the SADHS profile. This desire for a small family size is consistent with what has been observed in the field. Younger women did not commonly offer comments such as "God decides" and were able to express preferences for a definite number of children. An examination of the life histories shows that these "ideal" size preferences (most often ranging between one and three children) were a reaction primarily to the perceived costs involved in child-rearing. In addition to the numerous expenses involved in the day-to-day bringing up of children, such as feeding and clothing, women with high-school education spoke of having greater aspirations for their children (mainly with respect to education and better standards of living) than women with less education who tended to express fewer ambitions. Manto Mosele (58)[#14] made the following remark with respect to young people today:

> In the past, bearing children was a pride. The more children you had the more satisfied you were. Nowadays, life is demanding. Modern couples think of cost factors in bearing a child. We used to think that bearing children was a wealth. Children go to work and bring all their assets home. Now it is not the case. Now they go off on their own and live in their own homes. It was the case that children were invested in - not now - because, once they attain their goals, they go on with their own lives (e).

From my fieldwork it was evident that there was very little expectation that children would support parents in their old age. The chances of support, however, were seen to be somewhat more likely if the children were daughters rather than sons. This, however, did not appear to translate into any sex preferences for young women because, when the question was asked directly during individual and group interviews, no sex preference was expressed. Although no sex preferences were revealed, a "balance of children", at least one boy and one girl, was desired. Schoolgirls generally said that if they gave birth to two children of the same sex they would not attempt to have more children. They would be happy with that number but might adopt a child of the opposite sex later on.

Some of the views of the youngest women whose life histories were constructed can be presented here.

When I interviewed Minge Mkize (18) [#13] in 1998 she had 4 more years of schooling ahead of her. She wanted just one child but only when she was older and had completed her schooling. Minge came from a very poor family with 5 children. She wanted only one child because she saw many children as burdensome, particularly when resources were scarce. She maintained that she would rather have one child whom she could care for adequately.

In 1999 Sinah Makwela (22) [#1] had one child. She had to leave school when she turned 15 years old after discovering that she was pregnant. Since then she has had no more children. She told me that she did want an additional child - but later and only after she had found a job. Although she was in a visiting union she did not expect much support from her partner. Two children were ideal, given her expectation that she would be solely responsible for their financial upkeep.

Lindi Dlamini (22) [#15] had one child in 1999. She fell pregnant just after turning 19 years old and she went back to school two years later. Looking toward the future she expressed a desire for 3 - 4 children but only if she managed to find a supportive husband "who did not mess around". She said that she would not tolerate it if the man she married chose to have a second wife. She said that she would not have children because of the need for support in old age just as she did not anticipate that her children would be dependent on her for too long: "It is for them to look after themselves". A number between 3 - 4 was ideal because of the possibility of child mortality. She added, "in case one dies - I do not want to be left with nothing".

The desire for a smaller number of children by younger women can also be linked to their desire for more egalitarian relations with partners. In the group sessions (*Youth* group) there was much emphasis on the need for stable partnerships and for both partners to be involved in all decisions. As one person put it, "Table-talk is better". There is, however, some acknowledgement that power is vested in the one who earns money. As one schoolgirl suggested: "Power in the home depends on who is working. If the wife is working, she is the boss. If the wife is working and the man is not, she is going to undermine him. His status will be low (e)." The importance of this is perhaps that the recording of ideal family sizes expressed by schoolgirls at these early stages, who are generally not in unions, does not take into account possible changes in these preferences which may occur later on in life due to the nature of later unions and power differentials within them.

Education and the regulation of births

In Merafeng I came across a fairly high number of very young women who were using contraceptives, both modern and traditional. This was, to some extent, because the fieldworkers of the Planned Parenthood Association (PPA) had been active in promoting the use of contraception here, but also because many young women were becoming aware of how to gain access to contraception though the school's sex education and guidance counselling classes. Table 5 indicates the differences in contraceptive use between women who have had primary and secondary school education.

Table 5: Percent of women using contraception aged 15-25 years, by education: WS and SADHS

	Education level	Using contraception: SADHS	Using contraception: WS
15-25 years	Primary school	70.4 (1428)	76 (10)
	Secondary school	73.2 (3195)	85 (54)

Sources: South African Demographic and Health Survey, 1987-1989, recode file; Winterveld Survey, 1998, recode file.

The SADHS percentages reflect the proportion of sexually active women (15-25 years) who are using contraceptives. I did not ask questions about whether women were sexually active or not. From the high proportion of women in Winterveld who indicated that they were using contraceptives I have presumed that sexual activity begins early and that contraception is being employed more frequently in efforts to prevent unwanted early pregnancies. Different motivations for the high rates of contraceptive use are apparent. For schoolgirls the use of contraception improves the chances of completing schooling without the disruptions caused by an unanticipated early pregnancy. A girl who falls pregnant in primary school usually chooses and is advised to use contraception, particularly if she wishes to go back to school. Women with secondary-school education might be more inclined to use contraception partly because they have learnt more about how to gain access to contraceptives and also because the pressure to avert an unwanted pregnancy might be strongest when women are in high school. For women in their twenties, who are no longer at school, contraceptive use suggests a desire to space future births. This is particularly the case when unions are insecure and an additional child is regarded as an added and avoidable cost. Garenne and Halifax's (1999) depiction of "two peaks" makes qualitative sense here because it is usually after an extended birth interval made possible by contraceptive use that a young woman might enter into a union and becomes ready for another child.

Table 6: Proportion of women who would consider abortion, by education and age: WS

	Primary school	Secondary school
15-25 years	18.8 (3)	17.5 (11)
Over 25 years	9.8 (10)	23.4 (26)

Source: Winterveld Survey, 1998, recode file.

The SADHS did not examine the willingness of women to use abortion when faced with an unwanted pregnancy. Since abortion has only recently been made legal, many women in Winterveld were reluctant to talk much about it and reveal whether or not they had experienced an induced abortion. (Some women I spoke to counted an induced abortion as a spontaneous one - a miscarriage.) After the pilot study the question which aimed to examine whether women had *attempted* having an abortion was changed to determine instead if women would *consider* ending a pregnancy by having an abortion. Table 6 reflects very small numbers of women suggesting that they would be willing to have an abortion. In the course of the early fieldwork it seemed apparent that younger women with primary school education would be more likely to consider an abortion than those with high school education. This would probably be because women with primary school education might not be as exposed to modern contraception as women who have been to high school. On the other hand, older women with high-school education were more confident in expressing a willingness to end a pregnancy, rather than give birth to an unwanted child, than women with less education. This may also be an indication that abortions were prevalent among high-school girls in the past.

From the life histories it does seem apparent that abortions have been performed on young and older women, clandestinely, but that teenagers have been the main beneficiaries. (School toilets appear to be the place where some schoolgirls have attempted self-induced abortions, although assistance from traditional healers and certain elderly women has also been referred to.) Schoolgirls attempt abortions so that they can continue with their schooling and avoid reprimands from their families for unplanned pregnancies. How widespread this practice has been, though, was difficult to establish. However, the fact that virtually everyone interviewed knew someone who had had an abortion suggests that it has been relatively prevalent both in the past and the present.

Thus high-school education has a dual effect with respect to early, often unwanted, fertility. When they are in high school schoolgirls are most prone both to experiment with and to be coerced into sexual relations. School also offers a context that adapts behaviours, facilitates reduced desires for large numbers of children and offers opportunities to learn about how to delay and avoid early child-bearing. Some insight into national trends over the past decade is offered in Table 7.

Table 7: Early pregnancy: Young women aged 15-19 years who have given birth or who have been pregnant, South Africa, 1998 and 2003 Compared

Background details	Women who are mothers		Women who ever experienced pregnancy		Totals	
	1998	2003	1998	2003	1998	2003
Age						
15	2.0	1.1	2.4	1.9	468	294
16	5.2	3.3	7.9	5.2	458	275
17	10.7	9.6	14.2	11.4	444	272
18	19.8	11.9	24.6	15.6	474	295
19	30.2	22.9	35.1	27.3	406	247
Place of abode						
Urban	10.5	8.7	12.5	10.9	1,197	859
Rural	16.3	10.6	20.9	13.5	1,052	525
Province						
Western Cape	13.7	10.4	16.4	14.3	195	164
Eastern Cape	14.8	7.3	18.2	13.6	369	172
Northern Cape	15.2	12.3	18.0	16.1	44	28
Free State	8.4	12.2	12.6	15.4	136	100
KwaZulu-Natal	13.8	2.0	16.7	2.0	457	261
North West	11.0	10.6	13.4	14.3	164	97
Gauteng	8.9	11.2	9.5	12.3	377	269
Mpumalanga	18.8	12.1	25.2	13.1	190	91
Limpopo	14.9	14.0	20.0	16.8	318	201
Schooling						
No education	*	*	*	*	19	8
Grades 1-5	24.7	(5.3)	29.2	(9.5)	114	32
Grades 6-7	13.8	16.2	17.4	20.0	336	117
Grades 8-11	12.9	8.9	16.3	11.4	1,542	1,019
Grade 12	7.9	7.3	10.1	9.0	177	182
Higher	4.0	(6.9)	4.0	(6.9)	60	26
Race						
African	14.2	10.2	17.8	12.5	1,802	1,199
Coloured	15.7	6.4	19.3	11.7	208	114
White	2.2	(0.0)	2.2	(2.4)	162	51
Asian	2.9	2.2	4.3	2.2	66	20
Total	13.2	9.4	16.4	11.9	2,249	1,384

NB: Numbers in parentheses are based on fewer than 25 unweighted cases.
Sources: 1998 SADHS Report; 2003 SADHS Report

The effects of poverty and the domestic environment on early pregnancy

Although there appears to be a tendency for mothers and older women to refer to their teenage daughters becoming pregnant as a social problem of young people today, the life histories of mothers and daughters show that teenage and early pregnancy is certainly not a recent occurrence. Perhaps a key difference between past and present is that teenagers who fell pregnant twenty to thirty years ago were more likely to marry the fathers of their children. Having a child before arrangements for marriage were finalised was most often welcomed as a sign of fecundity. It led to the paying of bridewealth and the early birth of the child was seen within the institutional framework of marriage, resulting in the woman going to live with her husband's family at some stage (Murray, 1981). Today in Winterveld, a teenage, premarital or early birth most often does not lead to marriage. There are a number of themes that emerge when the stories of mothers and daughters are examined. Four themes are regarded as having specific relevance to understanding the responses of girls and their families to the possibility of early pregnancy. (The emphasis here will be on looking at the experiences of teenagers.)

Theme 1: The experience of teenage pregnancy and abandonment by partners adds to the burden of natal families and presents motivation for delays in future marriage and desires for fewer children.

Khanyi Mabetwa (78) [#4] had two children as a teenager before becoming accepted into her husband's family. Her teenage births were not frowned upon but were necessary for her acceptance into his family. She explains that the "gift" of birth was more important than the stage at which the birth occurred. Her first marriage, however, did not last long and she returned with two children to her parents' home. She married again for the second time - but only after a further birth out of wedlock. She had 10 additional children from this relatively stable second marriage. Years later in the 1970s, however, when one of her daughters, Louisa [#4], fell pregnant as a 19-year-old schoolgirl, Khanyi was deeply distressed. Although the child was valued as a "gift", it was fatherless and became an added responsibility for the struggling household. Louisa left the child with Khanyi and went on to find work outside Winterveld. Louisa eventually married and had more children seven years later. Although she had many relationships before marrying she had used contraception to prevent untimely births. Her eldest daughter, Miriam, remained with and was brought up by Khanyi and did not contemplate living with Louisa at any stage.

Bongi Msimang (43) [#5] was forced to leave school as a teenager because she had fallen pregnant. The father of the child deserted her and she was left to bring up her child, Mary [#5], alone, and without much support from her own family. Six years later she fell pregnant again and her new partner married her in a non-traditional wedding with few family members in attendance and no offers of bridewealth. When her daughter, Mary, fell pregnant at the age of 20 years she was also abandoned by her long-standing boyfriend. Mary was deeply upset at her boyfriend's disappearance. She had not tried to avoid falling pregnant because she had believed that a pregnancy would secure a marriage. Instead, her boyfriend and his family questioned the paternity of the child. None of them attempted to see the child after it was born nor did they offer Mary any financial support. In 1999 Mary lived with (and was supported by) Bongi and her stepfather. Mary believed that she would marry only when she was 30 and when she found a reliable partner. By 2007 Mary had not remarried, nor contemplated additional children.

Patience Khutsoane (48) [#9] and Nozizwe Radebe (66) [#3], whilst representing better-off families in Winterveld, both narrate stories about how their falling pregnant as teenagers forced them to drop out of school, marry their boyfriends and begin their duties as married women. Their daughters, Tebogo and Flora, respectively, also fell pregnant whilst at school, but some differences from their mothers' situations are noted. When Tebogo fell pregnant she chose not to inform her boyfriend but, instead, enlisted the support of another man who pretended to be the father of her child. Although she was not deserted she believed that the low-class status of her boyfriend would have added to the stigma of an early pregnancy. Before falling pregnant, Tebogo had never used contraception. After telling her mother about her pregnancy she fled home to escape her father's wrath and went to live with her grandmother. Her grandmother took over all child-rearing responsibilities and encouraged Tebogo to go back to school. Tebogo married her schoolteacher shortly thereafter, and had two more children after which she had herself sterilised. Flora, on the other hand, had tried to avoid falling pregnant by using contraception. Unfortunately she had used it incorrectly and consequently fell pregnant. On discovering that she was pregnant her boyfriend deserted her. Whilst pregnant she married another man (who pretended to be the father of her child) to avoid embarrassing her family. When the child was born she left him with her grandmother and went back to school. Flora's marriage lasted only three years. Flora, who turned 40 in 1999, has not had any additional children, although she entertained thoughts about a further pregnancy in 2003.

Although there is much diversity in the contexts and expectations of mothers and daughters who have had teenage births, in more recent years the consequences of these pregnancies have weighed more heavily on the family and family networks of the pregnant girls. In a poor locality such as Merafeng, abandonment is a survival tactic drawn upon to avoid dealing with the economic and emotional responsibility of parenthood, leaving the burden of upbringing with the girl's family. As Joseph, a teenager, explained to me in a group discussion (*Youth* group), "boys leave girls because they fear being fathers". Admission of fatherhood has financial implications which many boys and men seek to avoid. Although women have shouldered the burden of these responsibilities for many generations, younger women (particularly in the aftermath of a first birth and desertion) are more inclined to delay marriage and desire fewer children.

Theme 2: Early sexual activity which is prompted by the need for financial gains is being facilitated by encouragement to use contraception.

In the peri-urban locale of Merafeng child labour is not a motivation for high fertility preferences. Although originally sold as farming land, agricultural activities in Winterveld have been fairly limited. The common motivation for larger numbers of children as sources of labour, thus, has very little place here. Yet, despite this and the accompanying (and constantly expressed) low expectations of children, there is sufficient evidence of instances in which families benefit from the activities of their young children. Boys drop out of school in larger numbers than girls. They often leave Merafeng to do gardening or other odd jobs, returning when they have money to offer families or when they themselves are destitute and in need of support. Daughters also have their uses: from performing domestic chores and looking after younger siblings to bringing home money from sexual partners. With respect to the latter, given high levels of poverty and the fact that parents are often not around nor capable of supporting them, girls are often forced to find resourceful ways of feeding themselves and paying their school fees. Doing domestic work (I have been told) which is poorly paid and involves long hours of work does not bring as much as one can draw from a relationship with a man with money. Here are some stories illustrating elements of rationality in contexts in which girls and women experience much insecurity in relationships and livelihoods.

Josina Dlamini (43)[#15] had four children (three sons and one daughter). She had hoped for about 6 children but in 1990 after two miscarriages she decided that four children were enough and she then had herself sterilised. She did not, however, anticipate what was to follow. In 1994 her husband brought home another 'wife' who arrived with two children (one of whom he had fathered). The women did not share a good relationship and after much discord the second 'wife' ran away in March 1996, never to return. She left her two children behind. That same year, Lindi (Josina's 18-year-old school-going daughter), fell pregnant. Lindi's boyfriend, amidst accusations that he had impregnated two other girls, abandoned her and was never seen again in Winterveld. Living in circumstances of extreme poverty, Josina found herself responsible for seven children now. She sent Lindi back to school to complete her schooling. But she sent her back to school after making sure that Lindi had been taken to the clinic and had been given a contraceptive injection.

Josina said, "I did not want Lindi to fall pregnant. It was a disappointment. I have sent her back to school. She must finish her schooling and find a job. I trust Lindi. I cannot trust my sons. Boys grow up only to look after themselves. Look at this man who gave Lindi a child - where is he now? He is nowhere to be found (s)".

Lindi explained her situation:

My father wanted me to get married when I was 15 years old. He wanted me to stop school and find a husband. My mother did not want me to marry but to continue with my schooling. My parents did not argue about it. No, they hardly ever argued because my father came home during month-ends only. My mother decides on everything at home. She decided I must stay at school ... Many girls are falling pregnant in Winterveld because of the poverty. Sometimes it is because the boy gives you money. My boyfriend used to give me R10 each time we met. At school I used to struggle to pay my school fees. When they could afford it at home they would give me R5. I would not spend it. I would save it for my school fees. When I fell pregnant and he left me, I had to give up school and use all the money that I had saved - for the baby (s).

Lindi's story is just one of many. It is an enormous difficulty affecting the success of the AIDS intervention programme, Vulinqondo, in Winterveld. Amos Monyane at the Vulinqondo project said: "With the youth we have a problem of many partners. It is because of money. Girls go for men with money. They can be controlled by gangsters. They say to us, "we go for money", but we try and say to them, "don't go for money - go for safety (e)".

When daughters are able to bring in money from their sexual encounters mothers show little regard for "safety" and turn a blind eye to promiscuity. When I interviewed Sinah Makwela (22) [#1] and she suggested to me that her older sister, Sophy (25) [#1], was her mother's favourite, I passed it off as an indication of immature rivalry between the two sisters. Toward the very late stages of my fieldwork, however, the motivation for this favouritism became apparent. Although Lebo, Sinah's mother, presented herself as a stern parent who sought to rid herself of her two daughters because they were excessively troublesome, she did attempt at a later stage to win Sophy over. Sophy's life history reveals violent episodes: rape, abuse and beatings alongside much insecurity in finding work and earning a living. Her inability to find formal work saw her turn to sex work for money. On discovering this, rather than dissuading her, her mother had started to benefit from her hand-outs and buying of food.

The way mothers may benefit was also illustrated in another of my stories. Dora Mkize (40) [#13] had two teenage daughters, Minge (18) [#13] and Margaret (19) [#13]. Minge was approached by a tavern-owner in the area to take part in modelling contests in the taverns in Winterveld. (Locals refer to taverns not just as places where men go to drink but where gambling, illicit trading and much violence occur). Although Dora gave her approval she had been aware that her teenage daughter would be exposing herself to various risks associated with the trade. Her answer to the problem of keeping her daughter "safe" was to attempt to persuade her to use contraception. Margaret has been on contraception for about three years now but Minge is averse to taking the contraceptive injection, believing that it will make her fat and spoil her modelling career. Dora explained to me that Minge was being "very naughty" for not wanting to use contraception because she could easily "get into trouble". She stopped short of telling Minge to give up her modelling in the taverns. Minge explained: "I get R15 - R20 each time I take part. I have also won duvets, dinner sets and dishes. I give the money to my mother. My mother also takes my presents away and locks them in the cupboard (s)."

The fact that schoolgirls have sex for money is not a new finding - and certainly is not unique to Winterveld. What perhaps was a revelation to me was the frankness with which the issue was raised and discussed - and the sense that this was a practice widespread amongst the poorest sector of women. The important issue here is that early contraceptive use is on the increase not because parents have lost control over daughters, but because daughters are responding rationally to a lack of resources (often with collaboration from parents, particularly mothers) and in a way that has proved to be the most rewarding. In so doing, they constantly face the risk of unwanted pregnancies, sexually transmitted diseases and abuse.

Theme 3: Intra-familial dynamics and sexual abuse are factors contributing to increased contraceptive use.

Community workers talk of many instances in which they have had to "rescue" a girl from a situation in which she was being sexually abused by a stepfather or relative upon whom the family was dependent financially. Given high levels of female unemployment and participation in a predominantly informal economy, women in families often find themselves highly dependent on men. Sister Irene Mafoko at St. Peter's Clinic in Winterveld said:

> At times you find a mother knows the child is having sex with her husband - that he is using her. By challenging him they will be left without an income. She keeps quiet so that the husband can continue to look after them. Sometimes the child may report the incident to the mother. In some cases she may protect the husband even though she knows that it's true. The child is then helpless (e).

Step-children or children of an earlier union are often not afforded the same kinds of rights and privileges as children from a current union. Many go on to live with grandparents when the possibility of abuse emerges. Mary-Ann Stevens, the community worker instrumental in setting up programmes dealing with cases of abused women in Winterveld, said:

> Mothers come in early when the child is about 13 years to put them on contraception for fear of fathers raping them and of pregnancy arising from sexual abuse. In the mother's absence the eldest daughter is often

expected to replace the mother. Our response has always been to remove the child from an abusive situation - but we are learning about the problems of alternative arrangements for the girl and the many problems inadequate alternatives may hold (e).

Winnie Matwa, the Aids worker at the Sisters of Mercy (linked to the Roman Catholic Church), suggested that the risk of pregnancy was high within the family. She illustrated:

We are dealing with this case of a man with three step-daughters. He owned a tuckshop but he never gave them any money unless they had sex with him. The mother did not say anything because she was afraid that he would leave her. The first two daughters complied but the youngest refused to have anything to do with him. She never got any school fees so she has left school (e).

The painfulness of this reality struck me when I began interviewing Thandi [#8] and Pinky [#8] in an attempt to construct their life histories. Their story illustrates the kinds of dilemmas between mothers and daughters that could surface. Pinky Ramashala (19) was 16 when she first learned that her father, Petros Ramashala, was actually her step-father.

When I was young I did not know that he was not my real father. One day when my mother was not at home he told me that he was not my real father and that he wanted to have sex with me. I was very shocked. He said that I would find a boy and get a baby - then who would look after it? He would be supporting it. At first I did not want to tell my mother - but in the end I had to. My mother asked him and they started to quarrel. They were always quarrelling but this time they included me. He became angry with me. Later he found me and sjambokked [whipped] me on the legs. I was bleeding and in much pain. My mother reported it to the social workers. The social workers called the police. When the police came, they asked me, "must we take your father to jail?" I said "no" because he works for us (e).

Pinky had been asked to make a choice by the police. She chose not to have her stepfather jailed for fear that his incarceration would serve as a worse punishment for the whole family, since he was the only one with a regular income.

Shortly after that (in 1997) Pinky was in fact abused and raped by her stepfather. When Thandi learned of it, the family fell apart and Petros told Pinky to leave the house since she had caused all the trouble. In seeking advice from the social worker Pinky was told that she must choose where she wanted to go and what she wanted to do. She wanted to live with her grandfather (her mother's father) but Petros said he would only pay her an allowance if she stayed with his sister. She stayed there for ten months until she gave birth to a child and until the money ran out. Then Pinky went back home. By then her mother, Thandi, and Petros had developed an uneasy reconciliation. When Pinky arrived home Thandi had her taken to the clinic and put her on Nur Isterate (the contraceptive injection) for fear, as she put it, "Petros might rape her and she could have another child"(s). Shortly thereafter Thandi's marriage broke down and Petros left Winterveld. Pinky went back to school in 1998.

Of the 15 families interviewed, this was the only one within which rape had occurred and been contained. Although this story is included here to illustrate the theme of abusive relationships, I am not in a position to argue that such cases are common. Even if such cases are aberrant, I believe (from talking to key informants) that fear of such incidents occurring within families is encouraging contraceptive use. Schoolgirls who are in pursuit of a high-school education and have many financial needs (in addition to school fees) are most vulnerable to abuse.

Theme 4: Fear of daughters making similar mistakes, that is, of falling pregnant too early and of getting into unsuitable marriages, is making mothers encourage young daughters to take measures to prevent pregnancies.

Many mothers may not only be supportive of their daughters using contraception for fear of partners and husbands impregnating them but also because they did not carry the responsibility of child-bearing very easily themselves and they wish to aid them against making the same mistakes. In one of my case studies, Nomasonto (27) [#12], the daughter of a well-known father in Winterveld, revealed that she was only 13 when she first fell pregnant. Her pregnancy was regarded as a disgrace to the family and she was chased away by an irate father. She did not marry the father of her child but became, five years later, the fourth "wife" of a fairly wealthy man in Winterveld. When I began interviewing her, her distress was about the fact that her husband had taken yet another "wife" - a 17-year-old schoolgirl. She said, however,

> It doesn't bother me. The young ones are just after money. I am only worried about my own daughter. She is 13 years old now. She has started sex already. I am encouraging her not to run after boys. She must finish school and look for a job. She must get a baby when she is

married. I have not taken her to the clinic yet. She has only just started menstruating but I will take her soon (x).

Similarly, Phumzile Dlali (33) [#11], who has had three children by three different men (who all abandoned her subsequently, had her daughter sent to the clinic to be put on the injection before her 14th birthday. Phumzile explained: "My daughter is progressing and is clever in school. I told her that if she meets with boys she must not fall pregnant. Getting pregnant can spoil everything if you are too small. She is only in Std. 3 [5th year of schooling]. She must know what she is doing when she chooses a husband (s)".

In an illuminating report based on focus group discussions entitled *How parents communicate with their daughters and sons about sexuality in Winterveld*, Ratsaka et al. (1998) concluded that numerous barriers exist which inhibit communication between parents and children about sex, sexuality education and contraceptive use in Winterveld. They suggest that young people are keen to discuss such matters with parents but parents are often dismissive or reticent when talking about sexual or reproductive issues. Although there is sufficient indication of poor communication between parents and children in present-day Merafeng, parents (or younger mothers, rather) do offer daughters contraception advice, or urge them to avoid pregnancies. Whilst simply advising or telling daughters to use contraception does not necessarily involve much sex education or life skills training, such interventions usually represent a starting point for more meaningful dialogue about sexual behaviour in the longer term.

Sarah Gamede (43) [#14], now a schoolteacher, takes a different position from her mother, Manto Mosele (58). She said:

> I used contraception before my first child. My mother tried to save me with it. I was 16 years old at the time. She saw that I was friendly with the boys. When I missed taking the pills I fell pregnant. If she could have told me how to restrain myself I might not have had a child. My daughter is completing her high school this year. I am advising her not to use contraception and fall into this trap. I am teaching her about restraint and about meeting the right person. But at the schools they are advising them to go to the clinic. They are encouraging them to experiment with sex. I just don't like it (e).

From another life history a mother's anxiety about doing the right thing for her daughters becomes evident. Dudu Mabunda (65) [#10] spoke with some sadness about being forced to give up school when she was fifteen years old. Her mother had her married off to a man with money. "My mother said: "if you marry him you will be okay and I will only have seven other children to look after." My mother did not think I would achieve anything from finishing my education." So Dudu married and had seven daughters.

> My sister-in-law said, as my daughters were growing up: "soon those girls will be sitting with lots of babies". I was very hurt at that remark. From then on I had to ask the Lord for help in bringing them up. I had to be strict and careful with them. I did not want pregnant daughters. Prevention is better than cure. Each time I saw a boy in their company I had to establish: is he serious, is he playing? Who's his family? (e).

Dudu then went on to offer detailed accounts of her manipulation of each of her seven daughters, showing how she persisted to ensure that they did not fall pregnant before completing their schooling, that much bridewealth was paid, and that the men they chose were relatively well off. Dudu's preoccupation with keeping her daughters on the straight path does not reflect the norm in Winterveld. Most mothers do not appear to be as resilient as she was in offering both sex education and encouragement to use contraception.

There are two things in common about all the mothers referred to here. The first is that all (given their own experiences) were intent on preventing a possible future pregnancy of their young daughters. Getting daughters to use contraception or talking to them "about restraint" were all part of wanting to see them complete their education and achieve more in life. The second is that they were all from plot-owner families. Although it would be strange to suggest that property-ownership has a bearing on contraceptive use, it is apparent that families with more money are extremely unhappy when their daughters select partners who are poor or less educated. (In theme 1, both Tebogo and Flora saw fit to lie about the paternity of their children because the men involved were regarded as low-class.) With antagonisms and prejudices between plot-owners and tenants, a land-owner (as in the case of Dudu Mabunda) might not want to risk any of her daughters being forced to marry someone from an unsuitable background.

Short comment on wanted and unwanted fertility in Merafeng

It is not easy to judge when a teenage pregnancy is wanted or not. The 1987-1989 SADHS established unwanted fertility primarily by the number of negative responses to the following question: *"At the time you* became pregnant with ... (name of the youngest living child) OR (current pregnancy), did you want (more) children? (A further measure would be the extent to which completed family size exceeded ideal family size. This, however, is of less interest here since I am referring to women in the early child-bearing stages.) Responses to the question above showed that 59.3% of women under 20 years had had unwanted pregnancies. At the same time, with respect to the timing of *first* pregnancies (did they occur at the right stage, should they have been later or sooner or not at all?), two out of 10 women between 15-24 years said that the pregnancies should have been later, whilst one-third stated that they would have preferred the birth to be sooner (Du Plessis, 1996:40). Du Plessis (1996:40) suggested, "this is indeed a surprising result". This is because the SADHS results indicated that, although many young women claimed to have had births unwanted at the time they first became pregnant, these, in retrospect, were no longer unwanted. Thus, the data ironically showed that some women would have liked to have had these unwanted births sooner rather than later.

I discovered the lines to be fairly blurred when I attempted to study the responses of women in my fifteen life histories to establish whether teenage births outside marriage were wanted or not. Clearly, asking a woman (young or old) about whether a birth was wanted after a child had already been born cannot invite a clear-cut answer. An 'accidental' birth is not necessarily an unwanted birth. Although the younger women whom I interviewed (Tebogo, Flora, Phumzile, Nomasonto, Sarah and Lindi) talked with anxiety about the timing and circumstances surrounding the first birth, they did not express regrets about having had the child. Depending on family responses and on support from partners an accidental birth could turn into a celebrated event. Similarly, schoolgirls who fell pregnant deliberately because they desired an early birth, or to strengthen the bonds of a relationship or because it was believed that it would lead to marriage (as in the case of Mary, Sophy or Sinah), might change their minds about seeing the birth in a positive light. Desertion and poor economic means can make 'wanted' children become regarded as burdensome - particularly when new relationships are being pursued. Even in these circumstances it is not common to hear a young woman talk about a child that should not have been born.

Rather than the classification of "wanted" or "unwanted" births, the more important question for the qualitative work became one of assessing how this early experience of bearing a child shaped the thinking about the timing and context of additional births. Both young women who take steps to avoid falling pregnant and those who have early births learn important lessons in this initial stage, which lead to particular attitudes toward contraceptive use, marriage, relationships, family support and work-seeking efforts. These will be concerns of the next two chapters.

Conclusion

Many factors play a role in shaping the pattern of sexual activity and early pregnancy in Winterveld. Here, where many people live with poverty, social disorganisation arguments tell only part of the story. The larger part, I believe, can be explained by exploring the motivations of schoolgirls and young women, generally, as they initiate and sustain sexual relationships for money and other forms of support. Schools reproduce the constraints and risks of the domestic environment. Although schooling plays a role in changing attitudes toward child-bearing, its biggest contribution is to offer schoolgirls education concerning contraceptive use. Together with intervention from family members (primarily mothers) and lessons emerging from having or avoiding a first birth, early acquaintance with contraception could result in teenagers, schoolgirls and young women developing the means to wield greater control over child-bearing in the short to long term.

Notes

[1]   This is the actual name of the first school built in Winterveld.

Chapter 5

TRANSITORY PARTNERSHIPS, POWER RELATIONS AND PARENTHOOD

Introductory Comment

One of the central concerns of this study has been to consider transitions in marital and kin relations and how they shape child-bearing patterns in Winterveld. This chapter addresses this concern by drawing attention to what has been commonly referred to as the "distinguishing characteristics" of African marriage and family life (Phillips, 1953), and to reflect on their place in Winterveld social relations, given the vicissitudes that come with insecurities in the labour market and in intimate unions. I focus in this chapter on two broadly defined themes. The *first theme*, which emerged strongly in the stories of women, relates to the prevalence of violence, infidelities and discord within unions, and the particular consequences these have for the sustaining of households and conjugal relationships. Thus it has become necessary to consider the role played by gender and power - forces that are "difficult to incorporate into standard empirical models of demographic behaviour" (Greenhalgh, 1995:12) but which are essential for any contextualisation of changing fertility outcomes and family systems. A *second theme* relates to the changeable nature of "traditional" kin and family support networks. Older kin and "close" family members may assume responsibilities and assert claims on children in cases where biological parents are absent or attribute little importance to parenthood. In doing so, however, there are often expectations of reciprocity which, if left unfulfilled, lead to the neglect of children or the deterioration of kin relations in the longer term. In an effort to link with the previous chapter, the related concern would be to address the question of whether the involvement of kin (such as grandmothers) in the rearing of children (grandchildren) implies a level of involvement in "negotiations" around fertility decisions.

A note on spousal separation and the social context

For demographers studying fertility transitions, the significance of the living-together union, whether formally or consensually constituted, is that it represents a context of high exposure to sexual intercourse and thus involves high risks of conception. The age at which a woman enters into a union becomes an important determinant of the number of children she will have in her life-time (Bongaarts & Potter, 1983). Later ages at marriage have been associated with declining fertility levels in other parts of the world; a similar shortening of the reproductive age span is envisaged in Sub-Saharan Africa with increases in literacy and years of women's schooling (UN, 1995; Caldwell, 1982). As the previous chapter suggested, however, early sexual activity and child-bearing outside stable unions complicates assumptions about the relationship between entering into marriage, the onset of exposure to risk, and rates of pregnancy. This is in addition to demographers having long conceded that the marriage process in African societies makes unclear the point at which a couple is seen to be married (Murray, 1981: 119-128), when births are "premarital", or when a regular sexual union is seen to begin (Meekers, 1994). Statistics on the "married" sector of the African population and mean "age(s) at marriage" have always been unreliable in South Africa, and currently discrepancies exist between survey results. Although the 1987-1989 SADHS shows the mean age at marriage of African women to be 19 years, the mean age according to the 1985 census was 27.5 years and even older according to the 1991 census (27.8 years). This is because, while the demographic and health survey included consensual unions in their definition of "marriage", the census did not (Mostert, 1998: 159-161).

Apart from the age of partners at which unions are initiated, attention can be paid to customary practices within marriage which affect the natural "supply" of births, such as continuous breast-feeding and post-partum sexual abstinence, and to those more disruptive effects on potential child-bearing like separation, divorce and death. A key influence shaping marriage and family life in the Southern African experience, as already discussed in the previous chapter, has been the periodic separation of spouses due to the system of migrant labour (Timaeus & Graham, 1989: 385-388). Winterveld, however, is not a rural area from which migrants have traditionally left in large numbers for faraway places of employment, returning infrequently. It is a peri-urban area within close proximity to the wealthiest core of the country - the Pretoria-Witwatersrand-Vereeniging business districts. When farming began to offer increasingly less returns and the leasing of land and work outside the area became essential, relatively easy access to transport did not necessitate that working people live away from their residences for extended periods of time. Nonetheless, particularly since the 1970s and

1980s, there was much commuting or circulation between homes in Winterveld and alternative homes near places of work in Rustenberg, Pretoria or Johannesburg. Domestic units "in flux" and "stretched" across space (Murray, 1976, cited in Spiegel, 1996:26) necessitated by working household members having to live elsewhere to earn income and return periodically with remittances have been described in the life histories of women. Many of these references, however, are to households in rural areas prior to arriving in Winterveld. Since the 1960s, in-migration of tenants has led to "whole families" moving into the area primarily for the purposes of refuge and shelter, rather than single migrants arriving (without families) with the sole purpose of seeking employment in one of the nearby towns. Since locating in Winterveld, both plot-owners and tenants talk of detachment from other kin living in the outlying urban or rural areas.

Today, with increasing unemployment and retrenchments, smaller proportions of people migrate to work distances away and for extended durations of time. It is difficult to estimate the number of unemployed people living in Winterveld since the predominantly tenant population remains relatively mobile. In 1989 it was estimated that nearly 75% (of all men and women) were unemployed and, of those employed, 50% were involved in informal sector activities (Simone, 1998). In the WS sample of only women, over 50% were not earning money. Local residents (who are South African) refer to "the Maputos" (the Mozambicans) living in Winterveld as those who, as migrant labourers, continue to leave their homes for extended periods of time. An increasing number of men without formal work join women in informal sector activities, piece-jobs and limited farming activities. Some of them are, allegedly, becoming integrated into illicit activities. Thus spousal separation due to work-seeking efforts or migrant labour is arguably not the key factor contributing to marital dissolution or abandonment which could lead to declining fertility levels. The fragmentation of bonds and family structure is more likely a consequence of the stress generated within poor and contracting households as men and women struggle with each other for control over domestic decisions and limited resources. Unlike the case where working men can often be relied upon to return at some point in the future with a certain income, unemployed men, men involved in menial work or engaged in illicit trades show little inclination to be reliable supporters. It is not uncommon for them to desert their families and leave them destitute, thus abdicating familial responsibilities associated with biological fatherhood (see case studies e.g. Morrell & Richter, 2004).

Changes in the marriage system in Winterveld

The meaning of marriage

In Chapter 4 it was suggested that a variety of definitions of "marriage" existed in Winterveld. The issue of multiple meanings has been raised by other studies on family life in South Africa. In a study of children and family life, Kotze (1992:146) attempted to probe why a particular woman was regarded as a "wife" despite the absence of a marriage ceremony in Dixie, Gazankulu. He received the following response: "You know she stays and cooks at uncle's home." Staying and cooking (that is, without there being a marriage ceremony) were also criteria for being a wife in my fieldsite in Merafeng, Winterveld. Sometimes, despite not being married, the woman stayed and cooked for the entire family. Often the living together of a man and woman with other kin (even if it was intended to be short-term) resulted in mutual relationships of care, obligation and duty. When I once went to see Patience Khutsoane she complained that her eldest son was "disappointing me a lot".

From the Khutsoane life histories [#9]

Patience's eldest son was a taxi-driver but rarely brought money home because he spent a lot of his time with girlfriends. Not long after starting his taxi business he brought home a homeless girl, Zodwa, who had originally come from a large family. When Zodwa's mother died, their father admitted that he was not their biological father and ordered all the children out of the house. Zodwa met Paulina's son in town and was brought home as his girlfriend. Since becoming a part of the Khutsoane household she had been given numerous washing, cleaning and cooking responsibilities. Although Patience's son said that he did not want to marry Zodwa, Patience suggested that it was only because he could not afford to pay the bridewealth at that stage. In any event, Zodwa had no family to whom the bridewealth could have been offered. Patience's son was a heavy drinker and began to beat Zodwa up regularly. In September 1998 Patience took her son to the police. She was angry on that day. "It is a son's duty to look after his wife," she said (t).

"Husband" and "boyfriend" were also often interchangeable terms. A woman was likely to call a man her "husband" if they had a child together and if he offered some financial support, irrespective of whether they lived in the same residential unit or not. Another woman may refer to a man in a similar arrangement as being her "boyfriend" in order to emphasise that they are still to marry and live together at some later stage. Rose Malibane, a woman in one of my group sessions (*Ndlovu's* group), had never married (either through customary or legal means). She had two children from a "boyfriend" (as she called him - because he was married and had another family elsewhere) who visited periodically with generous amounts of money. She said that he gave her "courage and hope. I depend on him. He is my mother and father. He gives me money to buy everything"(s). The support he offered her afforded her some respectability in the area as an "outside wife". People referred to her as Mrs Malibane.

This chapter refers to, and interrogates the distinction between formally sanctioned "marriage" and informally constituted "living-together" unions. It was interesting to note that, of the 293 women in the Winterveld sample, about a third (97) claimed to have had a customary marriage and/or a registered marriage (though I believe that the number of registered unions was few). A further third (97) claimed to have been "married informally" or were at that stage involved in a cohabiting or consensual union and the remaining third (99) were either never married, or were separated, divorced or widowed. Of those in customary/registered marriages, 17.5% reported that their husbands were frequently away (for periods approximating six months) as opposed to 31.3% of those in consensual unions. This indication seemed to concur with my fieldwork observation which was that whilst most intimate unions appeared to be vulnerable to the stresses of life under poverty, consensual unions were particularly tenuous.

Women in the area were not shy to acknowledge that Winterveld unions were commonly short-term. The experience of falling pregnant, and subsequently being abandoned, was making younger women less willing, and less hasty, to enter into a potentially fragile union especially when a man appeared to be unreliable, a poor supporter, or displayed violent forms of behaviour. In the group sessions some of the younger women (many of whom had already had babies) suggested that they preferred not to marry, and that they would rather live alone with their children. Others expressed ideal-types of men in marriage - e.g. he must "not have another wife", he must "be educated" and he must be "democratic". The experience of rape and sexual abuse in early life was also a factor which made women reluctant to enter into a union, especially if its lasting potential was doubtful.

From the Mkize life histories [#13]

Dora Mkize talked about meeting her husband. "At first, when I met my husband, I was not fond of him. I never thought that I would end up with him. I was not that young. I was 20 years old. Because I had suffered before, I did not want anyone to marry me. I had been sexually abused. It was only after a long time that we married (s)."

From the Mabetwa-Makgoba life histories [#4]

Louisa Makgoba offered a reason for the long period during which she avoided men. "In 1970, during the time I was living at my grandmother's house, I met Phillip Makgoba ... At that time, my grandmother used to sell beer from home. Smanky, a man that used to buy beer from my grandmother, came to me one day and said, "I got a good friend who has no girlfriend. I think he would be the right one for you." At that stage Louisa was "not in love with anyone. I had no boyfriend. That was because I was tired of men. They make you pregnant and go." (e)

In Chapter 4, reference was made to the burdens placed on families as a result of early pregnancies. Children born of these unions often become the responsibility of the woman's family and her support structures. In acknowledging the prevalence of child-bearing out of wedlock, it would not be correct to suggest that a formalised marriage is becoming irrelevant for women in Merafeng, or generally in Winterveld. Although it would seem that an increasing number of unions (particularly of younger people) is short-lived and initiated without customary sanction, for many women, marriage (whether customary or registered in the courts) is valued as a rare commodity - often unattainable, but nonetheless desirable. The word "luck" comes up frequently when reference to "a proper marriage" is made. As learnt through the group sessions in 1999 and 2007 - women who have married with bridewealth and who "have signed" are regarded as both "lucky" and respectable. A woman who is married to a man who does not leave her, but who remains with her in the same house and supports her children, is treated with much respect.

A few distinguishing features of the customs and social practices associated with the African marriage system, and of relevance to an understanding of fertility transition and conjugal stability (noted in Merafeng), are referred to below:

Marriage with cattle or cash

In 1998 the *Recognition of Customary Marriages Act* was passed. In line with the enshrining of gender equality in the 1993 Constitution and in the Bill of Rights, it has sought to equalise the status of men and women in customary marriages. Of specific interest are provisions safeguarding the rights of women in polygynous unions, stipulations making the paying of bridewealth an optional practice in the validation of a customary marriage, and those requiring the obtaining of consent of the two prospective spouses to a marriage (rather than the consent of parents or other relatives). Although a customary African marriage is essentially about bringing together one man and one woman for the purposes of companionship, support and procreation, it has, traditionally speaking, combined the broader purposes of forging an alliance between families and kin. As Phillips (1953: 4) puts it: "[a]ny marriage is a matter of interest not only to the parents of both parties but to a wider circle of relatives, particularly members of the lineage of each. Every marriage requires the consent of some senior person, sometimes not even the nearest male relative but the lineage head." Customary marriage can be seen further in terms of a transaction between kin-groups whose negotiations can result in the setting of the bride price or the breaking off of a proposed union. In the peri-urbanised environment of Winterveld the authority of senior people has been undermined in recent times as younger people often do not consider "wider family interests" nor frequently ask for approval of their chosen partners. Older people (from the *Ikageng* group session) spoke with some disdain about how as family members "we can no longer intervene in the choices of our children". At the same time, it was conceded that "our parents never chose for us as well. We had the choice but it was according to custom. We could marry a cousin or a family friend." The insistence on marrying cousins or distant kin has long since declined, as has marrying "within the tribe". As Clara Molefe [#8] suggested: "When we were growing up we used to have views that we should marry within the tribe. My father married his cousin. My father had a cousin in mind for me. I was not interested" (s).

Winterveld, it is commonly stated, is a place where "different nations" have co-existed and interacted with relatively little conflict and tension over the years. Where tensions have come to the fore, these have been defined in class rather than ethnic terms. This is despite historical attempts to elevate the status of Tswana in relation to others, such as Ndebele and Shangaan. Partnerships and marriages between people of different ethnic origins are fairly common. However, when marriages turn sour it is not uncommon to hear parents reprimand their children for their choices by referring to these different identities. On meeting Johannes Rametsi [#8] in the aftermath of his daughter's separation, he said: "I told her not to marry that Shangaan"(e). When Flora Radebe [#3] reflected on her mother's bad relationship she said: "He [her father] was Zulu. Zulu men like a lot of wives. It was just his way"(s). When Sophy Makwela's [#1] boyfriend abandoned her, and he was protected by his family who supported his other girlfriend, she suggested that it was because he was Venda. More importantly, it was widely accepted that with much intermarriage and "mixing of the nations" various interpretations of customs and practices are being tolerated. Dudu Mabunda [#10] said the following about the marriage of one of her daughters:

> That family had sent us a letter saying they were coming. The traditions of those people are not the same as ours. When the Ndebele people bring *lobola* [bridewealth] they expect the girl to go with them. They wanted to take Maki [her daughter]. They said they had a big party planned that same day in Kromkuil. I did not want Maki to go with them after the *lobola* [bridewealth] was paid. They were disappointed, but I did not care. I said we must do things in a different way. All my children have had to first sign with the Minister (e).

(In addition to variously applied customs, local discourse suggested that marriage practices, sexual morals, and the behaviour of the youth in general has become worse "since Mandela taught them about their rights.") While many of the obligations and practices associated with the marriage customs of the different groups showed signs of change, for those who were formalising a marriage, the paying of bridewealth remained a tradition. Phillips (1953:14) suggests that:

> the indispensable element in the validation of marriage was the transfer of the agreed number of cattle from the husband's to the wife's group. Just as the transfer of cattle was necessary to validate a marriage, their retention by the bride's family presupposed that the marriage was in being and its obligations duly performed. Should a wife leave her husband and refuse to return he would claim the return of the cattle.

In the 1990s, parents or elderly relatives could still be seen to be playing a role as go-betweens. When two people wished to marry, the parents or elders of the boy often proceeded to the girl's home to ask her parents permission and to make arrangements. Often mature, respectable adults acted on behalf of a younger couple who might already have begun a relationship or have had a few children. Louisa Makgoba [#4] had four children before her marriage was formalised. She said that "his mother went to ask for *lobola* [bridewealth]. My mother called a few people to witness. In our custom a *madisella* [co-ordinator] is put in charge. The one bringing *lobola* will talk to him. They came and negotiated with my mother. The *lobola* was set"(e). In Louisa's case, as is increasingly the case in Winterveld, money rather than cattle was transferred. The most common reason given for this was the fear of theft. Some women claimed that it was no longer regarded as worthwhile to invest in cattle because they are stolen regularly and then slaughtered for their meat (though for the landless and most mobile sector of the population the retaining and offering of cattle are largely inconvenient). The most obvious deterrent, however, is that most people do not have cattle to offer prospective in-laws anymore.

Bridewealth amounts asked for by families can range from a few hundred to a few thousand rands. In reflecting on what was paid at the time of marriage many women will report on the amounts asked by their families as indications of their worth at the time. Clara Molefe [#8] said: "My father asked only for R400. I was cheap"(s). Thandi Ramashala's [#8] father also asked for R400 for Thandi's first marriage. He asked for R600 for her second marriage because she had had a child by then - and the bride-price was the cost of mother and child. At the higher end of the scale, I have been told, the family of a young, single girl can ask for as much as R5000. If she has had a child, however, a man will have to pay more to claim paternity. Sometimes, when parents ask for large amounts of money, men who cannot always rely on kin for financial support have to take time to accumulate sufficient money themselves to pay their own bridewealth. The couple may live together whilst the man begins a long process of paying off the debt accumulation in instalments. Amongst older people, mention is made of gifts which could be offered by the woman's family to the parents of the man at the initial stages of the marriage: (as lingerings of Sotho custom) these include a walking stick, coat, pipe, tobacco, an axe and a "straight" brandy for the father-in-law and a blanket, doek (scarf for the head), shoes and an apron for the mother-in-law.

A further practice, common in the past but difficult to implement at present, is that of paying "penalties" for "damages" caused to a girl and her family in the case of elopement or abduction (Murray, 1981:122). This was not commonly practised in Merafeng, partly because many first-time relationships end in desertion with little possibility that families can trace the man concerned after that. Even second-time elopements do not easily end with the paying of "penalties" or bridewealth. In Sinah Makwela's story her early pregnancy, elopement and non-payment of bridewealth became an embarassment to her, but her motivation for wanting it paid was not about forging alliances between families.

From the Makwela life histories [#1]

Sinah Makwela had a child when she was fourteen years old. Her boyfriend was jailed for theft not long after she fell pregnant and never saw the child. In 1998 Sinah said to me that she would like to marry her new boyfriend, Jimmy, at some stage - but before she turns 25 years old. They had talked about this - and Jimmy was willing to marry her. In fact, earlier in 1997, Sinah and Jimmy ran away from their respective homes, and "set up a home" in Merafeng. They did not mean to simply elope. They had intended to do the respectable thing and pay her father the bridewealth that he wanted. They "bought things for their home and started to put it in order"(t). Shortly thereafter, their home was broken into (in their absence) and they returned to find that everything was gone. After that they decided to go back to their family homes because they had no money, and nothing to live on. Jimmy said that he needed more time to save money for the bridewealth again. She said then that when they do eventually marry, she would like it to be legal, together with bridewealth (*magadi*). She would "pray for everything to be alright" (t). In February 1999 Sinah (and Jimmy) got into a fight with her father and was ordered out of the house. She did not go back to live with Jimmy because he lived with his family - "and they did not ask for her" (t). Instead, she lived with a friend getting handouts for food and clothes. Rather than seeing her rejection by her parents as a way out of paying the bridewealth, Sinah was more determined than ever that they should pay the money - partly to make amends to her family. Her need to pay the bridewealth was an attempt to reconcile with her father and pay him some respect by offering him money. In January 2000, when I visited Sinah, I learnt that Jimmy had not yet saved enough to pay for Sarah's bridewealth. Her family had by now little hope of getting any bridewealth, and had asked her to return home.

In 2008 when I last saw Sinah, she suggested that she still maintained a 'visiting' relationship because Jimmy had not as yet accumulated the required bridewealth.

Some mothers, in particular, Dudu Mabunda [#10], seemed to suggest that parents may ask for large amounts of money from prospective sons-in-law not just because of their financial need or greed but because they believed that it "added value" to their daughter and made a son-in-law reluctant to leave since he had paid an exorbitant amount. Dudu Mabunda attempted to make sure that high amounts of bridewealth were paid (in addition to the marriages being legally registered) before her daughters went off to live with their husbands.

The question of whether cattle payment or high bridewealth increased the stability of a marriage has long been an issue for debate (Phillips, 1953; Murray, 1981: 145-148). In Winterveld, I was also curious to establish whether "formal" and "informal" marriages could be distinguished as qualitatively different unions producing different numbers of children in the long term, that is, whether consensual unions are considerably more fragile than unions formalised by the paying of bridewealth. The South African demographic and health surveys use an all-encompassing definition of "union" to include a variety of living-together arrangements within which women are likely to be engaging in regular sexual intercourse. In focusing on women in unions (in the WS and 1987-1989 SADHS) it would seem that a higher mean number of children are born to women who have sanctioned (customary or registered) unions as opposed to those who are in consensual unions. Table 8 distinguishes between women under 30 years and over 30 years of age.

Table 8: Children born to women in "marital" and "consensual" unions, by women's age: WS and SADHS

Age	Currently married: *WS* Mean number of children born	Consensual union: *WS* Mean number of children born	Currently married: *SADHS* Mean number of children born	Consensual union: *SADHS* Mean number of children born
<= 29 years	2.1 (22)	1.3 (59)	1.8 (3674)	1.3 (1323)
>=30 years	3.4 (75)	2.7 (38)	4.4 (4690)	3.5 (486)

Sources: South African Demographic and Health Survey, 1987-1989, recode file; Winterveld survey recode file.

These results indicate that women in "proper marriages" bear more children than those in consensual unions. The validity of this assumption, however, is undermined somewhat by the fact that a "married" women might have spent periods of her life in one or more consensual union in which she bore children. Similarly, a woman currently living together might have given birth to all her children whilst in a previous formalised marriage. Small numbers of the women in the sample were divorced, separated or widowed in both the WS (16%) and the SADHS (9.6%). This also suggests that women are remarrying or entering into partnerships of various descriptions. The fluidity of marital status in Winterveld made it difficult to draw unambiguous associations between the structure of unions and relationships and the number of children born.

Nonetheless, it was regularly suggested that "*saambly*" (the Afrikaans word for "staying together" which is popular here) arrangements are more tenuous and less lasting than those, which have been formalised. Could it be as Dudu [#10] suggested, that bridewealth, in adding legitimacy to a union, strengthens (in some way) a conjugal bond, or is it the case that reluctance to part with the bridewealth makes married women experience pressure from kin to struggle through marriages and avert a separation at all costs? From the women's life histories the second scenario appears to be a common case. Given the poverty in Winterveld, bridewealth does not have to be high to keep parents bound to the terms of a marital transaction.

From the Motjieng life histories [#6]

Jacob was unaware that Freda was expecting a child until the late stages of her pregnancy. His response was that she should not worry, and that he would support the child. He did offer her some support because he was earning a regular income. Jacob's parents were of great help, always visiting and caring for their daughter, Sankie, when she was born. It was at the insistence of Jacob's mother that Jacob and Freda eventually married. The Sebolas paid a sum of money as bridewealth [*magadi*]. Freda's father had asked for money, because he did not want to delay the marriage by asking for cattle. He also did not ask for much money. The money was transferred only after the second child was born ... Sometime after the second child was born, Freda and Jacob started to have marriage problems. "Marriage was getting worse. He used to drink a lot. He used to kick the door in, and start insulting me. I began to suffer a lot. I told my parents and they said that I should bear with it. The *magadi* was already paid" (t).

Unlike Murray's (1977) depiction of the bargaining conducted by women in Lesotho for large amounts of money as bridewealth from the earnings of migrant workers, the bargaining capacities of older women in

Winterveld are constrained by the realities of an unstable labour market and high levels of unemployment. When they are fortunate enough to have the opportunity to bargain they often do so for meagre amounts. Despite the range that one could find here, payments were most commonly between R200 and R400 in the 1998-2008 period; mothers will talk of having "got something" even though it was not much and will contribute little to the household coffers. The transfer of "something" gives symbolic legitimacy to a union, and most often it is regarded as more respectable than a *saambly*-union.

The custom known as levirate, polygamy and multiple unions

(a) <u>The levirate</u>

The custom known as the levirate stresses the bond between two families (or lineages) initiated through marriage and the paying of bridewealth. Specifically, it implies that if a man dies his wife and children are to be inherited by his brothers or other male relatives. This ensures that they remain within the fold of and as property of the husband's family (Phillips, 1953:15). In the women's stories there have been quite a few references to widows being "taken over" by a husband's brother in the aftermath of his death. It would seem that this practice, which emphasises continuing guardianship of men in a particular family over wives, is prompted partly out of a sense of responsibility (of adherence to custom) and partly out of a desire to expropriate a brother's resources before these get taken over by the children, the wife's kin or outsiders. Sometimes if the widow was seen to be highly dependent on her late husband, the brother takes on a greater financial burden by attempting to support this family in addition to his own. In these cases the widow is likely to become an additional sexual partner.

Nhlapo (1991, cited in Ziel, 1997:54) suggests that the levirate remains one of the many traditional practices that discriminate against women. He maintains that these practices have had a place in agrarian subsistence economies and are now inappropriate in modern urban contexts. In Winterveld, when there are limited economic gains to be drawn from being "taken over" by a relative of a late husband or if the bridewealth has not yet been fully paid to the wife's family, a widow is likely to reject the custom and instead pursue a new relationship. An additional factor, and one of particular interest to the present study, is the way in which the responsibility of an additional partner (in accordance with the custom) may create insecurity in a man's first or primary marriage.

From the Makwela life histories [#1]:

Lebo had been familiar with the levirate custom. Her grandmother, Dina Aphane, had entered into one such union. As a teenager she [her grandmother] married Alpheus Aphane, had three living children, and was widowed in her mid-twenties. In accordance with the levirate custom, Lebo's late grandfather's cousin, Thami Mogoru, "took over Dina Aphane" as a wife a few years later. Thami Mogoru was a soldier and was often not at home, but her grandmother bore five children from this second relationship.

When Lebo was faced with her husband having to take over his brother's wife, however, she was most unhappy. She explained to me that about 3 - 4 years ago Simon's [her husband's] brother died, and Simon had to take over his brother's wife as his second "lawful" wife. Simon and his brother's wife then had some children together. Part of the unhappiness was about Simon's limited resources becoming spread between (at least) two households. In this case Lebo did not accept her husband's dutiful guardianship of his late brother's wife and proceeded to initiate a new relationship herself.

Lebo explained in more detail that since her husband spent a lot of his time with other women, she had begun to spend more of her time with S'bu, whom she loved very much. Lebo renewed her interest in contraception because of her relationship with S'bu. It also became apparent that S'bu took precautions (used condoms) in his relationship with Lebo to eliminate the possibility of impregnating her, and giving her (as a late-forties married woman) an illegitimate child. In March 1999, I was told, that this relationship was being threatened because Sbu's wife had left her homestead in Polokwane, to come and live with him in Winterveld. Lebo anticipated that she was going to be spending increasingly less time with him.

Although the levirate custom is said to be less predominant amongst younger people today, it still has a presence amongst those of Zulu, Ndebele and Shangaan origin.

(b) Polygamy

Goldman and Pebley (1989:212) suggest that "a common feature of African marriage systems is polygyny, a form of nuptiality in which some husbands have more than one wife". At the same time it is acknowledged that "polygyny is less of a feature in Southern Africa as compared to other regions" and that women in polygynous unions bear fewer children than those in monogamous unions (Pebley & Mbugua, 1989:339) since "time-sharing" of the husband between different wives leaves the wife less exposed to the risk of pregnancy. Local knowledge suggests that there are three categories of men who predominate amongst polygamists in Winterveld - these being (1) foreigners (Mozambicans and Zimbabweans) and (2) men with money - who can afford the paying of serial bridewealth and (3) "witchdoctors" or traditional healers. The Apostolic churches, the ZCC (Zionist Christian Church) and Church of Gospel (comprising mainly Zimbabweans) are known for permitting polygyny in contrast to the teachings of other churches in the area and Christian beliefs emphasising monogamy. A main motivator, however, for a polygynous union has been said to exist when a first wife is found to be infertile. In terms of customary rites a man is entitled to take a second wife if the first wife is barren. Sometimes the relatives of the barren wife "offer" another wife as a substitute, usually a younger sister of the wife. The experiences of women in polygamous unions (about thirty to forty years ago) are sometimes described in amicable terms and the relationships can be depicted as resembling those of co-workers and co-parents.

From the Skosana-Sibiya life history [#2]

Thoko Skosana's father, Stamare Mofokeng, and her mother, Dora Mphuti, were Sesotho-speakers. Her father had two wives. The elder wife was called "grandma" (in Sesotho, "Nkhono"). She recalled that they used to "live well" on the farm. There was only a problem when they did not get rain. No rain meant a lack of food, and nothing to plough. Dora, Nkhono, Stamare and all Thoko's siblings lived together in the same small homestead, though the wives slept in different rooms. Nkhono had two children, and one of her children died as an infant. Her father married the younger Dora Mphuti because Nkhono did not have more children. Dora gave birth to four children. Thoko was the last-born of Dora's children. It would seem that Dora and Nkhono had a very good relationship - cooking together and working together - almost like sisters. After Thoko was born her mother stopped having children. This is because her mother became quite sickly. It was said that there was something wrong with her womb, but they were not sure because she never had herself medically examined. Her father wanted more children, but her mother, like Nkhono before her, did not seem capable of bearing any more. Her father could have taken another wife if he chose to do so.

When Thoko married, however, *her* husband's motivation for wanting another wife did not make sense to her. It became a source of animosity in their relationship. The wives too did not have a very good relationship, and Thoko's feelings of rejection led her into an extramarital relationship.

> One day Mhlezi [Thoko's husband] came home to say that he wanted to marry another woman. Thoko was not shocked. She had suspected that he was spending time with another woman. She just wanted to know from him: "why do you need a second wife? I am getting children for you"(s). When he broke this news to her she was just about to have her second child. Shortly thereafter, Thoko gave birth to her second child. Thoko was about seventeen years old at the time. Shortly thereafter she began to do piece-jobs and work in town as a domestic worker. She would carry the last-born on her back and travel to town to work ... Mhlezi's parents did not object to his second marriage. They "took out *lobola* [bridewealth] so that he could marry the second wife"(s). They said nothing to her. They never asked if she was happy. She also said nothing because "I was stupid then"(s). Then one day the second wife, Minah, was brought to the farm. Thoko arrived from work to discover this other woman there. They did not have any *lobola* celebration. This woman just arrived, and it was the first time that she saw her. She learnt that "that girl was not staying far from the school [the night school that Mhlezi attended]. She was a much younger girl [probably about 15 years]" (s). When Thoko realised that they were all to share one room she felt quite violated. She then told him to:"take your wife and get out of this house"(s). They did not speak to each other after that. Mhlezi and his new wife moved to the back of the house. She recalled that her in-laws never asked about their squabble. Their relationship then deteriorated.

> Years later, whilst still living with her in-laws, Thoko began a relationship with another man. Having never used any kind of contraception at any point in her marriage, she now resorted to using withdrawal as a traditional method in this extramarital affair. She said: "I was living with my in-laws. It is not in our custom to have someone else's child and be living with your husband's family"(s).

Polygynous unions often invite extramarital relations on the part of women and extra-marital unions appear to encourage contraceptive use (both modern and traditional). In Table 9 the "union status" and contraceptive use of women in "polygynous" unions in the Winterveld sample is compared with that of women in the 1987-1989 SADHS sample.

Table 9: Polygynous unions and contraceptive use: WS and SADHS

	WS	SADHS
Proportion of women in polygynous unions	12% (35)	9% (900)
Proportion of women in polygynous unions who were "formally married"	57% (20)	81% (729)
Proportion of women in polygynous unions currently using methods	80% (28)	72% (623)
Proportion of all women using methods	72% (212)	60% (9709)

Sources: South African Demographic and Health Survey, 1987-1989, recode file; Winterveld survey recode file.

The 1987-1989 SADHS confirmed that a small number of women live in "polygynous unions" in South Africa. A large number of women in polygynous unions (45.6%) were over the age of 35 years. In the Winterveld sample, 31% of the women in polygynous unions were over the age of 35 years, whilst the largest proportion (48%) comprised of younger women between the ages of 26 and 34 years. The SADHS broadened the definition of polygynous unions by asking women in consensual unions whether their husbands had other partners. Most women in polygynous unions in the SADHS sample claimed to be in formal marriages (81%), rather than living-together unions. It is possible thus that co-wives were duly recognised in most of these unions after the following of customs concluding with the paying of bridewealth. In Merafeng, 20 "married" women and 15 women in living-together unions claimed that their husbands/partners had other wives/partners. Thus, although "polygyny is less of a feature in Southern Africa as compared to other regions", the blurring of the lines between marriage and partnership, the reality of high rates of marital instability and dissolution, and movements between states of "being married" to "living together" (and vice versa) is leading to notions of "multiple associations" being viewed as synonymous with polygyny.

Polygynous unions by their very nature suggest less frequent sexual relations for individual women, given the presence of other wives. The comparatively high proportion of women in polygynous unions using contraception may then seem a bit surprising. It could be that this predominantly older group of women is taking measures to control the number of additional children that they could have since they have already reached their ideal family size or it could mean that they have been persuaded to do so out of fear that their husbands would have a sum total of too many children to support; or they may wish to limit the number of children they could potentially have given insecurity in their relationships; or as in the case of Lebo and Thoko, contraceptive use, in the absence of husbands or partners, is to facilitate "extramarital" relationships and prevent the possibility of having children within them.

Elijah Nkomo (65) was a well-known personality in my fieldwork site. Although a household name through his involvement in community politics over the years, Elijah's popularity had a lot to do with him being a polygamist as well. In my interviews with him he admitted to having three wives and eighteen children. He once told me that if he were wealthier he would not hesitate to have more wives. Yet, the more I moved around the area conducting interviews, the more "Mrs Nkomos" I seemed to discover. Through my fieldwork encounters I learnt that Elijah Nkomo had at least six "wives" and thirty children. In interviewing Nani Nkomo (Mrs Nkomo senior) I became more aware of the continuing dilemmas of the wives of polygamists in contemporary times.

From the Nkomo life histories [#12]

When they first married, Nani did not anticipate that he [Elijah Nkomo] would turn out to be a polygamist. She had been aware that he associated with many other women but she did not suspect infidelity. He did not discuss the work he did outside the home and she chose not to ask. The first time that she had to deal with one of his other relationships was when Elijah came to her one day and admitted that one of his girlfriends was pregnant. She was quite clear about what had to be done. "I told him that he must go and marry this other woman and bring her home"(x). So he married this other woman, Lydia, and brought her home ... After that she became quite distressed to hear about many other "wives". He has "married" some of them [with bridewealth], but not all. "The biggest problem with having many wives is that he is not able to support them"(x). Nani complained that Elijah did not provide her with sufficient financial support. She supported her children with the money she made as a *sangoma* [traditional healer]. People paid her for healing them [in her work as a traditional healer] and for the herbal medicines they received. But she did not make very much money through this occupation. Besides, she has had to constantly watch her back. If she was not present all the time in the shop, the other "wife" would take the earnings and give her nothing in return. When she was not in the shop, the other wife usually claimed that there had been no customers, and therefore she made no money. There was little co-operation between the wives and much competition.

Elijah Nkomo was arrested briefly in 1999 for his involvement in certain political activities. Shortly before he was detained, Tumi Munyai, one of his wives (whom other wives referred to as a "girlfriend" because no bridewealth was paid) grew weary of waiting for him to pay his dues and left for Venda to marry another man. Nani was overjoyed because this "small *makoti*"[young wife, in this context] had become quite favoured by Elijah. When Tumi arrived from Venda, with photographs of her traditional and very expensive wedding celebrations, I asked her how "acceptable" it was for her to now have "two husbands". She did not see anything extraordinary about her having a husband (who had paid the bridewealth in Venda) and another common-law husband whom she saw infrequently in Merafeng. This was the first high profile polyandrous-type union that I was aware of in Winterveld. Unfortunately for Tumi, both the local men and women did not take kindly to her "double-union" status, and she became the butt of much ridicule in Elijah Nkomo's circle. When Elijah was detained Tumi called a public meeting of plot-owners, but the meeting was poorly attended largely because people were uncomfortable, I was told, about Tumi's status. "Who is she?", Nozizwe Radebe asked me. "Doesn't she have a husband? We hear funny things here." Although it was common knowledge that both men and women engaged in extramarital relationships, and sustained multiple unions, it was generally expected that men (who can legitimately marry more than one wife) could be open about these relationships but that women should display more discretion. The fertility implications of women engaging in multiple unions or being part of more established polyandrous-type unions is not considered seriously by studies of fertility or family life. I do not suggest that polyandry was a factor affecting fertility in Winterveld. It is nonetheless an issue, together with the implications of multiple partnerships, which should be probed if a more comprehensive picture of reproductive dynamics in peri-urban areas is to be developed (Hunter, 2002, 2007; Masanjala, 2007).

Unions and customs: breast-feeding and post-partum sexual abstinence

From the Skosana-Sibiya life histories [#2]

Thoko breast-fed each child until she discovered that she was pregnant with another child. She said: "There is this belief that if you are pregnant with a child the breastmilk is intended for that child, and it is then that you must stop. If you breast-feed a child whilst pregnant it will be as though you are feeding it with "dirty milk"(s). Thoko did not at any point attempt to deliberately use breast-feeding for spacing births. "We did not know anything about the value of breast-feeding"(s). She did not remember how soon after child-birth her menstruation used to return. She followed no post-partum customs and did not deliberately abstain from sex in the period after giving birth. She recalled that she became sterile immediately after her last baby was born and that she never menstruated again."I did not follow any customs. It was only when my husband was away that I was having a rest"(s).

Thoko's daughter, Martha, however, was advised by her in-laws to practise sexual abstinence whilst breast-feeding. Martha breast-fed her son for about three months. She knew that it was for a short period because the child "weaned itself" whilst still small by "leaving the breasts". After that it was bottle-fed. Amenorrhoea was short, as she menstruated quite soon giving birth. Although she was made aware of the breast-feeding custom which required post-partum sexual abstention, she did not tell her husband that she wanted to follow it because he would tell her what she could do and could not do [not the other way around]. She was scared of refusing him, she said, "in case he would rape me"(s). Sometimes her husband used to listen to her and "they could talk" - "but sometimes he was strict and harsh. He was in charge." It was not her task "to tell him about customs. It was for his parents to tell him." She believed that his parents did talk to him about it "because during the time I was breast-feeding, he was withdrawing"(s).

Unlike the many foreign women (Mozambican and Zimbabwean women) who appeared to make use of continuous breast-feeding as a natural contraceptive measure, local South African women, both young and old, living in Merafeng did not appear to have devised practices to sustain amenorrhoea deliberately through breast-feeding. Cultural beliefs held by all groups of women but particularly by Northern Sotho, Ndebele and Zulu-speakers, emphasising the harmful effects to the developing child (of the mother engaging in sexual intercourse whilst breast-feeding) usually encourage some period of post-partum sexual abstinence. A majority of women, irrespective of age or union status, both in the SADHS sample (54.7%) and the Winterveld sample (64.1%) appeared to practise sexual abstention after giving birth. These have no doubt been significant in sustaining longer intervals between births, especially when contraception is not used soon after child-birth. Some of the experiences of older women can be referred to.

Khanyi Mabetwa (78) [#4] explained that in the past there was no contraception and no family planning. She did not contemplate or take any measures to stop having children. She would have one child, then wait three months, and then fall pregnant again. She said that she did believe in the custom of abstaining from sexual relations whilst breastfeeding, but often she would engage in sexual relations with her husband, and he would practise withdrawal. Elsie Mashinini (81) [#7], on the other hand, claimed that she did not know where these beliefs about sexual abstention to avoid "spoiling of the milk" emerged from. She claimed that it was a "new belief" which women were subscribing to. Her understanding was that the only practice which they had in the past was a period of confinement in the mother-in-law's house. "We would stay for three and a half months. Then the mother-in-law would call the husband to come and see the child"(s). Clara Molefe (64) [#8] also talked about a period of confinement before her husband saw the child for the first time. Her period of confinement, however, was followed by a period of customary sexual abstinence.

From the Molefe-Ramashala life histories [#8]

"It was two months before my husband could see the child. I did not want to sleep with him for eight months after that. He listened to me. He "went outside" [he had an extra-marital affair]. I did not get cross because I wanted the child to grow up healthy. My mother used to frighten me by saying that "if you sleep with your husband while the child is small, the child's skin is going to be rough. Its legs will be thin"(s).

Sankie Motjieng (29) was a highly educated younger woman who followed very few traditional customs. However, she practised sexual abstinence for a long period in the belief that it would keep her daughter healthy.

From the Motjieng life histories [#6]

"My mother used to tell me - don't do it. I see now that it is true. My boyfriend's mother also told me. I breast-fed Beverly for one and a half years. In that time I abstained for one and a half years. When I took the child to the clinic everybody loved and admired her. I said "I can't do this [can't spoil the milk] to my child. People will laugh at me"(e).

Post-partum sexual abstinence is practised by many women, irrespective of marital status. It is most strongly practised when guidance from, in particular, mothers and mothers-in-law is forthcoming. The extent to which they can abstain from sex depends on their ability to communicate with their partners. Many women will talk about their husbands "going outside" as a consequence of their abstaining. That is why sexual intercourse with withdrawal is treated as exactly the same thing as abstention, despite it being a more risky abstention. In studying polygyny and marital infidelities among the Basotho, Spiegel (1991:154) was told by male informants that extramarital relations were a consequence of the demise of polygyny. He was told that, unlike in the past, men nowadays could not afford many wives, and that this was particularly problematic in the post-partum period when the wife has to practise sexual abstinence to avoid the spoiling of her milk. Spiegel also states that whilst Ashton (1952, cited in Spiegel & McAllister, 1991:163) suggests that "sexual activity had to be restricted to coitus interruptus" [withdrawal] his informants suggested "a total prohibition." In Merafeng a fair proportion of sexually active women, whether married or not, do abstain in the period after giving birth. For those who do not, withdrawal is common. Despite this, much "going outside" and infidelities are still evident.

Theme 1: Conjugal instability: a consequence of domestic struggles, infidelities and violence in unions

In the early stages of my fieldwork I did not anticipate that the issue of violence as a reflection of and contribution to the instability of households and conjugal unions would emerge so strongly in the stories of women. Despite its poverty, one witnesses a fair degree of goodwill amongst neighbours and within families in Merafeng (and broader Winterveld). By the time my initial fieldwork phase had somewhat petered out, however, it was quite evident, through comparing the trajectories of life experiences, that virtually all the women I had interviewed (both young and old) had encountered moments of violence in their lives - though to varying degrees. Whilst we could refer to institutional violence impoverishing daily life under apartheid, and the experience of assaults, harassment and detentions during the years of forced removals and influx control, the greater emphasis in the women's narratives centred on beatings, rape and sexual abuse at the hands of men in their families and with whom they related. But whether the violence is talked about as being in the "public" or "private" domain, numerous references to counterviolence in which women have been participants are also apparent. Men and women in Winterveld responded in the past to the violence of the Bophuthatswana government by colluding to kill collaborators, police officers and councillors. Today community tribunals may spontaneously emerge to discipline a thief or a rapist. In a similar kind of way, the women's stories suggest that endurance of violence often leads to particular kinds of response which may in turn be violent, e.g. when women gang up to beat an abuser or attempt to punish a man through denial, or theft of his resources. A woman may also react to a man's violence by attempting to punish him by refusing to cook, by denial of sexual favours, or by simply running away (Kotze & Van der Waal, 1995).

Two stories detailing episodes of violence over the life courses of marriage and family life are referred to here.

From the Molefe-Ramashala life-histories [#8]

When I first met Thandi Ramashala she presented a very positive picture of her marriage (12 August 1998). Describing herself as happy in her marriage and her husband as a good provider she added "a marriage is a lucky". She saw herself as being much better off than most of the other women with whom she worked at the Sisters of Mercy, and who were suffering, because they were poor and "without any husbands".

In a later interview (29 October 1998) Thandi admitted: "When we got married in 1982, I never saw the honeymoon with him. After a while he was staying with Letta Chilowane. When I was pregnant with Anna, she was also pregnant. Then Petros's [her husband's] mother went to see Letta and asked her: do you know that he has a wife? She said that she did not know"(e/s). Then Petros's mother came back and said to Thandi: "I do not know if he is coming back. You must go." [Shortly thereafter, Letta Chilowane's partner turned up, having been gone for about a year, to discover Petros living with her.] "Then another man turned up and hit Petros. It was Letta's boyfriend. He broke Petros's teeth. He came back at 2 o'clock one morning. There was blood all over. He told me all about it"(s). On the day that Thandi disclosed this, she also revealed her dilemmas concerning her daughter's [Pinky's] abuse at the hands of her husband, and how despite it all she had still attempted to save her marriage. She was particularly open because a few days before this interview Petros had packed his belongings and left their home.

Early one morning (12 January 1999) I stopped on the road to pick up a highly emotional Thandi. She was on her way to her youngest daughter's school. She had just heard from a friend of Petros's that he was on his way to take his daughter out of school in order to kill her. "Why would he do that?" I asked. Thandi explained that Petros had returned the week before. She had not anticipated that he would return, so she had let the house out. Thandi and her children then moved in with her elderly aunts who were living in a separate house on the same plot. So furious was Petros when he discovered that the house had been leased, that he attacked the man living in the house with a knife, leaving him injured. He then located Thandi at her family house and chased her around the house in an attempt to stab her. When the family intervened he threw bricks at them and injured his youngest daughter, Gift, in the head. The next day Thandi laid a charge against him for the attempted murder of Gift. Petros was then apprehended at his workplace, and formally charged at a police station. He was apparently very surprised that Thandi would report him to the police. Now he sent messages saying he was really going to murder Gift. We took Gift out of school that day.

In 2002, Thandi fell ill and passed away. People referred to the causes of death as 'stress' and 'sadness'. Her eldest daughter, Pinky, attempted to keep the family together in the aftermath, but squabbles over resources left the sisters fighting amongst themselves, sometimes violently. The sisters finally drifted apart after Pinky set Gift's bed alight after an argument one afternoon in 2006.

From the Motjieng life histories [#6]

Just as Freda began to earn her own money, her husband Jacob became unemployed. He lost his job because he was frequently absent (due to drunkenness). He had been working at the abattoirs. He was constantly accusing her of having affairs, and was becoming increasingly jealous. She could not say why he behaved in this fashion - "he was a *tsotsi* [a hooligan]". Then in 1978, everything came to a head. Someone suggested to Jacob that Freda was having an affair with her neighbour - a man younger than she was. "I do not know why he thought I was sleeping with that young boy ... my brother came home to tell me that they saw him [Jacob] with a knife on Christmas Day. He said to my brother, "see this knife. I am going to use it to kill your sister." After I heard that I ran away and hid in my uncle's house"(t). But Jacob did not come after her. Instead he confronted her neighbour with accusations of having an affair with Freda. A fight broke out on the street, and Jacob stabbed the neighbour to death. The stabbing, witnessed by people all around, invited what has become commonly known as "community justice". Jacob faced the wrath of people from the surrounding homes, as they kicked and beat him. They left him after they thought that they had killed him, and his elder brother rushed to his rescue. His brother, with the assistance of the police, took him to hospital, where the doctors managed to save his life. Freda never liked Jacob's elder brother. It was the elder brother who had made her life with Jacob worse by insisting that he should "beat me to discipline me" (t).

Someone came to see Freda to tell her that Jacob was in hospital. She was too scared to visit him in hospital. She knew his elder brother was helping him, so she did not see why she should be there, particularly in the light of what he had done. She was now tired of him, and did not want to see him ever again. Her father-in-law came to see her, and offered his support. He was sorry for his son's behaviour. Jacob spent a long time in hospital until he recovered. When he recovered he was charged with murder and was sentenced to a long prison term. He then disappeared completely from her life. "I started to breathe again ... I was now free"(t). He never attempted to make contact with them again. Her children today, she said, understand all that she went through. "They are not depressed about the situation. They are not worried about him ... They know he was a trouble-maker"(t).

Although the levels of violence in South Africa have been rated as amongst the highest in the world, there are few substantive sociological studies that attempt to offer explanations for the scale and nature of violent acts perpetrated, particularly within the domestic and familial spheres. The causes of violence amongst kin are varied and complex, and reflect embedded inequalities and tensions unique to family settings; in gendered terms, the abuse of women within households (both mothers and daughters) is an indication of their vulnerability and dependence on men in the family and their subordinate status within the larger institutions of society. Kotze and Van der Waal (1995:2) suggest that,"[p]eople learn, in their experience of social and political violence, to become emotionally hardened, on the one hand, and that violence is the only effective and therefore acceptable social instrument in situations of extreme competition and confrontation, on the other hand." There are many references in the literature to "a culture of violence" that persists in particular areas in South Africa to the extent that social life is described as one "in which violence becomes accepted as a norm ... its use is so widespread that acts of violence do not produce any sense of outrage" (Segel & Labe, 1990:255). Such a description holds little meaning for the experience of violence in the Winterveld context. Here violent acts do produce outrage, anger and much resistance, particularly on the part of women, both in the micro-contexts of domesticity and on the streets as evidenced by women's demonstrations at taxi ranks and in vigilante attacks on suspected child rapists in 2008 and 2009.

My purpose in this part of the chapter is to present a few more of the experiences of women illustrating the circumstances in which violence has occurred, and in which it has led to the deterioration of conjugal relations. In the Motjieng story and in some of the stories which follow, violence occurs in the course of accusations of infidelity. In most of the cases, the pursuit of multiple unions has as one of its motives the need to derive financial support from other men. But conflict over money also occurs as a result of struggles between mothers-in-law and daughters-in-law, children and parents, and women and their boyfriends.

From the Mashinini life histories [#7]

Elsie Mashinini had a tough life. She married at a very young age and moved into her mother-in-law's homestead. Relegated to the status of a servant, she experienced much abuse and starvation at the hands of the women in the house. They "poisoned" her husband's mind against her, and when he did not return for two years, she left for her own independent homestead ... When Zenele [Elsie's daughter] faced a similar kind of situation in her in-laws' home, her response was also to give up on her marriage and return to her mother's home. Zenele had married Vusi Mahlobo in 1960. He was a much older man, and she was his second wife. His first wife did not have any children. She moved in with his family and became a *makoti* [daughter-in-law] there. She was not "under a single authority"(s). Her husband was the boss but her mother-in-law gave the orders. Her in-laws were not good to her. Her mother-in-law was bad, she said, because she was allowing her sons to have girlfriends. Every now and then her husband would stay away for a long time and she would know that he was with other girlfriends. He would also give his mother money - and not her. She did not have enough money to send her children to school. Vusi used to beat her regularly on her mother-in-law's instructions, and chase her out the house. Eventually, she decided that the best thing to do was to leave her in-laws' home and go back to live with her mother. When she went back to her mother's house on the farm, her mother sent her children to school. She left her children with her mother and went off to look for a job in Pretoria.

Although Zenele had reacted to her husband's beatings and neglect by leaving his family home, her mother-in-law had played a significant role in manipulating the control and use of his money, and ensuring that Zenele was kept on a tight rein. She would take her son's wages and keep Zenele's demands suppressed through regular beatings.

Whilst Thoko Skosana (in the next story) was a compliant and long-suffering woman, her daughter Martha displayed much greater ability in taking charge of her reproductive life in the knowledge that with her husband deceased, she would most likely find herself in other short-term abusive relationships. Her particular concern was with violent men who were "disloyal" but who would also exploit her as a working woman, for her money.

From the Skosana-Sibiya life-histories [#2]

Thoko Skosana had all ten of her children while living with her in-laws. Her husband was often away, and she "felt trapped with his family" - sometimes feeling sad and confused and tempted to run away back to her parent's home. As the number of her children increased, the possibility of going back home became much slimmer. During these times, the church was important to Thoko. It used to help to go to church when her problems started. She attended the church her in-laws frequented - the Ethiopia church - and it was her "belief in God that made me stronger in accepting life as it was" (s). When it came to the number of children she eventually had, she can say that her in-laws "never put me under any pressure" (s). The only involvement from them was when it came to delivering the babies, and with the little support they offered in bringing them up. They never suggested that she should have more or fewer children. The number of children she ended up with was just a matter between herself, Mhlezi [her husband]"and God". "In those days", Thoko explained, "there was never any planning, and the in-laws never spoke to us about much." She simply "gave herself" to her husband and the births were a consequence of his "being around" rather than a matter of her choice or desire for more children (s). The birth intervals were close for the first two children, and she cannot say how spaced out the remaining births were. She was not unduly perturbed by her miscarriage and still-born births. She did not feel that she had to cover up by having another birth to make up for any loss. She saw it as a matter of "children who die go to God. It is just the way things happen"(s).

Martha Sibiya, Thoko's daughter, was widowed after being married for a short while. She never contemplated remarriage although she had many relationships after her husband's death. When she was giving birth to a child (whose father she barely remembered) she knew that she would find herself in that predicament again and was therefore prompted to "close herself up" (s). This was a good decision because "she never found a good man since"(s). The problem with men, in her experience, was that "men like to hit. I only seem to meet violent men.

Some of them hit because they are jealous. You have to watch out if you are late, or if you come home with less money. They ask: where is your money? Or, you came home yesterday at 6 pm, now today at 5 pm. Why were you late yesterday?"(s). After her daughter was born she had a relationship with a violent man. He used to beat her until she could take it no longer. "In the end, when you tell them to go - they take time to go ... I also did not want another husband because loyalty is a problem. They always find another woman. You never know what they're doing" (s).

Nomasonto Nkomo attempted to punish her husband for treating her badly, and for subjecting her to a poor set of living conditions, whilst at the same time bringing in another "wife".

From the Nkomo life histories [#12]

On 2 March 1999 I went to see Nani Nkomo. Mr Nkomo was in detention at the time and she expressed much distress about the fact that almost no-one had offered her any financial assistance. Her house was in disarray, and she looked very ill. She needed R41 to get to her son in KwaNdebele to borrow a larger sum of money from him. She had thought that her daughter, Nomasonto, would be able to get money from her businessman husband, but instead Nomasonto's marriage had broken down completely a few days before. Nomasonto had for a long while been unhappy with her husband bringing home a 17-year-old girl, and relations between them had soured. She began to spend longer hours outside the house running one of the shops which he owned. Then the previous week he apparently walked into the shop and accused her of having an affair with another man [a regular customer]. After a violent argument he beat her and then asked her to leave his house. He asked her not to pack because everything belonged to him - but simply to leave. Nomasonto went to her room and proceeded to set some of her husband's belongings alight. Her husband had her arrested for arson and she was jailed for four days until a neighbour paid her bail, an amount of R500. She then suffered from depression because she did not have R500 to pay him back.

Despite the dependence and pandering to men for financial support often shown, there is also evidence of opposition and non-compliance when women are ill-treated or subjected to excessive authoritarian behaviour. Stereotypical ideological constructions of "male role" and "female role", however, have not been sufficiently transformed. Amongst the poor women I've spent time interviewing, a strong sense of the man as "money-giver" or husband as "breadwinner" prevails despite the fact that support is often not forthcoming and survival is dependent on a woman's manipulation of her mother's pension or some other person's wages, if she herself does not earn any money. An image of women as being (not powerless, but) less powerful than men is pervasive in many cultures and societies. Within the African context, the marriage contract in which women are "exchanged" for money (a custom which women largely support) entrenches a sense of woman as man's property. In Winterveld, even without a contract, (by merely staying and cooking) a woman in a union is commonly viewed as a man's property by virtue of expected monetary exchanges.

The reality, though, of high levels of domestic violence in Winterveld should be seen, not merely as an admission of the subordinate position of women, but as an indication of numerous contestations at the household level. Violence, as in wife-beating, does not necessarily silence arguments about the use of money, about infidelities, and about support of children and other kin, but it often threatens the stability and duration of the union. Attempts by women to wield more power in daily decisions and to shift outcomes in their favour are not always successful, hence the continuation of minor disputes and more violent manifestations of conflict.

In the survey conducted in my fieldwork site, Merafeng, in Winterveld (WS) a question was asked in an attempt to assess power and decision-making in unions. Surveys, of course, are not the best instruments for studying the complexity and dynamics of power relations. Nonetheless, answers to the questions on "who decides on the following...?" are informative. They are important because they offered women an opportunity to rank their decision-making roles in relation to those of partners and others. Three out of the five sets of responses emphasised "joint" decision-making. Rather than an indication of egalitarian relationships, these responses given by women suggest an involvement in making (or wanting to make) these decisions though it may not always conclude in women's favour. "Joint decisions" are most evident on those contested matters of "how to use money" and "how to rear children".

Table 10: Decision-making in unions, all women: WS

Decisions	Man decides	Woman decides	Joint decision	Other decides
How money should be spent	13% (38)	34.5% (101)	51.2% (150)	1.4% (4)
Whether contraception should be used	6.6% (19)	58.5% (169)	31.1% (90)	3.8% (11)
How many children to have	13.7% (40)	39.7% (116)	43.8% (128)	2.7% (8)
What lessons children should learn	5.5% (16)	35.6% (104)	54.5% (159)	4.5% (13)
The allocation of household duties	3.1% (9)	50.9% (149)	43.7% (128)	2.4% (7)

Source: Winterveld Survey, 1998, recode file.

"Other" (understood to be primarily other family members) does not appear to play a major part in influencing the decisions of a woman or a couple. "Other" features more visibly in decisions on child-rearing, contraceptive use and to some extent with respect to how many children a woman ought to have. These interventions probably exist when very young daughters are involved. Men are most involved in "how many children to have" but are hardly involved in decisions on "whether contraception should be used". Almost 60% of women claim to be the decision-maker concerning whether or not contraception should be used. An indication of the tensions that could arise as a result of this can be seen by the following comparison: 59% of the married women and 63% of the women in consensual unions said that their husbands approved their use of contraception; 23% of married women and 22% of the women in consensual unions said that their husbands disapproved, whilst the remainder were unsure of their husband's attitudes. Of those whose husbands disapproved, 20.3% of the married women and 20% of those in consensual unions continue to use contraception (clandestinely).

This theme was intended to illustrate circumstances contributing to the deterioration of conjugal relations and dissolution of unions. It also focused on the difficulties women faced, in the context of family life, in gaining control over the various facets of their lives. Violence, domestic discord and non-egalitarian relationships have implications for fertility. The weakening of bonds, periods of separation (e.g. when being "chased away") and breakdowns of unions, suggest fewer opportunities to conceive and bear children than would be the case with unions exhibiting stability and continuity. At the same time, dependence on men, subordination in relationships and involvement with numerous men for support and companionship increase the risk of conception. In some instances, bearing children guarantees support. In others, unplanned children present new burdens. The key empowering factor for women contending with these decisions against the background of these insecurities appears to be the ability to determine when and with whom contraception should be used (Naidoo, 2002).

Theme 2: The perpetuation of domestic instability: the unreliability of kinship networks and the distribution of the social parenting process

Customs and social practices associated with marital definitions and transactions are changing over time, and some of these changes can be attributed to a recognition of the transitory nature of partnerships and the fluidity of unions and domestic arrangements. The micro-survey (WS) showing a fair proportion of women in my fieldwork site defining themselves as being in a union, either formal or consensual, also shows women having comparatively fewer children than seen in the national sample (SADHS). It has been contended, thus far, (in this and the previous chapter) that part of the explanation for lower fertility levels has to do with shorter-term relationships, abandonment and women's use of modern and traditional contraceptive measures to control and delay child-bearing. Social definitions of parenthood and claims on children within the ambit of supportive extended families are additional factors to consider if we are to understand the strategies adopted by women to rear children when their marriages fail or remain insecure. In taking a critical position with respect to demography's biological definition of fertility, Townsend (1997: 109) suggests that "births cannot be unproblematically attributed to the women who bore them if we are interested in either the causes or consequences of these births." The particular problem with seeing a woman's fertility in biological terms only is that her reproductive history (as in the number of children she has had over the years) becomes viewed as the only or main motivator for decisions on desired family size. The fact that these decisions are also influenced by the number of children she leaves to be reared by others, or takes on to rear for others, is often overlooked. In addition, demographic and health survey questions on desired family size are structured in terms of assumptions that the woman is the primary (if not the sole) locus of reproductive decision-making and that family members, and others who might play an important role in nurturing and rearing her children, are not active in influencing such decisions (Caldwell, 1985).

The meanings attached to child fosterage and the circulation of children between the homes of their parents, grandparents, and other kin and the implication of child circulation for future fertility considerations have persistently been raised by anthropological demographers. The specific question here is to what extent are the "costs" and "benefits" of bearing children being reassessed in the light of the fostering-out of children? In other words, does child-rearing by kin and the prevalence of familial support networks work as a disincentive to limit their child-bearing - because the "costs" are absorbed by other kin who derive and anticipate reciprocal benefits from children and their parents (Bledsoe & Isiugo-Abanihe, 1989; Caldwell, 1982; Page, 1989)? Or, conversely, as in the case of peri-urban areas like Winterveld, would the prevalence of fluid and unreliable support networks, and resistance by kin to assuming "traditional" and long-term child-rearing roles, serve to discourage women from having large numbers of children?

Anthropological studies have long illuminated the social processes of marriage in African societies in which men have made claims to fatherhood through the paying of bridewealth. Children have "traditionally" been valued in African societies - African societies being largely high-fertility ones. These statements tend to reinforce a belief that there is generally low interest in biological origins of children, and similarly that there is easy incorporation into social networks and kin groups which play supportive roles in their rearing. There are some suggestions in the stories of older women that biological paternity was never a source of stress in a marriage and that, particularly amongst those in Merafeng who originated from the surrounding farms, children were welcomed as sources of wealth. These experiences are not apparent in the stories of younger women. Given the prevalence of multiple unions and considerable insecurity in relationships there is much interest in biological origins of children and the questioning of paternity or the marrying of a woman who has had prior children may result in a man refusing to financially support (e.g. not paying school fees or participating in feeding) the children in question. In addition, as suggested in the previous chapter, there are circumstances in which a step-child can sometimes be expected to become "another wife" of the step-father.

Martha Sibiya's life history offers an illustration of how the birth of an additional child is valued in itself, despite it being fathered by an unknown person.

From the Skosana-Sibiya life-histories [#2]

After Martha's son was born in 1963, Isaac Sibiya [Martha's husband] and his family sought permission for their marriage. Her parents did not object to the marriage. They asked for six cows as *magadi* [bridewealth]. After the celebrations were over Martha went to live with her in-laws. It was not difficult to live with them because "they were very nice to me". She used to treat them like her own parents. Isaac's parents did not have many children themselves. They had only three sons. Isaac was the first to get married. [At that stage the family lived on a farm and all the brothers worked as labourers.] Being the eldest son, Isaac supported the family by doing work in town, bringing home an income of R2 a month. In 1965, Isaac was getting off a train when he tripped on the tracks and got knocked down by an oncoming train. He was crushed to death. "One day we got a telegram. It said that Isaac was dead. We were very shocked" (s). It was a devastating blow for the entire family. Not only had they lost a much-loved son but he was their primary source of income. After his death, Martha was at a loss and did not know what to do. Her in-laws did not want her to leave and certainly not to take her child with her. Her son was their first grandchild and "they did not want me to take him away"(s). She stayed with her in-laws for a few years. Eventually, though, they understood when she explained that "I had to find work and get on with my life"(s). They said that she could go but should leave the child with them. They did not want to lose touch with their grandchild. Isaac's younger brother too was no longer living with them so they very badly wanted to keep their grandchild with them. Whilst away, Martha had a relationship with another man, and fell pregnant. She did not inform this man that she was pregnant with his child ... After giving birth to her daughter she decided to take her to her in-laws' home. Her in-laws took the child over as their grandchild. They did not mind that this new granddaughter was not (biologically) their son's child. They looked after her with care for many years, and the child's paternity was never an issue. In 1999 her daughter was still unaware of the fact that she had had a different biological father. "She believes her father is Isaac Sibiya. It makes no difference"(s). It was a mutually benefiting arrangement. Her in-laws had wanted a daughter to bring up; leaving her daughter with her in-laws gave Martha the chance to look for work again.

The women I interviewed in Winterveld were able, most often, to distinguish between their biological and non-biological parents (non-biological parents were primarily grandparents who reared them). There was, however, still a sense that one can never be sure about who the biological father was. This uncertainty together with high levels of desertion from male partners has made the parenting role of women much more significant than that of men. In one of my group sessions with fourteen young people (*Youth* group I) I learnt that none of them lived with a biological father. This was not a fact that they considered troublesome because the mother role was considered more important. As I was told:

> Most of us who do not have fathers do not see it as a problem. We believe in mothers. The father does play an important role but it is the mother who is most important. As long as there is a mother at home, and she is earning money, then there is no problem. But if there is only a father and no mother, then it is not the same"... "We could experience many problems. Maybe the father will bring another woman. That becomes a problem. This stepmother will oppress us, especially if she brings her own children. Sometimes the woman will beat us and not give food (e).

From the Mabetwa-Makgoba life histories [#4]

> Louisa grew up as the daughter of a well-known and well-off family. "I was one of ten children. We are three boys and seven girls who are today alive. I cannot say which child has had which father. Maybe our mother was cheating our father. Since a woman stays alone in the house much of the time you do not know who is consoling her. There is a saying in Tswana, 'the woman is the one who knows whose children are whose'. The father does not know these things"(e).

Lebo Makwela's account of her fertility history, and her changing kin support base, bears a similarity to the many stories that I have heard about early births and the strength of the initial support structure which becomes increasingly fragile over time. In her story, her children became Makwela's children and she then became somewhat dissociated from her natal family. She was enormously frustrated in her middle age as her husband became less supportive and her unmarried daughters brought home children from absent partners.

From the Makwela life histories [#1]

> Lebo had two children whose fathers never knew of their existence. After her first child, David, was born, her father, who had been furious about the illegitimate birth, started to relax a bit and seemed quite

happy. In fact, her father assumed the "father- role" and bought her milk to feed the baby since she was not breast-feeding. She was heartened by the additional fact that many members of her family collaborated to assist her in bringing up the child. Her brother's wife bought clothes for the baby; "the baby had a good start to life"(t). Lebo's family resembled an extended family and comprised grandmother, father, mother, Lebo, new baby, elder brother, elder brother's wife, elder brother's two children, second brother, elder sister, cousin's child. Lebo left her child with her mother and went to look for work.

It did not take her long to find work. Her first job, at the age of twenty years, was in a small laundry in Marabastad, Pretoria town. At the laundry she did all kinds of jobs - receiving goods, doing administrative work and ensuring that the pressing machine and damper were in good working order. But she was not earning well, and eventually decided to leave that work. Whilst working she had had a brief relationship with another man, Willie, whom she met in Marabastad, and she now found herself pregnant again. Like the first pregnancy, she had taken no precautions, and had just been hopeful that she would not be so unlucky as to fall pregnant. It was another mistake. Willie had left without knowing that she was pregnant, and she never saw him again. In 1973, her second child - a daughter, Sophy, was born. She then spent time at home again, looking after two children, and being supported by her family ... A few years later (in about 1976) another family (the Makwelas) moved in next door. They were from Belfast in Mpumalanga, and were renting land, and living as tenants, in Winterveld. Soon Lebo and the sixth-born son of the Makwela family started a relationship, and she fell pregnant again. She had two children with Simon Makwela before they married in 1980. In 1980 they married formally, with the Makwela family paying the relevant brideprice, followed by a legal registration. It was only after this that Lebo and Simon moved out of their respective homes and set up their own home, finally living together in Winterveld. All the children took on Makwela's surname as they were now his children ... Since then Lebo no longer looked to her family as a source of support. Having married, they assumed that she and Makwela were responsible for the upkeep and well-being of their family. When Sophy and Sinah [Lebo's third child] fell pregnant and added their children to the responsibilities of their mother's household, Lebo was not particularly supportive. Lebo had had her last two children in 1991 and 1994. Her teenage daughters had also given birth - one in 1992 and the other in 1994. These were particularly difficult years. They also coincided with Lebo's growing reliance on a boyfriend for financial assistance rather than on her husband. She told me that she had often thought of taking her family to live on her father's plot (which has now been taken over by her brothers). She feared, though, that her brothers would demand that her husband buy things and would question him on his movements. She did not want any trouble. She added that "my brothers do not want my husband to get too familiar, especially because of his problem of not coming home"(t).

In the Makwela case, Lebo's husband did not differentiate between the children and all were treated as his own. Lebo's main complaint was his inability to support them financially. Although the paying of bridewealth connects the woman and her children to a man's family, in practice it does not always imply that there is no distinction between biological and non-biological children, or that they are afforded the same status. Three cases will be illustrated here. In Flora Radebe's [#3] case, she left her grandmother's home pregnant with a child from a prior relationship, to live with her husband (whom she married through customary rites); neither Flora nor her child were ever properly integrated into the man's family. He married someone else and she left him to live with her mother. She then sent her son to live with her brother whom she saw as better-off and therefore more capable of bringing him up than she was. Another case is that of Sarah Gamede - the daughter of Manto Mosele [#14], who as a non-biological daughter was mistreated and abused and moved from home to home to evade her step-father's wrath - and her own responses to parenting within her marriage. In a third case, Louisa Makgoba [#4] left behind children from an earlier relationship with her mother and went on to marry another man. Her mother assumed the role of parent, bringing up these children, and when her marriage collapsed, her new partner did not want the burden of looking after a child born to her during the previous marriage.

From the Radebe life histories [#3]

In 1980 while she was pregnant Flora met Wilfred Mahlangu whom she then married. He said that he would treat her child as if it were his own. "I sat down with my grandmother and told her everything. Only my grandmother knew who the true father of the child was. The rest of my family did not know, including my mother"(s). Her son, Sipho Radebe, was born on 15 July 1980. They lived together for three years (with his family) and then they separated. "My mother-in-law and father-in-law had passed away. I had just sisters-in-law. It was not tough, but an elder sister-in-law made life very difficult for me. She was usually accommodating his [her husband's] girlfriends. She protected him. At the end of the day she was taking my husband's monthly pay, not me. I had to ask this sister-in-law for money. Sometimes she used to say that there was no money. The others were okay. They used to stand up for me"(e). Sometimes her husband used to go away for long periods. She never knew where he was - but she realised that her sister-in-law often knew where he was. One day she saw this sister-in-law showing photographs of her husband with another woman to other relatives who were visiting. She knew then that her husband was serious about another girlfriend. Flora was not legally married. Flora and Wilfred had had a customary marriage. So when her husband chose to marry someone else she left her in-laws' home and arrived back in Winterveld. Her husband did not object to her leaving nor did he assert any claims on her son. She went to live with her mother and at first struggled to support her child. Because Flora and her mother were often preoccupied with work activities, and they had no other family living with them, Flora sent her son to live with her brother. When her son was growing up she was forced to admit to her son who his biological father really was. "I went to an early learning course. I learnt about communicating with children. You have to be sensitive. If you do not tell your child the truth he will learn by accident and he will never trust you again" (e). She arranged, as he became a teenager, for her son to see his biological father from time to time. They have not had any contact since with Mahlangu who played a short-term role as social parent.

From the Mosele-Gamede life histories [#14]

"My mother got married in 1967. My stepfather did not want my brother and I. So we were sent to his parents [her step-father's parents] to be looked after. They treated us very badly. They were very cruel. We used to get up at 3 o'clock. We would have to cook, clean and fetch water before school. We used to get thrashed. It was heart-breaking. Sometimes we used to go late to school. Once, the principal chased us away from school because we were so late. My brother died when he was fourteen years ... When I was sixteen years old I had a child. That boy left me ... In 1992 I met Peter Gamede. Before we could marry, I told him about my child and how hurt I would be if he treated that child badly. I did not mind not being married if that was the case. He kept up with the promise. He pampers the child. They are friends"(e).

From the Mabetwa-Makgoba life histories [#4]

Before deciding to marry Louisa, Philip Makgoba suggested that they have their own baby. Louisa already had a child from a previous relationship. "You know these African men - they want to have a baby before marriage"(e). In order to consolidate a marriage Louisa decided to fall pregnant. Her second daughter, appropriately named "Joy", was supposed to secure an intimate union that Louisa had hoped for for a long while. Joy was born on 12 January 1971. After Louisa gave up her teaching job she went to look for work in Rosslyn. She left her two children (Vivian and Joy) with her mother and said that she was going to look for work. Louisa eventually found a job at a clothing shop in Marabastad. She worked there as a shop assistant for three years. Working was a real struggle because Louisa was enduring much unhappiness at a personal level. It was three years after Joy was born and she was still not married. She fell pregnant for the third time and gave birth to twin daughters, Tiny and Sandy, but Phillip was still not ready for marriage. Much time had passed before marriage arrangements were settled. "By then, my mother did not want to send my two older children with me. She said that I should just take the twins"(e). When Louisa's marriage to Phillip broke down in 1994 she began a new relationship with Sam Mthetwa. Shortly after moving in, Mthetwa lost his job. Sitting at home during the day, he became increasingly conscious of the presence of Louisa's youngest daughter [Nolwazi] who appeared to be "idling at home". He said, "since she is useless, she must get out of his house". Nolwazi had to leave and live first with her grandmother, Khanyi. But Khanyi was not particularly keen to assume new responsibilities at this stage (she was now in her 70s), and Nolwazi then left to live with friends in Mabopane.

It is difficult to talk of fosterage and adoption of children in Winterveld in the conventional sense. Although there is much "fostering-out" as in children being sent to other kin to be looked after, or "fostering-in" as in children being taken in by a family to be reared, many of these arrangements are temporary and are relationships in which the care-taker expects reciprocation by means of money from working children or family members. Adoption is rare, though I have heard about childless women who have adopted children of women who believed that they had too many children to look after, or who did not have the means to support them. On one occasion someone offered Pumla (my interpreter) a child, because Pumla was childless, but Pumla's willingness to adopt a child was dampened when she learnt that the child being offered was mentally disabled. Disabled children and those deemed to be "not right in the head" are regarded as most burdensome, and therefore suffer considerable neglect. Most movement of children that I have observed appears to be around stepchildren who are unwanted in new unions and for whom the issues of responsibility and care become matters of dispute. Sometimes when children are given away, the woman bears more children in a different union as though she has had no prior children - similar to Louisa's case [# 4] with respect to her first two children. However, Louisa did not see herself as starting her child-bearing "afresh" nor did she deny the existence of her first two children. She was constantly reminded of her financial responsibilities to her mother for their upkeep. On the other hand, when men and women bring children into a relationship that is not particularly stable, as in Sophy's case, it has the effect of "settling" an ideal family size. In other words, it could make a woman and her partner feel that she need not bear more children since they have "acquired" an adequate number of children.

From the Makwela life-histories [#1]

Sophy told me that she could not bear to use contraception, but if she believed that she was pregnant she would go to the clinic to confirm it, and if it was confirmed - she would ask immediately for an abortion. She had never had an abortion before, but she knew it was legal and knew other women who had recently gone for abortions. None of her friends had used contraception. She would resort to an abortion because she did not want any more children. Marcos [her boyfriend] did not want any additional children either. He had one child, a daughter, from a previous relationship. So, together, they had two children. "Two is a good number ... we have one of each [sex]" (t). She said that she wanted to get married one day. "Marcos promises that once he finds a job we will marry." (Sophy's relationship, however, was quite insecure. Marcos went to jail shortly after Sophy discussed this with me, and she then turned to prostitution to earn a living.)

Page (1989: 401- 403) suggests that the combination of a high demand for children and high incidence of fosterage in (West) Africa appears paradoxical. At the same time she suggests that this paradox is "quite simple to explain". She explains it by pointing to the accommodating function of lineage within which the couple unit is subsumed. "In some cases where the broader lineage rather than the direct line is important, it is only normal that a wide range of kin may exercise not only joint responsibilities in children but also joint rights in them" (Page, 1989:402). There is much speculation in these circumstances of the kind of influence other kin (especially the grandparent-generation) may wield over reproductive decisions. The South African literature on family life in urban areas, whilst reflecting many controversies, tends to show that, whilst kin-based networks prevail and are often mobilised as a resource, these persist in "a more limited sense". Increasingly, the greater emphasis is on filiation (parent-child) links rather than kin in a more general sense (Manona, 1991). In Merafeng, I have not come across much direct intervention on the part of mothers or mother-in-laws to persuade younger women to bear particular numbers of children. (Table 10 suggests that women do not regard pressure from "other" kin as a key factor affecting decisions with respect to the number of children to bear and on the use of contraception). Part of the lack of involvement of older kin in the decisions of younger women is due to an attitude of accepting whatever comes. As an elderly woman declared (to much agreement) in one of the group sessions: "When it comes to having children it's God that decides. Only God knows how many children a woman will be able to have. It's God that knows, women have no say." With respect to their own daughters in unions it is also not uncommon to hear women saying "it is for them [the couple] to decide". Their willingness to play a supportive role with respect to caring for and feeding grandchildren, however, could serve, in an indirect way, to shape these decisions. Although it is common for older women to play a role in looking after children (grandchildren and children of other kin), reciprocity is often not enjoyed. Increasingly, there is a sense that much time is spent investing in rearing children - but these children and their parents do not give them much in return. Instead, they are exploited in old age for their pensions.

In one of my earliest interviews with her, Nozizwe Radebe [# 3] suggested that the wider kin support structures of the past do not apply in Winterveld.

> Children find older people burdensome ... unless they feel that they can control their pensions ... relatives do not help. Some parents get involved in their children's problems ... but many do not. But there is also a problem with children ... knowledge has increased. Children know too much ... they are now too big ... they cannot be disciplined (e).

Thoko Skosana [#2] spoke with greater warmth about interaction between older and younger kin. Her reference to "kin support", however, pertained to the coming together of family during wedding celebrations. She explained that now and then she did meet with her husband's relatives and they did throw parties. This was the case in 1998, when the youngest son of her late husband's brother paid his in-laws bridewealth. Except for seeing family during such celebrations, she lived in 1999 with just one son and one grandson (the son of her daughter who lives elsewhere). Apart from feeding them "out of habit" she told me that she did not see herself as being responsible for them in any way. She would get her pension and they would do odd jobs to support themselves. "They look after themselves, and I look after myself"(s). Thoko did not have any expectations that any one of her children would be of any real support to her, as she grew older (except perhaps Martha who lived closeby). Martha Sibiya attempts to watch over her mother as she gets older, but Martha was uncertain as to whether her children would watch over her in the same way. "Maybe they will be of help. Maybe they will make me cry. Here, old people get no help from their children - "but we can still hope"(s).

Perhaps the clearest indication of how financial constraints and the acknowledgement of limited reciprocal long-term support was affecting the willingness of older women to play the "traditional" supportive role to younger women came from the frank comments of Clara Molefe.

From the Molefe-Ramashala life-histories [#8]

In March 1999 when I went to see Clara she was quite depressed, claiming to be suffering with a "problem of the heart". Her problem was that her 28-year-old son was very troublesome. She told me that some time ago he had chased his wife and child away and then seemed to prefer the company of older women. Now she learnt that he had been arrested for car theft, and was an awaiting-trial prisoner. "I have been talking to him a lot, but he does not listen"(s). She said that she loved her grandson "but because of his father I do not know what to do"(s). Her son had never supported his wife and child; they had survived because she had given them food to eat. "The *makoti* [daughter-in-law] was staying with me when he was staying with other women in Atteridgeville ... I told her that I am a pensioner. I cannot support her. She must go and find a job. Then she left. She found a job as a domestic servant in Hartebeesfontein. She was better off. Then I told her to come back and take the child away"(s).

Given rates of mobility, and the unreliability of biological kin and kin networks to offer sufficient security to women and their dependants, limited friendship networks and "social groups" in some instances and in some ways reconstitute kinship-type links that serve mutually beneficial purposes (Spiegel & Mehlwana, 1997). Most of the women who were part of one of my group sessions came from a fairly close neighbourhood bound together in some part by Aubrey Ndlovu, the Community Policing Forum (CPF) leader, who lived in the neighbourhood. Aubrey Ndlovu played some part as he put it "in getting women to stop their idling" and play a greater role in supporting each other and their children. "It is the women who have to organise themselves. They are the educators of the children. Most of them here are gambling the little money that they have. They take the R2 and play with cards. Then they lose it and that is when their children do not get any feeding" (e). In 1999 I observed the existence of a loosely held-together support network in this sub-site of Merafeng. Women who lost money or found themselves destitute were supported by each other. If all else failed, Aubrey Ndlovu offered them food from his spaza (tuck shop) on credit. There was sometimes collective buying of bags of mealie-meal and sharing of food between households as women drew upon each other's time and resources. Often childcare became a distributed responsibility. Although there was some sense of "we take turns" looking after each other's children, the sharing became difficult since the children of the women there were of different ages, and therefore, required over time different kinds of support and feeding.

Family members who have conventionally played active roles in feasts and ceremonies are being substituted by neighbours and long-time friends who are represented in larger numbers in such functions there in "Mr Ndlovu's district." In June 1999, Safina Hlatswayo had a baby. I was invited to be there a few weeks later because a prayer was going to be held by Safina's "family". It was to be a ceremony that would introduce the baby to everyone. It was the first time that the child was to be brought out of the house to be seen by all. Whilst a fair number of people in the neighbourhood turned up, none of Safina's nor her husband's (biological) kin turned up. They were not expected to turn up because they lived some distance away in the Limpopo Province. In fact, a large number of people in this neighbourhood originated from Giyani, in Limpopo, and these origins appear to feed into shared notions of kinship. In this area, people have made kin of people who appear to share a few important similarities, central to which are origins and a "jobless" economic status. The process of creating kin becomes an important cultural resource and a way of resisting the stresses and responsibilities of a life amidst poverty (Spiegel & Mehlwana, 1997; Nkosi & Daniels, 2007). The involvement of women in sharing in each other's poverty and in watching over each other's children does, in small part, extend to monitoring each other's fertility. Through the groups it was evident that women in the area who had more than five children were regarded as "fools" or were "uneducated" in that they did not seem to know much about "prevention". Similarly, women with no children or just one child were treated with pity and much sympathy. It was in Safina's house that I asked Joanna Chauke about her views on Safina's new baby. She explained that:

> When there are no children, people are laughing at you. Sometimes people are insulting. If there is one child - people expect more of you.

Safina now has four children. She wanted only three. That last one was a mistake. Safina was using the loop, but it did not help. If Safina has another one after this, it will be a very big mistake. Maybe she must use the injection"(z).

Joanna, who spoke in the presence of Safina, showed much understanding of Safina's situation. In resembling kinship, neighbourhood networks often involve much chiding and manipulation. Since responsibilies of care are distributed, responsible advice, to avoid extra burdens that come with too many children, was also offered. I do not suggest that keeping a check on each other's fertility was commonplace or that such networks were numerous. Some kind of monitoring does appear to prevail when bonds between women in networks are fairly strong. These could relate to both biological kin or fictive kin. Many of these networks, however, sustain a fragile edge which breaks when people move elsewhere, when petty discord arises, or when some people become overreliant on the generosity and support of others.

Conclusion

Marital and consensual unions appear to be fairly fluid and insecure in Merafeng. Conjugal relations are easily unsettled by claims of infidelities, which often result in acts of violence in a milieu where men and women engage constantly with multiple adversity and material hardship. The disadvantaged position of women in the economic sphere, their expectations of male support, and dependence on men, lead them in the absence of regular partners to pursue and maintain various kinds of associations with income earners and men with money. Kin (in particular, parents and grandparents), equally subjected to the stresses of poverty, seem to play supportive roles to women, but simultaneously contest normative expectations of their child-rearing responsibilities, particularly when compensating monetary benefits are not forthcoming. With little intervention from other kin, fertility, it is argued, is primarily a matter of negotiation within a couple-unit, but ultimately it is the woman (prompted largely by insecurity) who empowers herself by manipulating her reproductive capacities through her use of modern or traditional contraceptive methods. Neighbourhood social networks can become involved, in small part, in influencing fertility decisions and in offering help in childcare and feeding, but this level of support can also be transitory and unreliable. With the contraction, rather than the spread of support across households and networks, there is considerable pressure on women to weigh the benefits of reproduction against the risks of poverty and marital dissolution.

Chapter 6

INTERGENERATIONAL REFLECTIONS: POVERTY AND 'REPRODUCTIVE DECISION-MAKING'

Poverty, unemployment and dependency in Merafeng

Poverty, it is often conceded, holds different meanings in different eras. Although early approaches to poverty simply equated the state of being poor with insufficient material resources, today more complex conceptualisations that take account of 'capabilities', 'livelihoods', 'social exclusion' and 'rights' have gained popularity (Bhalla & Lapeyre, 2004; Hall, 2003). Whilst many academics working in the field of poverty acknowledge, as Amartya Sen (1983) does, that "there is an irreducible absolutist core in the idea of poverty", there is, at the same time, criticism of the reductionism inherent in approaches focusing almost exclusively on basic needs or minimum requirements for physiological survival. As Kabeer (1994:139) states: "Human need is about more than physiological survival; it is also about living a healthy active life and participating in the life of the community. These are the 'beings and doings' that people value ..."

More inclusive definitions, such as that offered by Robert Chambers, strive to link both tangible and non-tangible aspects of socio-economic hardship. Chambers's (1988:8-9) linking of 'poverty proper' and physical weakness (the tangible aspects) to isolation, vulnerability and powerlessness (the intangible aspects) holds importance for South African studies in that he places emphasis on the connectedness of material wellbeing to socio-economic and political rights. Intangible needs might include a desire for incorporation and participation in the institutions, political processes and social networks of society. Barriers to inclusion (as was evident in apartheid society) impacted on the abilities of groups and individuals to have access to state resources, to pursue independent livelihoods and to exercise full citizenship rights.

Although contemporary analyses of poverty in South Africa tend to place a lot of emphasis on economic determinants, there is much interest in the ways in which enfranchisement and the acquisition of rights has led to the shifting of chronic poverty (Aliber, 2003). In other words, poverty in South Africa is generally conceived as more than material hardship and as involving simultaneously the inability to wield power, agency and control personal destinies (Kabeer, 1994; Du Toit, 2005). Thus, much current writing on poverty in South Africa centres on analysis suggesting that people's lives have changed – and simultaneously that they have not. Clearly, South Africa in the late 2000s boasts a greatly altered political landscape from the one that prevailed more than a decade ago. Legal racism no longer exists and democracy has replaced the segregationist doctrines of separate development. There is freedom of movement and expression in place of influx control, pass laws and detention without trial. Notwithstanding this, anecdotal evidence consistently reiterates that for the poor not much has changed in terms of the larger socio-economic context the government sought to confront in 1994 (see the recent work of Schlemmer, 2005).

In offering a synopsis of hard poverty data, Landman (2003:1) maintains that there is now some consensus amongst analysts that (on average) about 40 percent of South Africa's population is enduring poverty with the bottom 15 percent facing "a desperate struggle to survive". Seekings and Nattrass (2002:2) identify the three principal classes in post-apartheid South Africa as being first, an extremely wealthy and multiracial elite or upper class, (2) an intermediate 'middle-class' group incorporating professionals and the organised working class, and (3) the marginalised (or underclass) including lowly paid farm and domestic workers and the unemployed. The increase in the numbers of people without work and material resources remains a central factor influencing the resilience of poverty and inhibition of change efforts. In seeking to make sense of the impact of hardship on the lives of the poor, I was particularly concerned in the midst of fieldwork, to capture subjective definitions of poverty in the manner drawn by May and Norton (1997). In concluding their earlier study, May and Norton (1997: 99) argued that "poverty is perceived to encompass a number of key dimensions with income not mentioned" and that the wealthy in these [largely poor communities] are "a modest elite who have managed to achieve little more than a working class lifestyle".

In my interviews in Merafeng "money" or "income" was mentioned regularly as the key determinant of who was perceived to be "wealthy" and who was believed to be "poor". The "elite" in Winterveld were consistently identified as the formal wage-earners who had "more money". These include teachers, nurses, clerical and retail staff and certain categories of domestic workers (those working for cleaning companies or employed by wealthy individuals). Wage-earners were often talked about as being the "affluent" in the area alongside the land-owners, taxi-drivers and shop-owners. Elderly women land-owners, who lived relatively isolated existences or who endured ill-health despite being housed in attractive homes, were not regarded as wealthy. Although outsiders would immediately note the differences in the quality of the houses in which land-owners and tenants live, type of housing was rarely mentioned as an indicator of poverty. Lack of water resources and electrical supply were regularly mentioned as determinants of poor living conditions. Both land-owners and tenants with whom I associated often talked about themselves as living in poverty. In one of my first group sessions, women land-owners, whom I considered to be comparatively well-off, described themselves as coming together as a group to "uplift themselves and rid themselves of poverty" (*Office* group). In a group session with women tenants (*Ndlovu's* group) in 1999, who appeared to be much poorer, I received the following answers (which I list as separate statements) in response to the question, "what problems are the women experiencing?"

> The main problem experienced is crime. There is a lot of housebreaking. Even children are stealing. It is mainly the children who do not even go to school. They do not get enough food. Parents are not working. There is a lot of suffering. No money, no food, no education, no water, no electricity.

> We have heard that water and lights are coming. We will be very happy. We are tired of using batteries to get the television switched on. We have had enough of poverty. Even water is going up to 50c for 25 litres.

> Husbands are not working. So there is little money. You can just buy porridge and then the money is finished.

> Rape is a big problem. Women are scared to go out in the dark. After eight o' clock they are all in the house until the next morning.

> The other problem is that women do not have husbands. Many are the breadwinners. There are many broken families because fathers leave their children. The women survive by doing piece-jobs. They do washing for other women.

> The main worry is poverty.

> Before you can do anything, you must have food. Many women are illiterate. If these women can be grouped together and get some training then they can do something. Then they can help the others (s).

Although, in this short extract, some of the issues contributing to the poverty and insecurity underlining women's lives are illustrated, the inability to find the money or means to feed and support children is the most obvious factor aggravating poverty. There was a strong sense of wanting a husband or male partner for support. In other interviews I detected much dependence on pensioners' earnings and on child welfare benefits. I became aware, in the course of the fieldwork, of a number of women who had relied heavily on "blue card money" (unemployment benefits) and grant money and who became quite demoralised when some of these welfare benefits were withdrawn. In Merafeng thus women's experiences of "poverty" would include the inability to walk outside their homes after eight o' clock, low levels of transferable skills and the constant worry that "fathers will leave their children".

In 2006, group discussions highlighted similar descriptions of poverty. As two women in one group emphasized:

> The problem I am experiencing is no work. Winterveld is poor. There are no lights and no tarred roads. Also crime is high... [Q: What kind of crime?] There has been a lot of rape recently... Burglary too.

> I am suffering to bring up my children. I got no money and sometimes there is no food to feed them. I haven't got money for clothes for them ... when they get sick I have to wait at a clinic. There is no money to take them to a doctor.

Chambers offers a "hierarchy of basic needs" in which the satisfaction of "basic survival needs" is seen to be essential before the satisfaction of security needs and the need for self-esteem (Kabeer, 1994: 139). Kabeer, however, suggests that, in studying the ways in which women experience poverty, one has to take account of the extent to which social needs such as self-esteem are being met alongside tangible, physiological needs. She suggests that: "for poor women, the notion of self-esteem itself might be more closely tied to the ability to feed their children than to middle-class ideals of female propriety, which would hamper their survival strategies" (Kabeer, 1994:140). Thus, one has to explore how these non-tangible needs are being defined and what meanings they hold for different groups of women. Part of my interest in this study has been to examine the meaning that reproduction holds for women, in relation to other needs, at different stages of their lives. In the course of fieldwork, the ever-increasing need for money, income and employment were the urgent needs expressed by women in addition to them wanting to "get some training" so that "they can do something".

How does having children connect with survival strategies? Does access to employment, as in the conventional sense, reduce the need for children? Does having more children secure support for a woman from her partner and his kin? What needs are met through reproduction and which needs are hampered? Survey evidence with respect to the association between employment and fertility is offered below.

Findings of macro- and micro-surveys

In October 2008, exactly a decade after the 1998 National Poverty Hearings in Cape Town, the well-respected Archbishop Njongonkulu Ndungane toured all South Africa's provinces and summed up his observations by stating that South Africa is in "a state of emergency". He painted an unhappy picture of deepening poverty and desperation shaping people's lives in all the provinces and their inability to find work. As in most developing countries, South Africa exhibits a shortage of skilled labour and an oversupply of unskilled labour. For younger African women with low levels of skill (living in areas such as Winterveld) it has always been extremely difficult to find formal work. This has, in more recent times, been worsened by the fact that the formal employment growth rate has been declining steadily since the 1970s: from an annual growth rate of 2.9% in the 1960s, it dropped to 0.7 in the 1980s and has been negative since the 1990s. Between 1990 and 1995, with shifts from labour-intensive production to capital-intensive processes, an average of 82 000 jobs a year were lost (Erasmus, 1999:28). Job creation has been slow since and the social inequality gap has widened. The Gini coefficient in 2001 was the highest in the world at 0.77 (HSRC, 2004).

About 52% of people in the NorthWest Province (in which Winterveld is located) are living in poverty and the vast majority of Winterveld's population is currently extremely poor. For most of them, hopes are pinned on the growth and development of "informal sector activities". The informal sector encompasses a very wide range of activities which include selling goods (such as fruit and vegetables), services (such as shoe repairs or tuck-shops) and small-scale manufacturing (of items such as furniture and clothes) (Bozzoli, 1991:15). Earnings in this sector vary considerably but are generally lower and less guaranteed than salaries of formal jobs in the private or public sectors. People usually turn to this sector after they have been retrenched or after they have found it impossible to find what are conventionally regarded as "proper jobs" (May et al., 1998:15). Although precise numbers are difficult to establish, the 1995 October Household Survey (OHS) showed that about 1.7 million people were in unregistered businesses or had categorised themselves as working in the informal sector (Erasmus, 1999). It's difficult to attain reliable recent estimates as poor people move in and out of the informal sector, particularly since they engage in these activities alongside pursuing formal work.

The number of women seeking work, and participating in the labour force, has increased significantly in the recent past. Erasmus (1995:35) suggests that in the North West "female participation rates increased by 20% between 1980 and 1991". In the Pretoria-Witwatersrand-Vereeniging area (the business district in which women in Winterveld most commonly seek work) the female participation rate increased by 12%. This occurred at the same time as the male participation rate decreased. Larger numbers of women were seeking formal work or independent earnings, as the previous chapter suggested, on account of economic pressure associated with supporting households and children, given reduced concomitant spousal or familial support. Work for women in Winterveld was heavily concentrated in the more menial tasks, in selling activities and in domestic labour. Earnings were generally lower for women doing unskilled and informal sector work than for men (May et al., 1998:15). In the 2005 - 2008 fieldwork period it was very difficult to raise conversations about anything other than work and income earning possibilities. Women wanted to find ways of earning money and making a living.

What has been the work pattern over the decade of research? Only about 30% of women in the 1987-1989 SADHS responded positively to the question, "Are you now working to earn money?". A similar question in the survey (WS) conducted around my fieldwork site showed that 47% of women earned money. The comparison, however, is limited not only by the respective sizes and types of the samples, and the different time periods in which the surveys were conducted, but also possibly by different understandings of what constitutes work and what earnings were involved, e.g. it appears that informal sector work activities (which were subject to many restrictions at the time of the SADHS) might have been under-estimated. In addition, whilst it appears that more women in Winterveld work, their average earnings may in fact be considerably lower than the earnings of those identified as workers in the SADHS. The SADHS did not ask about the amount of income earned. Amounts would be useful to allow for speculation on the necessity for supplementary sources of income, and thus assess how much more independent a working woman was likely to be in comparison to a woman who was not earning money. The SADHS did, however, attempt to probe categories of work performed, and tried to establish the work status of women before and after first marriage. These questions were intended to establish whether women gave up work after marriage, and then relied on support from a husband, and whether that had implications for child-bearing. Arguably, since definitions of marriage are themselves variable, and women often enter into more than one union, and there might be numerous reasons why women could find themselves jobless after "marriage", answers to such questions are not very meaningful. Table 11 depicts the age groups into which employed and unemployed women in the WS sample fell. (Because the numbers are very small I did not attempt to distinguish between those actively seeking work and those "staying at home". My experience in Merafeng was that most women without work were keen to earn money in informal sector activities, short-term jobs or formal employment.)

Table 11: Employment status, by age:WS

Age	Employed	Unemployed
<=25 years	26% (20)	74% (58)
26-34 years	59% (65)	41% (45)
35+ years	51% (53)	49% (51)

Source: Winterveld Survey, 1998, recode file.

Although the sample size was small (N=293) the results appear to correspond with fieldwork observations in that the youngest group (those 25 years and under) was identified as the group enduring the highest levels of unemployment and the middle group (those 26-34 years old) as the group most active in "earning money". An open-ended question established that selling activities and domestic work predominated, although a small number of shop-workers and skilled workers were also included.

All women were asked about their "household incomes". At the time of the survey (WS) it was believed that a composite figure reflecting household earnings would be a better indicator of an individual woman's access to wealth and resources than her independent and often meagre earnings. Fifteen women said that they had no knowledge of what was earned by household members. About half the women who offered estimates of household earnings claimed that these earnings were below

R800. About 63% of employed women and 39% of unemployed women claimed that their household earnings were above R800. I do not suggest that these calculations on the part of women are accurate nor that household earnings are non-variable over the months. Given increasing rates of male abandonment and male unemployment, household earnings are becoming more and more dependent on the earnings of women. This places immense pressure on women to find ways and means of surviving economically. Being employed, it was apparent, implied greater control over domestic and personal decisions, and far less dependence on others and greater decisiveness in making major decisions.

Since the 1990s there has been greater illumination of domestic discord and intra-household inequalities particularly when women are not contributing toward common coffers or if they lack the power to control the purse strings of others (Posel, 1997:49). Since a woman in these circumstances might feel little sense of "ownership" over the process by which household income is eventually distributed, increases in the earnings of other household members might not be a critical factor determining or changing her desires for children. Thus in the course of fieldwork it seemed apparent that when women controlled independent sources of income they were in greater command of general, including child-bearing, decisions. Table 12 shows the association between women's employment and reproduction at the macro-level.

Table 12: Desired children and children born, by age and employment status: SADHS

Age	*Employed* women: mean no. of children desired	*Employed* women: mean no. of children born	*Unemployed* women: mean no. of children desired	*Unemployed* women: mean no. of children born
<=25 years	2.9 (829)	1.1 (1132)	3.0 (4000)	1.0 (5765)
26-34 years	3.5 (1214)	2.4 (1610)	3.7 (2386)	2.6 (3332)
35+ years	4.4 (1079)	4.5 (1406)	4.6 (2211)	4.7 (3073)

Source: South African demographic and health survey, 1987-1989, recode file.

When the SADHS results were studied to establish the relationship between work and child-bearing it was found that occupational category had a bearing on reproduction eg. unskilled workers have higher fertility than skilled workers (Du Plessis, 1996). In Winterveld a concentration of women would be in the occupational category "unskilled worker" or be listed as "unemployed". Thus to facilitate comparison it was found convenient to group women in terms of the employed and unemployed. The results of Table 12 show that the reproductive outcomes and desired fertility of employed and unemployed women are not very different. There is, however, a slight indication that unemployed women (particularly at later ages) bear more children than working women. More significant implications are also captured by looking at whether and how soon women would want to fall pregnant again. The SADHS shows that employed women were considerably *more unhappy* about falling pregnant "soon": 69.6% in the under 25 year age group, 60.6% in the 26-34 year age group and 68.9% in the over-35-year age group said that they would be unhappy about falling pregnant "in the next few weeks". Unemployed women in the same age groups were *less unhappy* about falling pregnant soon - 51.9%, 24.9% and 23.2% respectively. This result concurs with the analysis suggesting that, in the absence of work opportunities, women may be more willing to have larger numbers of children as "insurance" and as safeguards against "risk" in the future (Cain, 1982). In stating this there are two issues worth mentioning. The first issue is that a very high number of women (about 25% of all women in the SADHS sample) were unable to visualise an "ideal number" of children. The stereotypical view is that this group represents largely older, illiterate women with fatalistic and "pro-natalist attitudes" predominant in environments where "lineage takes priority over conjugal bonds" (UN,1995:60). However, in the SADHS, the "indecisive" group cut across all age groups, but were representative of largely unemployed women (73% were unemployed). When unemployed, women appear to be less able to talk in "precise terms" about family size. The second issue is that there are limitations to using macro-surveys in South Africa to adequately illustrate the effect of African women's employment on the proximate determinants of fertility when African women have endured little security and considerable changes in work status. "Current" work status (or a single categorisation of occupation) does not illuminate the numerous and different kinds of work women may have done or the durations of time spent unemployed. Correlations between "current work" and "number of children ever-born" exclude a sense of wavering motivations, linked to various transitions in work and family life, intervening at different points in a person's life. This makes the results of both Table 13 and 14, in the final analysis, quite difficult to interpret.

Table 13: Desired children and children born, by age and employment status: WS

Age	Employed women: mean no. of children desired	Employed women: mean no. of children born	Unemployed women: mean no. of children desired	Unemployed women: mean no. of children born
<=25 years	2.8 (20)	1.3 (20)	2.6 (58)	0.8 (58)
26-34 years	3.1 (65)	2.0 (65)	3.1 (45)	2.2 (45)
35+ years	4.2 (53)	3.6 (53)	3.7 (51)	3.5 (51)

Source: Winterveld Survey, 1998, recode file.

"Current" employment status can be used to make particular points about "current" (and possibly changeable) desires for children in Winterveld. Table 13, which draws on the very small sample size of the Winterveld micro-survey, does not reveal significant differences in child-bearing between employed and unemployed women. Thoughts expressed about additional children and the timing of these births are perhaps more revealing. About 30%, 43% and 77% of employed women, in the under 25, 26-34 and over-35-year old age groups respectively, claimed that they did not want more children whilst a larger proportion of unemployed women, 33%, 62% and 86% in these age groups, did not want further children. Unemployed women (over 25 years of age) were also using more contraception (66%) than employed women (59%). Of those women (predominantly in the 26-34 year age group) who expressed a wish to have more children, most wanted children after two years. The qualitative interviews showed that when women found work they tended to talk about children as becoming more affordable. Having another child might become a fairly immediate need of a woman who has been delaying having additional children in the belief that she could not properly support them. Prolonged spacing of births might occur among the unemployed as they wait for better financial times in which to bear children. This can be illustrated by reference to Sankie Motjieng's story.

From the Motjieng life histories [#6]

Freda Motjieng was regarded by neighbours [in 1999] as an alcoholic. In my first attempts to interview her I was told by Mama, a neighbour, that I should come early because by midday Freda would most likely be drunk ("she will be busy drinking the Chibuku"). Freda did not work throughout the week any longer. She had a domestic piece-job on Thursdays only. Despite being critical of Freda's drinking, neighbours admired her resolve in placing a high priority on her children's education. Freda had three daughters in their mid- to late-twenties. All of them had completed their high school education successfully. None of them fell pregnant at school. Sankie and Lena both had babies a few years after leaving school. Although completing their schooling, none of them, however, managed to find good or stable jobs. They have all done piece-jobs and part-time work . At the time of my interviews only Lena worked. Freda said then, "Lena is the only one who works full-time. We all depend on Lena these days. I am worried about Sankie. She lost her job last year [1998]. She does not seem to be able to find another job again. Sankie suffers with headaches all the time because she is not working. She is very depressed"(t).

Freda told me that she wished that her daughters could return to their studies. She thought that perhaps they needed more education to get decent jobs and improve themselves. She knew that the neighbours thought that it was something special in the area for a poor woman to have all her daughters matriculated. She was proud of her daughters but disillusioned that they could not find work.

Sankie (29) explained: "When I finished school I wanted to be a social worker but I had no money. I had a teacher in school who was very good to me. He wanted to sponsor me for tertiary education. He promised to help me even before we wrote our examinations. I did well in my examinations. I got a matriculation exemption. My best subjects were English and Geography. After that he said I should come to his house and speak to his wife. Unfortunately, his wife said "no". She did not want him to support my studies or give me money. His wife was also a teacher, and they had no children, but she did not want him to help me. I was very disappointed. Of all my disappointments in life this one was my biggest disappointment"(e). Sankie said that she saw this teacher in 1999 and he was very disappointed that she had not progressed academically. In 1993 her grandmother's younger brother had also offered to help her "but he did not keep his promise. I used to keep telephoning him until I gave up hope." Sankie talked about her younger sister, Lena, who was supporting the family. Lena was working at a carpentry place. Her work entailed varnishing the planks. "She does not tell anyone what she earns. She does not support the family like I used to. She buys things only if she wants. We do not know what she does with her money. Her child does not have clothes ... the child is struggling now. She is no longer at pre-school. If you ask her why - she says she does not have money. Lena and her boyfriend separated recently. We see that he does not come home anymore". At that stage, communication between the sisters had deteriorated and they no longer talked much about anything. Sankie said, "Lena is stubborn. You cannot ask her why the father of her child has left. If you ask she will say, "you are full of rubbish". She will also say, "women of your age have their own homes". Then you regret asking. I cannot talk to Lena. It is better to talk to my younger sister, Nomsa"(e). Attached to Freda, Sankie and Nomsa's mud and tin home is another smaller "room" cleverly structured and made of mud and wooden planks. Lena built a room for herself separate from the rest of her kin, possibly as a sign of independence but also to avoid dealing with their demands and the pressure of responsibility.

Sankie's boyfriend, Samson, lived in Makaunyane nearby. She said, "maybe we will get married if his job pays him well. Then we will move out on our own." She also talked about her thoughts on having children. "I wanted to get another child now, so that by the time I am thirty years I will be sterilised, but I do not have money. My boyfriend was not earning much. Now he is gone to his brother at Bushbuckridge [in the Northern Province] to get a driver's licence. Maybe then he can work as a driver. There are many chances for a job then. He was working last year but he is retrenched now. In April [1999] he must reapply; he could get a temporary post"(e).

Sankie explained why she wanted only two children. "Life is not like those old days. Two is enough. Samson and I talked about this before. He is happy with two children. He has no parents. He lives with his sisters. The sisters used to talk to me. They said that Beverly [Sankie's daughter] is getting too big [she was 8 years old] and I should have another child. I said, "money talks". It is too much money to bring up another child. I am lucky that this child of mine was never sickly. Since she was born she has never been to a doctor. Her only sickness was coughing. I took her to the clinic for some cough mixture. I need to save all my money to prepare for the next child. If I find a job I will have another child ... I still take the pill but I need to be careful about how I take it. Samson wants me to have another child now. I said I do not want another one now. He feels that he will get work soon ... Last year we agreed to have another child this year [1999] but I did not know that I was going to lose my job then"(e).

Although Sankie was in a fairly good relationship she did not trust Samson's promises of finding a job soon, nor could she rely on members of her family for financial support. The crucial issue delaying her willingness to have another child soon was her concern, in view of her unemployment, about whether she could afford to support another child. It could be argued that Sankie's case brings out the combined effects of both youth and high school education on reproductive decisions in poor environments; decisions which might be differently taken by older women with lower levels of education. Some indication of these associations evident amongst women in Winterveld is offered in Table 14.

Table 14: Desired children and children born, by mean age, education and employment status: WS

Educational level	Mean age of women: *employed* women	Mean no. of children born: *employed* women	Mean no. of desired children: *employed* women	Mean age of women: *unemployed* women	Mean no. of children born: *unemployed* women	Mean no. of desired children: *unemploy ed* women
No education	40 years	3.7	4.8 (13)	42 years	3.0	3.7 (19)
Primary school education	38 years	3.3	4.3 (38)	36 years	2.7	3.4 (48)
Secondary school education	31 years	2.0	2.8 (87)	27 years	1.6	2.8 (87)

Source: Winterveld Survey, 1998, recode file.

Here the oldest unemployed women with no education do not appear to have (on average) very high numbers of children. Although the desire for larger numbers of children seems to decline with decreasing age, and with increasing education, it could still be argued that access to some kind of employment could play a role in making children both desirable and affordable. It is noteworthy that the means suggest that older women in all these educational groups would ideally want to have more children than they already have - probably when financial circumstances make it possible[1].

In his discussion of empowerment and fertility transition in Antigua, in the West Indies, Handwerker (1993:41-52) argues that, although women's educational levels had increased dramatically over the years, education "by itself" had "almost no impact" on the sharp decline in fertility. It was the *conjunction* of new employment opportunities and the demand for a more educated (skilled) labour force, linked to structural transformations in the national economy, that influenced a reorientation in women's thinking about family sizes. As the economy shifted from agriculture towards tourism women found work opportunities and freed themselves from dependence on men and from the necessity to invest time in having many children. Since child-rearing was now regarded increasingly as a "consumption" activity it made sense for women to want fewer children given expectations that it would cost more to bring them up. In particular, high costs were involved in educating both sons and daughters and in sustaining a higher standard of living. As in Handwerker's description of the women in Antigua's move toward having smaller numbers of children, education itself can explain little of the decline towards smaller family sizes in Winterveld. It may well be that a massive pool of readily available jobs could have a similar effect on Winterveld's women. The reality of many years of lowly paid and scarce work opportunities, however, seems to show that the conjunction of work and education influences behaviour somewhat differently. Formal jobs or work that brings in larger amounts of money free women from dependence on others (e.g. partners and kin). At the same time they also offer women opportunities to fulfil themselves in meaningful ways, to look more prosperous, and to strive towards better lives. The "good life" may have been long in coming and may be short-lived.

As additional but related points, although the expressed desires for children in Winterveld were consistently low, it is possible that they were low because women did not often want to "wish for" a number far different from the number they anticipated that they were likely to end up with. It would seem as well that when (comparatively younger) women have tried to have additional children, under these poverty-stricken circumstances, child-bearing was often not motivated by thoughts of future security. Given the demands and "risks" of everyday life, security in old age was usually furthest from the minds of women still in their child-bearing years. There are a number of factors, apart from affordability, that intervene in taking the simple choice out of women's hands. The most obvious of these is reduced fecundity as a result of sexually transmitted diseases (STDs), which are widespread in Merafeng. The motivations of women are varied but a further explanation as to why working women might want more children is that they have an opportunity to take advantage of more prosperous times to fulfil themselves as women and also quell suspicions of disease and ill-health. In 6.4 a closer look at these issues is offered through intergenerational stories. I offer these stories because the contrast between "old" and "young" offers some indication of institutional change and persistence which has a bearing on reproduction and the constitution of families in present-day Winterveld.

Contrasting the experiences of different generations

Older women's views on life, work and reproduction

In Chapter 3, I referred to Winterveld's origins as a farming territory in the period between the late 1930s and 1940s. Some time after the first wave of landowners settled in the area, a second wave of tenants arrived at different intervals between the 1960s and 1980s. Most of the women in my stories grew up in families which arrived in different periods. They participated in predominantly agricultural activities, in which their families were engaged, but at different stages of their lives, and for different reasons, they left their homes to seek paid work in Winterveld or in nearby Pretoria and Johannesburg. The older women whom I interviewed, primarily in their mid-sixties to early eighties, talked in different terms about land ownership, access to livestock and wealth in general. Although their descriptions of family structure and relationships, of time spent in their in-laws' homes and in relatively independent residential units, were also varied, many of their experiences as women, and thoughts about reproductive and child-rearing responsibilities, appear to be fairly similar.

Whilst some women lived on trust lands prior to arriving in Winterveld, most of the older women spent their childhood on white farms where their fathers (and families) worked as labour tenants. The rural environments from which the women came are depicted as environments in which kinships bonds were fairly strong, where labour efforts were largely collaborative, and where there was little shortage of food.

From the Mabetwa-Makgoba life histories [# 4]

Khanyi (78) was very young when her great-grandfather (her mother's grandfather), Piet Gololo, was alive but she remembers some things about him. He was born and brought up in Zebediela [in the Northern Province]. As a child she respected him as the most senior man in the family. Although people in Zebediela planted all kinds of vegetables on their farms, Piet Gololo only planted mealies. "He planted fields and fields of only mealies". Khanyi's maternal grandfather was Johannes Gololo. He was also a mealie-farmer but he tried his hand at fruit-farming as well. "In those days everything grew well and there was no starvation" (t).

From the Mosele-Gamede life-histories [# 14]

Manto Mosele (58) was born in Makapanstad. "It is on the other side of Hammanskraal. It is a tribal area made up of a number of villages and controlled by a chief, Hendrik Makapane. We lived in the chief's *kraal* [living quarters] ... My father was an industrious man. Although he was a farmer he did carpentry and bricklaying. Because he was involved in building houses in the villages he was exonerated from doing ploughing for the chief. There were big fields of mealies. The women were kept busy all year round especially at harvest time. They had to spend time putting crops in bags. The mealies were ground at the big mill ... My father used to rear pigs, horses, donkeys and cattle. He had a lot of cattle because he used to be paid in cattle. He used to sell pigs at the Pretoria market. That was the life we used to experience ... I was an only daughter but I had to work tough jobs as well. I did the same jobs as my brothers"(e/s).

Khanyi arrived in Winterveld as a young woman, the wife of an enterprising man who bought four plots and set up a number of shops, whilst Manto arrived as a young girl of about eleven years when her family settled there as prosperous landowners. Manto attained a higher education and went on to become a school principal in Winterveld.

The many accounts of life on the white farms, from about the 1940s to the 1970s, differed quite considerably. Experiences were shaped by the generosity of the farmer, whether he was a "good man" and the extent to which his wife made demands on the women for domestic services. Although some women talked about living on a particular farmer's property for long periods of time, most experienced much movement from farm to farm as farm owners replaced labour when farming became increasingly mechanised and because farm owners experienced greater financial constraints.

From the Khutsoane life histories [# 9]

Patience Khutsoane (48) was a comparatively young woman. She recalled her father telling her about life on the farms. "My father used to talk about the farm life before they started to live in the township. They used to plant vegetables and mealies. It was not expensive like the township. They had their own cows. The farmer gave you a small plot to grow your vegetables. My father used to do most of the work but my grandmother used to help him. My grandfather used to look after the farmer's cattle ... Until 1968 my father was still under the white farmer's control. The relationships were good then. My grandparents never earned money. Each month they would get 80 kg of mealie-meal"(t). Paulina's father and uncles eventually left the farm to work in town.

Skosana-Sibiya life histories [# 2]

Martha Sibiya (55) grew up on a farm. She said that "farm life was most enjoyable", but added, "this was also because we did not know any other life". The most important thing about growing up on the farm was that "food was plentiful" and there was "no suffering". Her mother, Thoko (70), however, referred to unsettled early years with contrasting experiences. She said, "every year we would move to a different farm because by the end of the year we would be told by the farm owner that there was no more work." She remembered the frequent uprooting. They would have to pack their things and leave. Then they would stop at another place. Her father's job used to be, generally, looking after sheep, planting mealies and planting tobacco. "The homes on the farms around Groenstad were very small. We sometimes had just one or two rooms in which to live. But we did not *live* in them. We used to go there only to sleep. When my father worked in the fields, my mother and I sometimes helped him, but our responsibilities were to assist the farmer's wives on the different farms on which we worked. For this we got paid R10 a month. In those days R10 was a lot of money and we could buy many things" (a/s). (In the Mashinini life histories [# 7] Zenele (56) also talked about domestic labour on the farms about forty years ago. She claimed that as a young woman she was paid R1.50 a month. Her mother, Elsie (81), was paid 15 cents a day. She added, though, that this was good money. "In those days you could buy a dress for 10 cents, trousers for 20 cents and sugar was 2.5 cents. We could live well on that money") (s).

In the 1950s and 1960s, against the background of a deteriorating agricultural economic base and the rising costs of essential goods, more men sought work outside Winterveld. Women assumed larger roles both in keeping farming alive and in selling agricultural produce. In a group session (*Ikageng* group) I was told:

When Winterveld was in its early days it was mainly the men who went out to work. Women remained in the area. They were ploughing and surviving by using donkeys and oxen. Men used to go out to work and stay away. But not all were staying in Johannesburg. Younger men were out but coming home fortnightly. Women were bringing up children. When the women ploughed they would work together. If a man decided to stay at home and work, he would sometimes work for about three families. Women would help him. They would fill the crops in many bags. In April or May the women would leave their children with responsible elderly people and then try and sell the produce at the locations (s).

It was common practice to use child labour for farming. Some of the women who attended some early years on farm schools talked about schools operating in terms of three-monthly cycles. There were no school activities during sowing or harvesting time; the expectation was that children would be released from schoolwork to participate in farming activities. In a group session (*Ikageng* group) I learnt that, in Winterveld, around the 1960s:

> Sometimes the school would be approached to send schoolchildren to help with the sowing. The schoolchildren would be sent out of the school to help. Later the school principal would be sent some reward. Mainly a contribution to the school fund (s).

From the Mosele-Gamede life histories [# 14]

> Child labour was a part of life. We were taught the value of hard work. On Saturdays children could spend long hours fetching wood, doing washing and ironing. After that they did their homework (e).

The stories of the older women suggest that child labour made an important contribution to most households. In terms of Caldwell's (1982) argument, fertility remained relatively high because the direction of "wealth flows" were from children to parents. With many of the men being absent for periods of time women involved themselves in a range of work activities and there is no clear sense, in the very early days, of a gendered division of labour. Large numbers of children were thus desirable both as labour resources and as insurance and protection against difficult times. Although there were costs involved in clothing children and sending them to school, expenses for day-to-day living were not regarded as exorbitant. As one woman in a group session (*Mama's* group) complained: "Bringing up children was not very hard. For some it was not tough. We used to milk the cows. We could make porridge for the children. Life was not expensive. Now they say the cost of living is too high for many children. I do not believe it" (s).

Extended family networks and collaborative "community" efforts at farming are regarded as positive features of the 1940s to 1960s. Older women, however, tend to express dual sentiments toward them. On the one hand, families played economically functional roles in child-rearing and in serving as a safety-net or cushion against potentially hard times.

On the other hand, it was the weight of family structure and intensity of relationships, felt by both unmarried women and married women (in the mother-in-laws' homestead) which encouraged the seeking of employment in larger numbers. Whether they remained working within the confines of the household or negotiated time to work elsewhere, for periods of time, women talk about their working lives, peripheral or more long-term, as not compromising their child-bearing and child-rearing responsibilities.

In her description of the movement of young Bafokeng women in the 1920s to 1940s into domestic service, Bozzoli (1991:22) suggests that:

> "[t]hese were young women who sought both to live respectable Bafokeng lives by retaining their identities and connections with others from the same area, and also to increase their independence by working away from home and earning a little money. Both employment in domestic service and informal-sector activities helped the women pursue all of these aims ..."

Similarly, for women who derived earnings from work (mainly domestic work), work was important as a means of gaining some money with which to buy personal items as well as to assert some independence from the tediousness of family and agricultural life. As farming became less meaningful as a source of livelihood, however, households began to rely, to greater and lesser extents, not just on men's but women's wages as well.

There are a number of *themes* apparent in the older women's stories that are relevant to an understanding of their reproductive experiences:

Theme 1: Diffidence, and a lack of power, to negotiate family size with migrant husbands

In the previous chapter reference was made to contestations, often of a violent nature, at the household level. Although many of the older women encountered disputes and problems in their marriages they were wary of talking about them. For example, Thoko Skosana [#2] and Elsie Mashinini [#7] both indicated that they had experienced marital problems but avoided criticising their late husbands. Instead, they spoke with much respect for their husband's attempts to support them, and were grateful for the fathering of their children. The oldest women whom I interviewed also tended to see themselves as subordinate to their husbands and subject to their control.

From the Dlali life histories [#11]

Lucy Lebepe (61) said, "In my house my father was the boss. After marriage my husband was the boss. I was taught never to speak back. We learnt that women had to be at the mercy of men ... There was no such thing as choices in those days. If you try and abstain [from sexual relations] he will ask: "Why? Have you got another man?" The old people will advise you and say you must respect your husband. You must do his washing. You must cook for him. When he hits you, you must not hit back. I took their advice"(s).

Child-bearing thus was simply part of women's lot and often viewed mainly as a consequence of men being around. Women looked forward to their men being home on their periodic visits. I was told that men would attend to family matters, hand over the larger part of their earnings and wives would most likely discover themselves to be pregnant at some point after their departure. In a group session (*Ikageng* group) one woman described the pattern of life after she married.

He had a short time with me. He only came when he had two weeks' leave. My husband was the breadwinner. He just gave me money and went away. I organised the home and brought up the children. He spent two days travelling, and twelve days resting at home. When he was at home he was the boss and he listened to all our complaints (s).

Another woman said:

When the men came for those short times they just came to make the women pregnant ... This is how we have lots of children. There was no planning (s).

Another woman explained:

We were breast-feeding sometimes for three full years because the husband was not usually at home ... I was breast-feeding one of my children when my husband lost his job. He was at home then and not working. I then could not breast-feed for more than one year. That is why the time [birth interval] between that child and the next one is only one year. Husbands are the ones who know about impregnation. The wife just finds herself pregnant. Control comes from the husband (s).

The dependent positions of women within their families and marriages, and their perceptions of themselves as mothers, above all else, shaped their identities as women and made it "normal" and "natural" to strive for large numbers of children.

Theme 2: Negative attitudes toward modern versions of family planning

The older women expressed quite negative attitudes toward family planning. Since it was believed that "control comes from the husband", an admission from a wife that she was trying to control her own child-bearing would have most likely been criticised as un-natural. Traditional methods such as post-partum abstinence, long periods of breast-feeding or withdrawal were not thought to be in the same category as the injection or the pill because they were practiced in accordance with prevailing customs. Modern contraception was regarded as something foreign to African cultural practice and was considered to be the cause of both infertility and promiscuity. Whilst being disinterested when it was being introduced in the 1970s, a few older women admitted to having become more aware of the effects of contraception since their daughters had begun using it.

From the Nkomo life histories [# 12]

Nani Nkomo (58) said, "I worked as a *sangoma* [traditional healer] ... I had 8 children. I never had to use contraception. I thought it will make me sick. We used to say that it will make us infertile." In a later interview she said, "I speak to my children about contraception. These days it is bad outside. Most of my daughters use them. Only two daughters fell pregnant while they were at school ... These days four or five children will do. The cost of living is too high. Before we used to have many children because we were not suffering ... We had many children because we hoped that many would look after us" (x).

From the Mabetwa-Makgoba life histories [# 4]

Khanyi Mabetwa (78) said that she had never tried to influence her children's views on family planning. She believed, though, that she should have spoken up because one of her daughters used the injection as a young girl and became "affected". Khanyi said: "My daughter is now forty years old. She cannot conceive because she used the injection when she was very young. She has gone to many doctors but it is of no use. She does not want to try traditional medicine. We are church-goers so we do not want to use traditional medicine"(t).

The aversion to family planning or contraceptive use was strong not just because it was "foreign", and potentially harmful to women's bodies, but because it was wrong to "hope for" fewer children. As I was told in a group session (*Ikageng* group):

> We cannot hope for less children. Maybe we will get babies or not. We would not have been happy to know about family planning. It is not nice. Even our husbands were not in favour. Unfortunately, today, schoolgirls learn about family planning. They use it and then they do not get babies ever ... We African people want a lot of children. That is why we are so many (s).

Older women such as Manto Mosele and Nozizwe Radebe both, coincidentally, used modern contraception after having five children each. Manto had three miscarriages. She had also suffered trauma after her eldest child had died at the age of fourteen years. Nozizwe had had one miscarriage and one still-birth. The fact that both used contraception after having five children each was not, they contended, on account of them having acquired higher levels of education or because of what micro-economists might refer to as "middle-class tastes". Whilst both would have preferred to have had more than five children, both were diagnosed as having medical problems, making it risky to their health to have too many conceptions. Thus, in certain cases, deliberate avoidance of pregnancy through contraceptive use was regarded as reasonable if it was being used to protect the health of the mother.

Theme 3: Desires for larger numbers of children and no sex preferences

When asked - if she could choose again - what she would think was a "good number" of children Khanyi Mabetwa (78) suggested that "thirteen children was a good number". Khanyi had given birth thirteen times but only ten children had survived. She would have wanted all thirteen to have lived until adulthood. She did recognise that her children were happy with having fewer children than she had had. Most of them tried to have two children each except one son who had six children, and one daughter, Louisa, who had five daughters.

It was rare for the older women to talk in terms of wanting fewer children than they had given birth to. Women often talked about wanting as many as "what God permits" and "what husbands want". Some of the views were captured in a group session (*Ikageng* group):

> It is hard to say who prefers more children. You cannot say whether it is the husband or the wife. Both were happy with a lot of children ... We

gave birth at home. I never went to a clinic before giving birth. There wasn't anything then (s).

Many children can be good for support but there has been little support. In those days more babies were always wonderful. It was bad if you did not have children. People were laughing at you. I was so happy with many children. I thought that they were going to look after me. Now they are all gone. They are looking after their wives (s).

For some women, bearing more children served the purpose of stabilising a tenuous marital relationship. Women who found themselves in polygynous unions often tried to compete with the other wives and win the husband's favour by having more children. A more recent example of this was Nani Nkomo's [# 12] admission that "I was having children to encourage my husband to stay. He was popular with other women. I wanted him to stay with me" (x).

In bearing children, older women expressed virtually no preferences for sons or daughters. Once again, they did not appear to "wish for" sons or daughters. This is arguably the case because, given the large numbers of children born, women invariably gave birth to some sons and some daughters. Of all the older women interviewed, only Dudu Mabunda [#10] had all children of one sex. Dudu Mabunda (65) is younger than Elsie Mashinini (81) and Thoko Skosana (70). Dudu has had a more urban-based upbringing with access to higher education whilst the other two women grew up on farms. What they have in common are the facts that all of them married as teenagers and all have seven (living) children.

From the Mabunda-Thobejane life histories [# 10]

I have seven children because I kept trying for a son. Mr Mabunda wished for sons. In my opinion one should be happy with whatever is in the house. A number does not matter. But Mr Mabunda was being teased by his family. They would say, "You have only daughters. Now your surname is gone." If I had a son earlier I might have had fewer children. After my seventh child I said we had to stop trying. My parents-in-law were upset. My marriage was not upset (e).

Nani's and Dudu's motivations for wanting additional children probably bear a resemblance to those of other women in Winterveld, but Khanyi's comments below capture, I believe, the central fears of women of her generation.

From the Mabetwa-Makgoba life histories [# 4]

It was not the number of children that worried us. We were worried more about how to keep the children fit and alive. Even when they were growing up I could not leave them alone or with strangers. I would get visions of bad things happening to them. Sickness was a big worry. I would also fear coming home and hearing someone say that they were knocked down by cars or something. That is why I was happy when my mother was here to watch over them (t).

Theme 4: Many children as a response to fears of infertility and child mortality

Although there is much debate about the changing structure of households and kinship networks (Amoateng, 1997, Amoateng and Richter, 2003; Russell, 1998; Murray, 1981), families are often depicted as becoming, over time, progressively smaller due to the fewer number of children being born to individual women. Thoko Skosana, Elsie Mashinini and Khanyi Mabetwa, however, suggest that their own families, as young women, were larger than those of either their parents or grandparents. There are two main reasons offered for this. In the past it was not uncommon for women in polygynous unions to have as few as two children. When other wives have already had large numbers of children, a third wife, for example, is under little pressure to bear as many children. A further and more obvious issue would be the high levels of child mortality experienced in the past.

From the Mashinini life histories [#7]

Elsie remembered her grandparents on her mother's side. They were a monogamous couple. They had only two children. She was not certain why they had had only two children but she knew that some of her grandmother's children had died. By contrast, Elsie's mother had had nine children - two of whom died of illnesses when very young. Elsie had seven children after two had passed away. Her younger daughter, Zenele (56), had had eight children but only four survived. Zenele explained, "I have never been interested in family planning and such things. I wanted about ten children ... It is heartsore when children die. Two died as a result of illnesses. One died in his sleep. I do not know what happened to that child. Then ten years ago in 1989 my one son was killed by the boyfriend of another woman [in Winterveld]." Zenele articulated the reasoning of (older) women who have lived with the fear of child mortality. She said: "If you have many children there is a chance that some will die. From those who live only a few will be of help to you in later life"(s).

Given the centrality of women's reproductive roles to being regarded as good wives, women who had few children exposed themselves as being less fecund or were sympathised with because it was assumed that they were in poor health. Thoko Skosana [#2] grew up in a household in which her mother and her father's first wife were both regarded as being sickly with "womb problems". Khanyi Mabetwa's [#4] mother had only two children. She was said to have become sterile after giving birth to her second child. Martha felt a sense of pride in having had as many as ten children. She claimed that she had created a "real" family for her children. This was unlike her own situation. When she was a young woman, her only sibling, an older sister, died after "inhaling fumes". "Who can I now talk to when I have problems?", she asked.

Miscarriages sometimes resulted in feelings of anxiety but were not accompanied by the same kind of guilt which still-births (when the "child is whole") brought. Through hospital negligence Nozizwe Radebe once suffered a still-birth.

From the Radebe life histories [# 3]

The doctor thought I was going to make a case. I was so upset. But still-births, they say, are caused by the ancestors ... Immediately after that I fell pregnant again to make up for the loss of the child who died. That's when Flora was born (e).

From the Skosana-Sibiya life-histories [# 2]

Martha was shocked. She said: "I never expected to have a still-born child. When they told me the child was dead I did not understand. [She blamed herself.] I asked myself, "What did I do wrong?" I went to Heidelberg Hospital because the baby was late in arriving. At the hospital I was advised to have future children through caesarian section. At first I did not trust them. I went to a traditional healer for advice. She gave me some herbs as protection against future still-born children (s).

A study of the sentiments of older women on child mortality, and of perceptions of themselves and their fecundity, offers a lens through which fertility and its determinants can be more fully explored. In Greenhalgh's (1995: 23) critique of demography she suggests that demography's assumptions and biases appear to be "almost pre-feminist". She cites as an example the view that "only women aged 15 -

49 are reproductively "dynamic" and thus worth studying". This focus on older women is intended to illuminate, in part, fears and tensions about self-perceptions and unfulfilled reproductive roles which have been experienced by older women and which continue to persist as "clusters of habits" to shape the life experiences of younger women. A prevailing fear among women in the past was that of being diagnosed as infertile or sub-fecund.

From the Ramashala-Molefe life histories [# 8]

[Clara Molefe (66) and her sister Dimakatso Molefe (56) live together on a plot in Winterveld. Clara and Dimakatso claimed to have come from a long line of women amongst whom "barrenness is common". Although Clara evaded the stigma that comes with being infertile, Dimakatso was childless and lived a reclusive, isolated existence.]

Clara talked about her life and experiences. "My family worked for the white farmers. We were labour tenants. My mother also sold pottery ... I never went to school. During the day I used to grind the mealies and fetch water. In that time we used to mix soil to patch the floor. I used to cook as well ... I married when I was "big". The man I married was working in Germiston. I met him when I started working in town. My friends were going to town to work. They were dressing well. I needed money for nice dresses. I asked my parents for permission. They allowed me to go ... At first I slept on the train platform ... I had bad experiences as a domestic worker. I worked until I got a pension."

Clara eventually "divorced" her husband. At the time of the divorce she had had two children. "He treated me badly and was not supporting me." Clara explained what she thought was a major problem in her marriage. She met and married her husband in Germiston after having relationships with many other men. She had never used contraception but her earlier relationships, she claimed, did not result in any pregnancy. Her many relationships left her "very sick". From her account of it it is possible that she was afflicted with a sexually transmitted disease and that it affected her fecundity.

"I had my first child shortly after marriage. I was very happy. I wanted children. My husband was happy. The second child came *fifteen years later*. I don't know why. My husband was still living with me but his family were complaining. Because I was taking so long they said that this means that the first child was not his. I was hearing this"(s).

When asked whether she would have wanted more children in that marriage, Clara replied: "I cannot say. Children are from God. I cannot think of a "number" ... I was scared of my husband. I could not discuss such things with him ... I never knew of family planning ... After my husband left I used to earn a living sewing aprons and wrap-around dresses. I was working as a domestic worker. I used my employer's machines ... I did not have another husband. I did not care. What are you going to do with a second marriage? I can have a boyfriend. It is better if he lives in his own house ... I had two other children from this one boyfriend. He helped support me ... He was driving a motor car. I was eating meat with him. He was a very good man ... He left because he was married. His wife had other children the same age as mine"(s). Clara had hoped that he would not leave, but that he would stay and support her, because she had had his children. This was not to be.

Clara's younger sister, Dimakatso, did not have any children. She considered herself to have been condemned from the time she was born. She said, "My mother was not expecting me. My father used to say that my mother has a "... poison"[sickness due to bewitchment]. He went to the traditional healer to say that she is not fertile. Then they said that she is pregnant. They did not know how I could be born. My mother was not healthy. They said she was not menstruating ..." Dimakatso described her early years on the farms. "My job as a child was cleaning, gardening and looking after the cattle ... One day I was "robbed" by my mother's sister. I heard that I was "sold" to a man who I did not know. My mother's sister said: "That man who comes here - he's married to you."... We stayed together for five years. In those five years I had two children. They both died when they were babies. I was shocked when the first baby died. I breast-fed the child for long. I was not meeting with my husband ... It was not a natural death." Dimakatso believed that the child was bewitched ("She was killed by my mother's sister's child"). "I went to a *sangoma* [traditional healer] and they said that she was "poisoned". I fell pregnant immediately after that. The child was still-born (it was a "whole person"). We did not try to have children again. My husband was disappointed. It spoilt our relationship. He helped me clear my things and I went back home." On arriving home she was taunted and humiliated by relatives. Dimakatso then left to find work in town. She did have another partner later on but did not fall pregnant. When Dimakatso's grand-niece, Pinky, had a child, Thandi (Pinky's mother) tried to persuade Dimakatso to take the child as her own. Having lived with the childless stigma for so long, Dimakatso said, "It is too late for that. We cannot try to replace those children who have died"(s).

Younger women's views on life, work and reproduction

My purpose, in reflecting on the experiences of older women, was to focus on child-bearing during times when kinship structures were seen to be strong, when child-rearing responsibilities were distributed, when marriages were less fluid and when, as some of the women suggested, "life was not expensive". "Costs of living" were rarely given as reasons for having fewer children. For older women, the presence of many children was valued in itself; children were also regarded as important sources of labour and insurance, and determinants of well-being and social esteem. In this section the overview of the experiences of younger women (primarily in their twenties to forties) show some similiarities but many differences from their mothers' situations.

In Chapter 3 the political and economic struggles that marked different phases of life in Winterveld were discussed. References to the rapid expansion of the population, due primarily to the movement of people from the surrounding areas into Winterveld, and to the extreme tension experienced during the days of the Bophuthatswana regime were made. The kind of survival strategies women have adopted to fend off increasing hardship, to compensate for weakening kin structures and insecure relationships were also discussed in previous chapters. These include dependent relationships, multiple unions for financial gain, involvement in low-reward informal sector activities and short-term work in town. Women who saw themselves as suffering the effects of poverty and unemployment were using contraception to delay child-bearing and have fewer children in the long term. The experience of poverty was all-encompassing and included a sense of urgency about wanting to find secure and rewarding work.

Work has been scarce in Winterveld. There are few shops and businesses which offer employment. Farming did not appear to be a feasible livelihood option for young women. Gardening jobs were regarded as being mainly for the most destitute people who were usually seen digging trenches and tending to patches of field, primarily on the church grounds, as a source of livelihood. Increasingly this kind of work, which serves mainly feeding functions and reaps minimal financial rewards, was regarded as work for older people and for foreigners. Many of the women doing gardening on the church grounds were Mozambicans living in the country illegally. Literacy levels of women have increased over the years and, as a result, the younger women preferred to look for clerical ("office jobs") rather than domestic jobs. Although a large proportion of women (younger and older) continued to work in the area of domestic labour, younger women, unlike their mothers, arguably, were less inclined to see domestic work as a life-long preoccupation. Short-term and *ad hoc* domestic work was the norm. The popularity of informal sector selling activities varied. In Mr Ndlovu's district I did not sense that younger women from poor families felt any discomfort in working out schemes to sell vegetables or in sitting for long hours at a roadside stall. In other parts of Winterveld I have seen younger women cautious about, or reluctant to get involved in, selling activities, suggesting that selling was not real work.

Living in an area where large numbers of people are unemployed may lead to what is commonly referred to as "search inactivity" (Erasmus, 1999:4). This refers to a situation where people wait for jobs to find them rather than go out and actively seek out jobs. It is not unusual to hear women talk of "looking for work" but note, at the same time, that they never leave the house to look for work; often they do not display the confidence or have the means (daily bus fare) to go out and seek employment in the towns. It is also not unusual to observe reliance on vague promises ("I got a promise for a job"). Many women have in fact benefited from "work having found them". For example, the lives and statuses of Thandi Ramashala [#8] and Winnie Matwa (a key informant) were significantly changed when they were recruited by well-meaning entrepreneurs. The huge cheap labour pool available is sometimes drawn upon by small businesses and by fly-by-night operators from outside the area. Loosely held together, informal, social networks do prevail amongst the youngest cohort of women in Winterveld. As ex-school or peer group networks they tend to shape and reinforce perceptions of what are "better" or "worse" jobs. It was also through them that women were able to learn about available jobs, or alternative (and irregular) ways of making money as well as to find the resilience to cope with unemployment and poverty.

Tenuous links between work, fertility and "feelings of well-being"

In studying the myriad of experiences of young women in Winterveld in order to establish ways in which "socio-economic factors" or, specifically, access to work (or more money) shapes their willingness to bear more children, one comes across a variety of responses.

From the Khutsoane life histories [# 9]

Tebogo Khutsoane (28) grew up in a very protective and money-conscious family. "My grandmother used to say that "you must not trust a person who does not have anything"... In fact, my grandmother disapproved of my mother. She did not think that she was good enough for my father. My mother came from a "lower socio-economic grouping"(e). Although coming from one of the more privileged families in Winterveld the early events of Tebogo's life do not appear to be any different from those of other younger, and poorer, women in Winterveld. A teenage pregnancy interrupted her schooling. She gave up school to care for her child. The child died of an undiagnosed illness. Tebogo believed that she had been "bewitched" because she had not disclosed the true identity of the child's father (he was from a very poor family). In 1991 Tebogo went back to school. In 1992 Tebogo married her teacher and had another child. She left school again. In 1993 she went back to school in a third attempt to complete her high school education. On discovering a short while later that she was pregnant (yet again) she attempted a back-street abortion. It was an unsuccessful attempt. Nonetheless, Tebogo went on to pass her high school examinations and gave birth to her second child. Tebogo then contemplated going to university. "Going to university required a lot of money but I had too much of pride to ask my husband or my mother for money. In 1994 I stayed at home and applied to different places for university funding. Then I eventually got a bursary from the Public Service Commission and a place to study Nursing Science at the University of North-West"(e). Before beginning her studies Tebogo decided to have herself sterilised. She was twenty-four years old at the time. Her reason for doing this was that she had had two children. Her husband had also had two children from a previous marriage. In 1999 Tebogo completed her Nursing Science degree. When I met Tebogo again, in January 2000, she said that she had been unemployed for about eight months. The five years that she had spent studying had also taken its toll on her marriage, and she was now separated from her husband and living with her mother, Patience, in Winterveld.

Tebogo's child-bearing ended prior to her attempts to upgrade her studies. Her decisiveness in putting a permanent stop to future child-bearing was linked firstly to a perception that she had four children (this included two of her husband's from a previous marriage). Secondly, and more importantly for Tebogo (whose early life was marked by different kinds of trauma and feelings of humiliation) she now sought an adult life which offered her more esteem and security. (Unfortunately the breakdown of her marriage and prolonged unemployment status were both unanticipated.)

Sarah Gamede (43) was sterilised at the age of thirty-five years shortly after giving birth to her second child. Her first child had been born nineteen years earlier when she was just sixteen years old. After her teenage pregnancy Sarah went back to school, completed her studies, and became a schoolteacher. She later married Peter Gamede, a fellow-teacher, in 1992. In surveys, Sarah (and Tebogo) would be captured within a younger cohort of educated women who would most likely be argued to have delayed child-bearing and had fewer children as a consequence of more years of education. This assumption would not be totally accurate however because it was an early pregnancy that delayed the completion of her education (and not education which delayed fertility). Nonetheless re-entry into school did delay her decision to marry and have a second child. She told me that her second child was born only after her career had stabilised and after she felt secure in her marriage. The main issue for Sarah, rather than her own preferences, was her husband's fear of poverty.

From the Mosele-Gamede life histories [#14]

I have only one child with my husband. My daughter was born in 1994. We discussed many things in courtship. We discussed children ... My husband had eleven brothers and sisters. Now some have passed away. How he grew up affected him. He struggled. They did not have much. That family struggled. He is quite happy with few children (e).

Now note another story:

From the Radebe life-histories [#3]

When I first interviewed Flora in 1998 she worked long hours as a travel consultant for Dixie's Travel Agency in Pretoria. Her tasks were varied but she dealt mainly with aliens who wanted to remain for longer periods in the country. The priority areas were re-entries, work permits, passports and IDs. For this she earned only R750 per month. Her transport costs per month were about R200. Her actual income in hand was therefore lower. Her employers first paid her R1000 a month then reduced it to R800 before it dropped to R750. Flora accepted lesser remuneration rather than face retrenchment. She was understandably very frustrated with her work. She said at the time:"I need to buy beautiful things for myself. I cannot manage to buy anything with the way they pay me" (e). She was quite sure at the time that she would not be having another child because she was happy with one child. "It has been hard to bring up my child [he was eighteen years old at the time] ... having another child will be a burden" (e/s).

By December 1999 Flora had resigned from her work and obtained qualifications to set up her own travel agency. She was planning to run her business from home. Through various schemes Flora was accumulating the start-up capital for this small business venture. On the brink of being self-employed and now almost forty years old, Flora said the following: "I am owing myself one more child. I am not yet settled. It was not good to have just one. I will be happy to have one more. If I do not, I will accept having just one" ... When asked again what her "ideal number" of children was, she responded: "The "ideal number" of children to have is two. It does not matter, though, it depends on God and if God allows me to have one more ... I am having a relationship now. It is not a bad relationship. It has been going on for about a year now" (e/s).

By 2003, however, Flora's home business had collapsed, her relationship had ended and she no longer contemplated an additional child. Flora's case illustrates the fluidity of the reproductive decision-making process and its contingency upon a range of personal and economic dynamics. However, it is important to emphasise that Flora's self-confidence and anticipation of prosperity increased quite significantly after she became self-employed. It forced her to re-evaluate aspects of her life, including her prior thoughts on relationships and child-bearing. Had her relationship sustained itself, she might well have been happy to bear another child. Work, in this sense, offers opportunities for women to fulfil what they might consider as previously unfulfilled reproductive roles.

From the Mabunda-Thobejane life histories [# 10]

Kebone Thobejane (44) is the eldest of Dudu Mabunda's seven daughters. She was, however, the last to get married. Dudu had taken special care in screening prospective sons-in-law. She needed to be convinced that the man whom Kebone eventually married was going to offer her "special care". Kebone was caned (on the head) by a music teacher shortly after beginning high school. She had a "breakdown" and a series of epileptic fits after that. With a domineering mother, and treated like an invalid, Kebone became increasingly reclusive. She failed high school three times. All six of her sisters became professionals, either teachers or nurses. Before marrying, Kebone did a fair amount of work outside the home: she once worked in a supermarket; she also did dressmaking and typing. Kebone married when she was in her late thirties. She has had no children and is pitied in the area as an "infertile" woman. "Before marriage I did not have too many boyfriends. It was strict at home. My mother used to say that if I fall pregnant I must look after myself. I will be on my own. I started using contraception when I was nineteen ... I love children but I do not have a child. When I am with other people and they boast about their children I keep quiet for fear that they will ask: "where is your child?" I'm happy with Mr Thobejane. He says, "be proud of who you are".

Dudu, however, was unhappy with having approved Thobejane as Kebone's husband. Kebone's inability to have children has led to much animosity, accusations and counter-accusations between the Mabundas and the Thobejanes. Dudu told me that: "Thobejane comes from a barren family. People have told Kebone to adopt a baby and bring it up. He does not want to hear about it."

Kebone is not sure whether the fault lies with her or her husband. She said: "Recently I went to the doctors. They said I am fine. When it was his turn to have himself checked he complained of back-ache. Doctors gave him pills for back-ache. He did not explain the real reason for going to the doctor." She claimed that if the fault was hers it is because of her early use of contraceptives. She added: "If he is infertile another man could give me a baby - but I would not like that"(e).

Kebone was fortunate in one sense. She did not come from a family living in extreme poverty. If she had she would have, most likely, experienced ostracisation and some degree of public humiliation. Nonetheless, her infertility since her marriage made her reclusive and reluctant to socialise outside the home or seek work. It has also made her increasingly dependent on her husband. It may well be that the cause of Kebone's inability to fall pregnant lies with her husband. Such an admission, however, would upset conventions which suggest that "barrenness" is a "woman's problem" - and it is with her that the ultimate blame should lie. Irrespective of whether or not younger women choose to have fewer children, "too few" as in Flora's case or "no children" as in Kebone's case affect the way others view them, and the way they, consequently, view themselves and their "social acceptability" as women. In this sense, the fears of younger women are quite similar to those of older women, referred to earlier. Their sense of economic hardship, however, is arguably much stronger.

Land-owners in Winterveld represented a diverse group of people who reflected considerable differentials in terms of wealth. What appeared to be relatively consistent, though, was that female-headed households were much poorer than male-headed households. Lucy Dlali (61) [#11] owned a plot but survived through domestic work earnings in bringing up her family. Since turning sixty in 1998 she relied solely on her pension. In 1998 Lucy complained about Phumzile's (her daughter's) complacency in relying on her for money.

From the Dlali life histories [#11]

When I first met Phumzile Dlali (33) she was unemployed. She was always at home and said that she did not want to "go around looking for a job". Phumzile was one of those women who were now weary of looking for work and weary of being unemployed. Apart from cooking and cleaning in her mother's home she used to do washing for other women in Winterveld. In 1998 Phumzile told me that she earned R1.50 per month for washing clothes for a better-off family in Winterveld. Phumzile's three children had been "accidental", a consequence of poor contraceptive use in relationships, maintained largely for monetary reasons, with three different men. All had abandoned her shortly after she gave birth. Her most recent boyfriend, she said, was also unreliable. "He's got the same character as the rest (s)."

In February 1999 Phumzile was invited by a group of women to help them sell tupperware at Mabopane Station. Whilst selling she was approached by a bus-driver who also owned a shop in Lebotlwane (near Warmbaths). He was looking for someone to work in his shop. He offered Phumzile R250 a month. Phumzile left home and worked in his shop for three months. But the work was full-time and she was not allowed to go home during weekends. When the owner did not allow her to take time off, to visit her family during their ancestral feast, Phumzile resigned from her work. She reminded her employer that she needed time off - "I've got children to look after." Although disappointed with the low pay she was not unhappy about the work experience. "On my side it was okay. No-one gives me money at home. [Lucy buys food; Phumzile gets no money for her private use.] Now I will look for a job in Marabastad or in town"(s).

Phumzile did not complete high school. Her work experiences were limited, unrewarding and short-term. She relied on support from numerous relationships and on her mother. Bearing children, rather than serving to win her financial support, led to her abandonment. Now under pressure from her mother, and because "no-one gives her money", Phumzile was no longer able to stay at home, dependent and complacent. Her working experience in Lebotlwane, although low-paying, gave her some confidence to seek better paying jobs elsewhere (for her own support and well-being).

From the Makwela life histories [#1]

Lebo (48) told me that she had thought seriously about building a career around water projects in Winterveld. Since 1997 the Rand Water Board (referred to locally as RDP Water) sought to use local labour to lay the foundations for Winterveld's development. The jobs entailed digging trenches and laying water pipes. She was contracted in 1997 (with her daughters, Sophy and Sinah) to dig and close the trenches for the water pipes. It was manual labour but they earned some money - "at first we earned R250 per week. Sometimes we would find a reason to "pull two day's money" by doing extra loads" (s). She later underwent some training, and bought books on pipe-laying, hoping that she would be regarded as skilled enough to gain sub-contraction work. Her intention was to get a contract and hire and manage the work of other people who would do the hard labour jobs, that is, laying pipes and digging water canals. Unfortunately, she was turned down. Lebo complained that she would have been awarded the tender if she had paid a bribe.

Although Sophy (25) and Sinah (22) joined their mother in hard labour jobs they have had no intention of pursuing such work "as a career". In fact, both felt quite embarrassed to do that kind of menial work. Their choices, however, were limited. Both were unskilled, having dropped out of school at the junior secondary level. Sophy did not want to consider working as a domestic worker, although in 1996 she did work as one for two weeks. "Things were going well at the employer's house until I allowed the gardener inside the house when the employers were not around. When they arrived they said that an expensive watch-bracelet was missing. They asked if I had allowed the gardener inside. I said, " yes, but that I did not know he was going to steal". They said I must stop working and must come back the following week. When I went back the following week they told me that they did not need me anymore because "they had found another girl"(s). Sophy left humiliated, and vowed never to do domestic work again. Her next job was with her mother and sister at the RDP Water Project. They did this job from September to December 1997; and from January to April 1998. Later in 1998 Sophy was raped and beaten by four men. Shortly after that she left for Johannesburg to find work. She failed to find "a decent job" and later turned to sex work which was apparently more financially rewarding than domestic work. Sophy supported one son who in 1999 was six years old.

In 1999 Sinah was also "looking for a job" but she admitted that she "would not leave the area". She did not want to leave Jimmy, her boyfriend, who lived close by. "I will be staying here for Jimmy's life ... I was once in Johannesburg for three weeks. When I came back I heard that Jimmy had had an affair with another girl"(s). Sinah was distressed on hearing about Jimmy's affair. After that, she decided not to leave Winterveld to look for jobs elsewhere. When I first interviewed Sinah, in 1998, she said that she would like to eventually have three children in all. She was not using contraception because she suspected that she was sub-fecund ("I don't catch easily"). In any event, Sinah had claimed, "If I fall [pregnant], I will be happy". However, in 1999, after Sinah was made to leave home, and Jimmy did not welcome her into his family home, and she became both emotionally confused and financially destitute, a possible pregnancy was considered to be "the worst thing". In 2008, when Sinah and I last met, she talked about her great efforts to sustain her relationship and her acceptance of the fact that she had borne only one child.

Like Sinah, Lindi Dlamini and Mary Msimang were also twenty-two years old at the time of my initial interviews. They also fell pregnant before completing their schooling. In 2000 both were looking for work. Just as Sankie Motjieng had indicated earlier that she would prefer to have another child only when she could afford to, Lindi and Mary wanted to have children only if they found appropriate work. They did not rely on families or on their partners. In 2008, Sinah, remarkably, still sustained her relationship with Jimmy, but had not had an additional child.

From the Dlamini life histories [#15]

Lindi said: "My main aim is to find work. I will want to be about thirty years old when I marry. The man I marry must be educated. He must be supportive and not 'mess around'. Educated men do not have second wives." Lindi had been using contraception since having her first child. "I would like to have about three to four children. Two girls and two boys or two girls and one boy." Lindi, although a South African, had a Mozambican mother. I found that the fears of child mortality were particularly strong among Mozambican women living in the area. Thus Lindi explained that she desired three or four in case of child mortality. "If some die, there will be others"(s).

From the Msimang life histories [# 5]

Mary said: "I want to have a career. Marriage is something for later ... When I fell pregnant my boyfriend said the baby was not his. His mother and sister were talking for him. He gives them money. They did not want me to have any of it ... I am bringing up my daughter myself ... I need money for her food and clothes ... I think two children is a good number of children. I do not have a preference for either boys or girls. We can all do the same things these days"(s).

The stories of younger women like Phumzile, Sophy, Sinah, Lindi, Mary and Sankie were different in many respects. They were similar in that all had children from earlier relationships and all had subsequently had negative and insecure work experiences. All as well had strong needs for independent work to live better lives. In these stories of poorer women joblessness acts somewhat as a deterrent, making women protect themselves against future pregnancies. Bearing children as a means towards securing support from men does not appear as a strong motive for sustaining relationships in the long run; contraception is used precisely to avoid pregnancy in these insecure relationships. For Sophy, liaisons with men were pursued unambiguously for money. For the other women both the nature of the relationships, and the extent to which financial support was forthcoming, varied. Although younger women talk with some pride about the birth of children, they display greater control and are more selective about the timing of future children than their mothers were. There are a number of general *themes* that emerge in the stories of younger women that can be referred to.

Theme 1: The conjunction of insecure relationships and absence of stable employment is shaping a pattern of lower fertility

The inability to find a secure means to earn a living, against the background of unstable relationships and weakening kinship bonds, presents a particular kind of crisis for young women within Merafeng. Daily struggles to survive increase awareness of the costs involved in bringing up children. In Caldwell's (1982) wealth-flows theory lowered fertility is an indication of the progressive nucleation of families as the costs of children become higher than their anticipated productive contributions to the household economy. Despite acknowledging responses to the burden of costs, it would be difficult to argue that families in Winterveld are becoming "nucleated" or necessarily "child-centred" in the sense suggested by Caldwell. The younger women in my stories have borne smaller numbers of children but remain primarily a part of female-headed households or of fragmented extended families. Given signs of child neglect (limited feeding, late entry into schools, early end to schooling etc.), the movement towards smaller numbers of children emphasises an emerging "woman-centredness" or rather the strategic placing of women's needs and economic survival before societal prescriptions for "child-centred" households and for investment in childbearing and rearing.

As one woman in a focus group in 2006 emphasized:

The women here suffer a lot. Some are doing piece-jobs. Some are getting grants. Some use the money for children – some not. When mothers are not here, grandparents can use child grant money for children ... sometimes these young women forget that they have kids. Many of them don't want them because they cost too much (s).

The fact that life circumstances for most women in Winterveld are not improving, but remain harsh, offers some credence to Lesthaeghe's (1989) views on how living with economic hardship may result in definite attempts to limit and control child-bearing. Rather than smaller family size being associated with signs of upward economic and social mobility (Caldwell & Caldwell, 1993), it is being linked in Merafeng with resistance to poverty (Naidoo, 2002).

Theme 2: Positive attitudes toward family planning enhance ability to assert control over when children are born

Perhaps the strongest differences that I found in my interviews, between older and younger women, have to do with attitudes toward contraceptive use. Unlike the older women, younger women have grown up at a time when contraception has been actively promoted and is readily available at schools, clinics and family-planning centres. Caldwell et al. (1992; 1993) place much emphasis on the relationship between fertility decline and contraceptive use in countries with stronger economies in Africa such as Botswana, Kenya and South Africa. It is suggested that underlying the demand for contraception "is education and the rise of the modern economy" but it is also maintained that "[n]evertheless, most contraceptors say that an important factor in their practice is the hard economic times. This claim would be more convincing if there were more "stoppers" (Caldwell et al, 1992:237). (That is, a more definite response to economic hardship, in Caldwell's view, would be evident if women were, in greater numbers, putting a permanent end to their child-bearing). Economic realities and the maintaining of simultaneous and serial unions often invite ever-changing responses to questions on "desired numbers of children" in Winterveld. Increasingly women who want to end the possibility of future births have themselves sterilised. Women on reversible methods of contraception, on the other hand, have the option of stopping their use of contraception, when better times prevail, to allow for a possible pregnancy. In many of the stories, however, prolonged use of contraception in an attempt to space or delay a future birth has meant and is amounting to the halting of child-bearing - as these better times fail to appear.

Since 2005 there has been talk in the area about some women becoming less concerned about contraceptive use. "These days it's 50-50" said Eunice Mphelo, "Some control. Some fall pregnant for the grant"(e). A state child grant is now offered for indigent, unemployed parents with dependent children. For desperate women, the small monies offered represent an income-earning possibility. Thus, whilst positive attitudes prevail, there is some negation and debilitation of contracepting practices given the incentive of child grants and societal norms about women's sense of worth being defined by reproductive outcomes. More time is required to properly note revisions to existing social rituals due to the popularisation of the child grant.

Theme 3: Intention to have smaller numbers of children is introducing questions of sex-preferences

Unlike older women who might have been hesitant to "wish for" many or few children, or sons or daughters, younger women appear to be more decisive about having fewer children. This decisiveness, however, as has already been suggested, is driven somewhat by the acknowledgement of unstable unions and by a lack of financial resources, but undermined very recently as already stated by the presence of child grants.

It is possible that younger women who have fewer children might begin to regret this precisely because of the absence of a son or daughter. Rose Malibane (29), a woman in a group session (*Ndlovu's* group) has had two sons. She wanted to "try for a daughter". Her "husband", though, did not want her to have any more children. He had had three children elsewhere. "He is worried about support. I know I cannot think about another child until I find work"(s). In other interviews, women in their forties also showed signs of regret especially when they had not had any daughters. Evah Jiane (42) and Elizabeth Mabena (45) were both part of a group session (*Ndlovu's* group). Evah said, "I did not want more than two children. Now I think if I was younger I would want more children. I have missed not having daughters. I have only two sons. The older one is a *tsotsi* [hooligan]. The younger one does community work. Both do not earn money"(z). Elizabeth said, "I am worried about having only sons. I have no daughters ... I am now too old to have children ... I tried to adopt my sister's child two years ago. Before I could fetch her she was knocked down by a car and killed in town. This is one of the things that makes me lose my mind"(s). The point here is that since there is space to re-evaluate child-bearing when financial circumstances improve, some women might be willing to, and often do, bear children at later stages in their lives to make up for perceived familial 'shortfalls'.

Theme 4: Persistent fears of mortality and disease create uncertainty about child-bearing and child survival

Child mortality was said to be one problem that had, for years, been under control in Winterveld. On a trip to Kromkuil Clinic in 1999, I was told, "We no longer have a problem of child mortality ... mothers have been taught about oral hydration treatments. When babies have diarrhoea they can be treated at home and at the clinic"(e). Sister Mafoko at St. Peter's Clinic also said at the time:

> Child mortality is not really a big problem anymore ... mothers have been educated on how to take care of children. They come for immunisation against measles. Without immunisation measles kills, especially if the child is malnourished ... child communicable diseases have been reduced in Winterveld ... Parents know that children will have problems attending schools if they are not immunised (e).

Prior to the spread of HIV infection, fears of child mortality had lessened. The central fears of women seemed to be that of contracting sexually transmitted diseases which could affect their ability to conceive a child and carry it to term. Women sometimes also speculated about their own fecundity and whether they were "healthy", "fit" or "too old" to bear children.

One of Scheper-Hughes's (1997) findings in her study of child mortality in a poor, Brazilian sugar plantation town (Bom Jesus da Mata) was that large proportions of women gave up breast-feeding in favour of bottled milk and milk powder. She stated that:

> [t]he culture of breastfeeding was lost over a very rapid period in modern northeast Brazilian sugar plantation life. What had changed radically was poor women's beliefs in the essential goodness of what comes out of their own bodies, which they now saw as dirty, disorganised and diseased, as compared to what comes out of clean, healthy, modern objects, like cans of Nestle's infant formula ... (Scheper-Hughes, 1997: 217).

Although describing a different social context, women's perceptions of themselves as unhealthy or potentially "diseased" can affect their willingness (and not just their ability) to bear children. A woman in one of my group sessions (*Ndlovu*'s group), Gladys Semela (40), and her sister, Kgaugelo (38), both claimed to have been afflicted with sexually transmitted diseases at different points in their lives. Gladys had two children. She gave one of her children to Kgaugelo because gonorrhea had made her sterile and childless. Neither Gladys nor Kgaugelo, however, was unhappy about the arrangement. They saw their bodies as "dirty" and "diseased". Kgaugelo acknowledged that children born from her body (if it was possible to conceive) would have been equally diseased or deformed. She said that, "when I go to the hospital I see cripples and mongols. Yesterday I saw a child with a big head. I don't want such a child"(s).

The pattern of lower fertility in my fieldwork site was largely a consequence of women using a variety of methods to assert control over their bodies. I was aware, though, that disease frequently intervened to increase the likelihood that many poor women living there would have fewer children. It was for this additional reason that it made sense to learn that many women were likely to take a chance and bear a child precisely when it was logically inconvenient to do so - when they found work. Not only does work offer means of support but it offers the opportunity to counteract the belief that a woman is sub-fecund or incapable of having children.

My initial fieldwork, however, took place at a time when AIDS had not yet taken a drastic toll in Winterveld. By 2002, child mortality was no longer being talked about as something of the past, but a tragedy of the present. Whilst arguments on how the current conditions and high levels of affliction might encourage women to seek to have additional children have been raised (Levin & Dubler, 1990; Cooper et al., 2007), AIDS in Merafeng appears to have an enhanced "fertility depressing" effect (see also Potts & Marks, 2001).

Responses to the Problem of AIDS

South Africa has currently the largest number of people living with HIV and AIDS in the world (Anarfi, 2003: 33). Notwithstanding the magnitude of the crisis, political, scientific and community responses to the AIDS pandemic in the country have been slow and insufficient (Kistner, 2003). In Winterveld, although health workers at family planning clinics and in hospitals and health centres spoke with concern and anxiety about the increasing number of people being diagnosed as having AIDS, I did not develop any strong impression that ordinary people were beginning to take protective measures in any consistent way. In the period between July 1998 and July 1999 I came across very few people who knew of others suffering from or who had died of AIDS. In my interviews women would refer more frequently to high blood pressure, tuberculosis or diabetes than they would to AIDS. Health workers, however, pointed out that when people did die of AIDS this was rarely reflected on death certificates. Doctors often only indicated that the patient died of tuberculosis or other AIDS-related diseases without reference to HIV or AIDS. This was (and is still) done because people want to bury their dead without stigma and with some dignity in the eyes of the community. There is still a lot of confusion about what causes AIDS. There was also an obtrusive sentiment prevalent amongst local people and health workers at the time that foreigners (particularly Zimbabweans and Mozambicans) were bringing the disease into Winterveld. At the clinics nurses suggested as well that a large proportion of the AIDS patients were "foreigners". As Eunice Mphelo at Vulinqondo (an NGO promoting AIDS awareness) said, "We have a high influx of outsiders. Those people are bringing the disease. We see them when we do our visits. They don't use much modern medicine. They go to the traditional healer and they are told that they are bewitched". At the Kromkuil clinic nurses suggest that, whether foreign or not, "some don't believe AIDS is there". People would prefer to suggest that "it's *makgome* - which is like when you did something wrong and now you are getting punished". Given this lingering sense that AIDS is related to "bewitching" and wrongdoing, it was not surprising for me to hear of an instance when "the community" turned on a Mozambican man living with AIDS and killed him out of fear that they would be affected by his "curse".

In January 2000, on a brief visit to Winterveld, I found that two of the women whom I had previously interviewed were more aware and curious about the spread of AIDS. Dudu Mabunda [# 10] told me about "two families who had died of AIDS". She was concerned about the ways in which one could contract AIDS. "How does a whole family die of AIDS? Can you catch it like the 'flu"? (e) In discussing how AIDS was spread, we considered possible reasons for how "whole families" could have died until Dudu suggested that it was most likely a consequence of intra-household (sometimes incestuous) sexual relationships or an indication of just how widespread AIDS had become over a short period of time in Merafeng. Where intimate economies, or multiple liaisons, persist the magnitude of HIV/AIDS becomes acute, and there are dire consequences for economic survival and the reproduction of domestic units (Naidoo & Misra, 2008). In this period Lebo Makwela [#1] also confronted me with news that had disturbed her. Cidi, the shebeen-owner, had AIDS. Cidi, a woman in her early forties, was apparently now "as thin as a rake". It was well known that Cidi enriched herself not just by selling liquor but through sex-work. Lebo's concern, like that of many of the other women in the area, was that "she used to take my husband's wages". For Lebo, who was herself engaging in an extra-marital relationship, the possibility that both she and her husband could be HIV-positive was now very real. In yet another brief trip in July 2000 I learnt that mainly young people were beginning to die in rapidly increasing numbers, one of whom was Lebo's eldest daughter who passed away in 2001.

Since HIV is spreading at an alarming rate amongst the youngest cohort of the population, strong emphasis has been placed on sex and AIDS education in the schools. Mary Msimang (22) [#5] said, "My sister, Thobeka (13), told me that nurses now come and advise them. They are teaching them about AIDS at all school standards. They also teach them about contraception ... In my time we never learnt about AIDS. We only learnt about contraception"(s). There are limitations, however, to adopting an AIDS-awareness strategy that does not target older groups with the same enthusiasm as it does schoolchildren. Sexual relationships do not restrict themselves to men and women of similar cohorts; schoolgirls often have relationships with older men. Winnie Matwa, the AIDS worker at the Sisters of Mercy, said, "we are getting a few teenage girls who are HIV-positive. They are being told that they can never get children. They get angry but we tell them that if they have children - those children will be dead. Then they listen"(e). Although young people (men and women) expressed fears of contracting AIDS virtually no one I had spoken to in the course of my fieldwork had been in a relationship in which condoms were used consistently.

From the Mabetwa-Makgoba life histories [# 4]

Louisa said: "My daughter, Tiny, [a student] talks about AIDS. Last year they were researching at the clinics. She told me about how AIDS affects people. They were at Taung in the Cape, Mpumalanga and even in Gauteng. She was even trying to motivate Nolwazi to be careful about AIDS. We are all becoming aware of AIDS. My sister at Old Mutual tells us about how you cannot get approval for policies if you have AIDS. I try to talk to James about AIDS but he does not listen. If he comes back after being away for a few days I am afraid to sleep with him. He may tell me lies. We Africans got this tendency of accepting lies ... We could be furious for a few days and then we get over it ... I use female condoms now. I saw some [male] condoms in James's sock-drawer the other day. I was amazed. He does not use it with me. I do not know if he uses it elsewhere. Men feel that condoms are something that you do not use with your wife. It is only for when you have sex with someone other than your wife. The taxi-drivers here will also tell you that condoms are for when you take a prostitute to the hotel because you do not know what diseases such a woman is carrying" (e).

Louisa talks to her daughters about partners. "They must try to have stable boyfriends. You do not just say: "I love you". You must live with a man for about six months to see if the relationship works. Learn about the man. You could end up marrying a freak. At the end of the day you could have AIDS ... I even tell them to avoid pregnancy and to avoid AIDS. They should keep condoms with them all the time. I say to them, "if he does not have any you must give it to him". Have your own discipline. If you cannot, don't have sex"(e).

Given South Africa's history of migrant labour, it is generally conceded that long-term spousal separation and geographical mobility have played major roles in facilitating HIV transmission. It has been common practice for migrants, who were housed in single-sex hostels on the mines, to have girlfriends in town (in addition to wives elsewhere). Sex-work around the Rustenberg mines has become financially rewarding work for impoverished Winterveld women. Campbell et al. (1998) suggest that sex-workers who want to avoid contracting AIDS find it difficult to persuade mine-workers to use condoms because they will simply lose clients to other women who do not make such demands. In discussing the views of miners on health and sexuality, Campbell et al. (1998) emphasise the ways in which condom-use is affected by social constructions of masculinity. A central issue raised by mine-workers was the role of "flesh-to-flesh" sex which they regarded as important for maintaining a healthy mind and body. In this context condoms were regarded as impersonal, "a waste of sperm" and undermining to attempts to keep themselves healthy. In my group sessions (*Mama*'s group) women also talked about the necessity for regular flesh-to-flesh sexual relations to prevent "sickness" and "madness". Ill-health was thus blamed simultaneously on infrequent sexual relations and on frequent "messing around".

At the clinics staff complained about the problems endured when attempting to treat STDs. STDs (such as gonorrhea and syphilis) were rampant in Winterveld. When a woman came in for contraception she was usually also examined for STDs. If she was found to have an abnormal discharge they would ask to see her husband and/or other partners she might have been with recently. They would not offer her treatment on her own. Most often her husband would refuse to come for treatment. Sometimes she would disclose a range of partners. Sometimes her husband disclosed multiple unions. Often when men and women were found to be HIV-positive they would not come back for treatment. At the Kgabo Clinic, the matron, Mrs Nkutshweu, said:

> There is the denial issue. If a person is diagnosed as HIV-positive he moves elsewhere for diagnosis. In fact, half of the people whom we diagnose as HIV-positive are already being treated by a traditional healer for their symptoms. People start with traditional medicine then move to western medicine. Then they become impatient with modern medicine and go back to the traditional healer (e).

Shifting Conditions and Reproductive Dynamics

The experience of extreme poverty and the reality of increased mortality, amongst other crises at the level of households, it can be conjectured, places enormous pressure on families and individual women to work towards smaller family sizes. On this point, the Department of Health (2004) report based on the 2003 South African Demographic and Health Survey (SADHS) refers to a "precipitous decline" in South Africa's fertility rate – the total fertility rate (TFR) stood at 2 in the period covered by the survey. Substantive analysis of the factors driving this "precipitous decline" is still to be developed. What remains fairly constant, though, is the high level of early pregnancy. In Merafeng, the explanations for teenage pregnancies and increasing HIV infection rates are being framed progressively around what adults claim are youth perceptions of their "rights". As one parent said in 2006:

"This weekend six young people are being buried. Us older people are very worried but we can't say anything. The more you try and control your children, the more they say they have their rights. They'll take you to the charge office… The only thing killing these kids is their rights! They don't know that responsibility goes with rights. When that thing [HIV] comes, they go with their rights".

In the aftermath of the death of her daughter, one of our key informants said:

"There is nothing that anyone could have done to save [MM] in the end ... But I am worried about my other children. I can only talk to [Lydia] and Thandi about this and not the others. When I try and give advice and ask about whether they are taking precautions they get angry and say: "You mum, you think we're all going to die".

Warnings emanating from the older generation derive partly from their growing concerns about their children's health, but they also reflect anxieties about assuming greater responsibilities for the care of the young and the maintenance of households (Schatz & Ogunmefun, 2007). With the high numbers of young people dying, orphaned children find space in grandparents' homes and multi-generational domestic units. In Winterveld, where family networks are fragile and debilitated, children are helped by Tumolo (an NGO) or housed in the Good Shepherd (next to the Sisters of Mercy). Similar to the context outlined by Varga (2003) in her research on adolescents in KwaZulu-Natal, pregnancies weigh heavily on the girls' familial networks, and the nexus of interpersonal relationships and inter-household resources that she accesses. They compromise further "personal, financial and professional goals" (Varga, 2003:168) that could have been achieved. Thus, in the aftermath of a first birth, young women, as I learnt in the early stages of fieldwork, were notably more cautious in averting possibilities of further unplanned pregnancies. The high levels of contraceptive use of women in their twenties and thirties, contrary to what one anticipates in poor areas, had been quite striking in this period (1998-2003).

Over the past five years, community discourse about pregnancy has become much more complex. Increasingly, the talk about contraceptive use and the dissuasion of pregnancy is constructed alongside acknowledgement of girls' accessing of the child grant. In August 2007, Dudu Mabunda was heckled at a pay point for child grants as she preached to young girls, some still in their school uniforms, about the problem of teenage pregnancy. They said to her: "This is our right. Mbeki is giving this to us. What have you to say?" Another woman informant told me: "You know, I helped these people at Garankuwa to write up grants. You'll see girls of 20 years with 4 children. I once asked such a girl: "Why don't you stop? She said: "this is the last". Later I saw that she was pregnant again". If one were to ask questions about how the provision of child grants are changing people's lives in Winterveld, it would usually lead to animated conversations about how young women are accessing grants, gaining autonomy and resisting calls from family to 'avoid accidents'. The early stage of a woman's life ("the dangerous time") is usually considerably affected by attempts to understand and gain control over her body. Although contradictory, views about the 'right to use contraception' currently share the same space and are intersecting with strong sentiments on 'the right to access the grant'; both reflecting defensive and creative strategies of women seeking to navigate through and survive the excesses of poverty.

Transactional sex, as Masanjala (2007) maintains, offers a ready "livelihood opportunity" for unskilled and disadvantaged women. Arguably, the meanings associated with 'transactionality' are broadening somewhat in Merafeng to incorporate thinking about and manipulation of state-administered child grants. The talk in the area is that child grants can generate incentives not only for teenagers but also for older women to bear additional children. Whilst this growing public perception is dismissed by researchers drawing on quantitative data (Makiwane & Udjo, 2007) there is sufficient grassroots dialogue about such a reality to warrant further investigation, particularly in poverty-ridden settings. With regard to the macro-picture, Makiwane and Udjo (2007) point out that 0,27% of all South African children were grant beneficiaries in 1999, but this percentage increased to 45% in 2005. To consider the impact of this on the ideological and material frameworks of people's lives I raised a number of key questions in focus groups between 2005 and 2007. At first I was taken aback, but grew progressively less surprised to hear women talk about others they knew who were having babies to increase the monthly grant amounts they already receive. Whilst the grant represents small monies (R200 per child in 2007), it was still referred to as offering women 'something', especially if more than one child was counted. In one focus group, the following comments were quite telling:

AB points to CD: "She's got 2 children. She wants more … to get the grant" (All look at her) CD responds: "Yes, I want 4 to get more [grant money]".

EF speaks up: "I am two months pregnant. I got pregnant for the grant. I got 3 [children] and this is my fourth".

GH states in the middle of the discussion:

"I want more money. There is no money and there are no jobs. I struggle to bring up my child. I cannot take my child to the doctor when he is sick. This one grant is not enough."

IJ says assertively: "Me, I like the grant. If there is no grant I will have no more [children]… I want 12 children". (Others murmur, hinting that this is a defiant exaggeration)

KL says: "I have one child. For two years I did not apply for the grant because my mother was supporting me. My mother passed away last month so I will apply now for the grant". When probed further she said, "Yes, I will have another child for the grant. This money is not as much as the old age pension".

AB says: "My child's father doesn't want to pay maintenance anymore. He said: "You've got the grant money. Use that." I know some others [other men] who give only R100 and tell you to add the grant money to buy food".

In responding to questions about contraceptive use, the women suggested that while it is still high on women's agenda, they are beginning to use it inconsistently. As IJ claimed, "Some still use [contraceptive methods]. Now a lot don't want to prevent because of the grant." With regard to how men are reacting to women's access to grants, MN said: "One boyfriend said: "he's going to make lots of kids. The government is helping him to maintain the kids. He will make them with different women". Whilst the terms of transactional sex usually dictate that women access men for money, the child grant offers an additional (and state-sponsored) route for the sustaining of livelihoods, one that men can indirectly benefit from. In the eyes of men women's growing autonomy is both welcoming and disconcerting. In focus group discussions in 2002 young men spoke with much regret about sisters and girlfriends who had to carry growing familial responsibilities and who were forced to earn money by eliciting sexual favours and by risking infection and pregnancy (Naidoo et al., 2004) In more recent focus group discussions in 2006 men talked about women's emerging strength and about men's limited power to monitor what their partners do and how they manage their resources. How do such politics and livelihood strategies affect peoples' responses to the possibilities of infection and to the AIDS epidemic in general? Whilst it is clear that there is community-wide concern about rising levels of mortality, I was struck by the casualness of comments from the women's focus groups. In response to a question probing just how concerned they were about becoming infected, some women in one focus group responded sharply:

"If there is 5 boyfriends, some use [condoms] and some don't. So I will still get infected."

"Ay, I'm used to AIDS. I am free with it. We don't worry about it anymore".

"She's talking the truth. Some are doing this [unsafe sex] and are not [anymore] worried about AIDS."

Clearly, such attitudes and perceptions of AIDS-related misfortune are deeply embedded in the constraints of domestic space and networks of struggling communities. With reference to women's struggles to make personal and reproductive decisions, Levine and Dubler (1990: 343) emphasise that the: "most crucial element in poor women's response to AIDS is their perception of its danger relative to the hierarchy of other risks and benefits present in their lives and the lack of resources to make alternative choices… many women are willing to take the risk because the alternatives [impoverishment, nil resources] may seem worse". Additionally, they suggest that the exercising of 'reproductive choices' is influenced by a moral, economic and a social world in which, increasingly, "women make decisions with other women about babies who will be largely raised by women" (1990: 343). This description has much relevance for the Winterveld case study, and undoubtedly, for many other similar hardship-driven South African social and economic contexts.

Conclusion: Focusing on the Study's Contributions

Re-visiting the primary research concern

How does the experience of poverty shape over time, the stability of unions and 'reproductive decisions' of women? Feminist economists have long observed that while both men and women bear the brunt of poverty, they, arguably, experience and are often expected to respond to it differently (see e.g. Kabeer, 1994:141). This appears to hold true for Merafeng. Sometimes unemployed or poorly paid men become dependent on the earnings of women or working children. Squabbles over prioritising how money should be used often occur in these situations in which resources are stretched and always insufficient. Thus, in growing numbers, as the life histories of women have shown, men respond to economic insecurity and domestic strife by abandoning their families and abdicating their primary feeding and child-rearing responsibilities to women. In circumstances where women are not abandoned they often complain that their partners squander money, or use much of it on their own needs, leaving them with little to maintain children and see to the needs of a household. Stress within households is generally aggravated by violent, abusive behaviour and accusations of infidelity. Households without the daily presence of men are common and the sustained experience of poverty keeps affective bonds fragile and relationships subject to the constant threat of dissolution. In their excellent paper on 'Friends and Family: Social Cohesion in South Africa', Chipkin and Ngqulunga (2008: 68) maintain that present-day South African society is frequently strained "in the area of affective relations"... "friends very quickly become enemies" [and] the "family is a site of profound contradiction: on the one hand it is a place of ferocious gender violence; on the other hand, it is today the key institution through which attempts are being made to moderate the effects of growing unemployment and poverty".

In the present study, the life histories of both older and younger women indicate that while domesticity has always been subject to various kinds of pressure, the structure of households and support networks have become gradually more fragmented over the years, particularly evident in the 1998-2008 period, as local and world economies enter into a recessionary phase and as local state institutions grapple with problems of delivery. In these fragmented times it has been customary for women to bear children in more than one union. Young girls are often criticised but generally not disowned by their families for having a child out of wedlock. The birth of a child is sometimes quietly celebrated, even if the pregnancy was unanticipated and its timing inconvenient. The high levels of early sexual activity and rates of pregnancy, accompanied frequently by male desertion, however, have led to increased contraceptive use among the unmarried and very young. The themes outlined in Chapter 4 emphasised that contraceptive use increased among sexually active young girls as a means of gaining more control over when and with whom they bear children. In some instances early pregnancy (outside marriage) represents an attempt to strengthen the bonds of a relationship or to ensure financial support. Many women have learnt, though, that an attempt to elicit financial support for a child can be a frustrating and futile exercise. Increasingly, as a response to indigence, contraception is being used to avoid pregnancy whilst facilitating relationships for pecuniary gain. This might suggest vulnerability to disease and exploitation from an early age, but it also implies efforts at strengthening feminine abilities to influence the context and timing of births.

In Chapter 5 it is argued that marriage is difficult to define, that unions are generally short-lived and that many women who have children do not enter into formal unions. At the same time, the chapter refers to circumstances in which marriages are formalised and bridewealth is paid. Women are always central to the planning and organisation of weddings, bridewealth negotiations and festivities. In an environment in which family life is fragile, women who manage to secure 'good marriages' with 'good husbands' are admired as "respectable" and regarded as being "lucky". Women with less luck, that is, those without husbands, with children to support, jobless and in poor health and with little assistance from relatives, have to find the resilience to contend with their hardship. A woman will most likely try to avoid the financial burden of having another child if she is uncertain of her ability to support and care for it. In *Negotiating Reproductive Outcomes In Uganda*, Blanc et al. (1996) argue that more needs to be understood about how reproductive decisions are made and whether these "decisions" can be seen to be stable fertility goals. In studying the processes by which men and women arrive at the number of children they have and want to have, they argue, as I have done in this chapter, that fertility ideals change over time, and that economic impediments are pivotal in the social construction of low fertility desires. Unlike the Merafeng case study, their study reveals that most couples were in formal marriages. Thus it is within the framework of formal marriage structures that negotiations between men and women, but also disagreements, misperceptions and power struggles shaping reproductive decision-making processes become evident. Blanc et al. (1996) do not make marriage the focus of scrutiny and do not explore contexts in which re-evaluation of child-bearing decisions occurs, given the insecurities associated with tenuous marital bonds and multiple unions. **Table 11** in Chapter 5 shows that women in the area suggest that a small number of men involve themselves in decisions on how many children they ought to have, or on whether or not they should use contraception. Whilst some men assert their preferences, it is more often the case that child-bearing is left as a decision and responsibility of women. For women, the strength of the conjugal, intimate union emerges as an important determinant of reproductive decision-making.

Uncertainty about a partner's ability to render support might lead to long periods of waiting. It is for this reason that birth intervals are often irregularly spaced and some years apart as women wait for when they find work or a trustworthy, romantic union. When women find themselves in dependent, stable unions for long periods of time, it is sometimes in their interests to bear many children in the hope of strengthening these relationships and guaranteeing long-term financial support. Dependency might also translate into efforts on the part of women to bear children in serial unions in the hope of gaining support and remuneration from different men. The relatively low levels of male interest in high fertility and in child-rearing, and the comparatively greater pressure on women to support, clothe, feed and educate children have led to many women in Winterveld devising ways of avoiding pregnancy and bearing progressively fewer children.

Concerns about affordability explains the long birth intervals or, in some cases, having fewer than the desired number of children. Another factor is reduced fecundity as a result of sexually transmitted diseases (STDs) that are widespread in Winterveld. Thus women who work or who find themselves in financially better circumstances or in stable relationships might desire additional children if it is believed to fulfil non-tangible needs such as self-esteem. When the "unyielding sameness of making do and surviving" (Simone, 1998:289) gives way to a deterioration or improvement of economic circumstances, it introduces reappraisals of reproductive decisions and changes with respect to the continuity of unions. The fluctuating nature of reproductive decisions and the tenuous nature of family relationships are, above all, a response to the experience of poverty in its broadest sense. Transactionality in the Merafeng context usually relates to women's usurpation of male resources in exchange for sexual favours; it remains to be seen whether manipulation of state monies (in the form of child grants) will redirect prevailing practices towards desires for high fertility.

The experience of growing up and living with poverty has shaped the lives of women within the Winterveld area in important ways. Although subjected to the constraints of their social environments and their socialisation as women, poverty has trained them to become increasingly reflexive agents who constantly seek ways of empowering themselves by 'regulating' their environments, other people and their own reproductive capacities. Reproductive decisions will become less changeable when affective bonds and intimate unions themselves are subject to less change and when men and women enjoy the security which comes with experiencing such things as reliable material support, improved infrastructure, amenities and quality of life. For this to be realised, Winterveld will have to experience a broader transformation in which poverty is alleviated, employment becomes available and the development processes are initiated with much greater vigour than has been seen to date.

Linking findings of the Winterveld case study to a theory of hardship-driven fertility transition

The previous chapters have attempted to capture women's thoughts on and experiences of child-bearing. (See as well summarized life histories in **Appendix 1**). In most of my interviews, younger women (between their twenties and forties) expressed stronger desires for fewer children than their mothers did. In assessing such generational differences qualitatively I would regard them as offering a clear indication of a much broader trend towards wanting smaller-sized families. For a variety of reasons which include the increasing costs of maintaining families, younger women within my fieldwork site, who were reaching the end of their reproductive years, appeared to be considering two to three children as a relatively appropriate family size. In the group sessions women who had borne five or more children were often talked about as irresponsible and "uneducated" and sometimes faced wider social disapproval and reprimand. In the initial phases of my fieldwork, younger women had few fears about child mortality, a fact empowering them to gain greater control over potential child-bearing. Some fertility differences between mothers and daughters whom I interviewed can be reiterated. Khanyi Mabetwa (78) [#4] bore ten children whereas her daughter, Louisa (47), had five. Although Louisa had as many as five children she had had them in different unions. She might have had fewer children had she not been using child-bearing partly as an attempt to secure a marriage. Patience Khutsoane (48) [#9] had eight children in a dependent marriage but her daughter, Tebogo (28), had only two living children before having herself sterilised. Nozizwe Radebe (66) [#3] had five children but her daughter, Flora (40), had just one child. Flora was considering having another child because she was beginning to believe that one child was not enough. While these cases suggest varying motives they do not appear to contradict established analyses which argue that individual women are seeking smaller family sizes than their mothers and that South Africa is undergoing a fertility decline of considerable significance (Caldwell & Caldwell, 1993; Handwerker, 1991:56; SADHS, 2003).

The obstacles to fertility decline in sub-Saharan Africa have most commonly been argued to be a lack of economic development and the prevalence of norms and customs promoting pro-natalism. The signs of declining fertility in some African countries in the 1990s have revived modernisation arguments which link the decline to improvements in economic and living conditions in conjunction with health programmes and increases in women's education (Robinson, 1992). Fertility decline is also seen as occurring in those African countries with comparatively stronger economies (Caldwell et al., 1992). With specific reference to the South African case, Caldwell and Caldwell (1993) speculate that fertility will decline more significantly in post-apartheid South Africa as black people, who endured barriers to social and economic advancement in the past, now find themselves experiencing upward mobility. Significant declines in fertility are also dependent, in their view, on the easing of social and economic constraints that make people value children as a source of wealth and insurance. South African demographers often refer to different fertility regimes prevalent in the country, defined by racial/socio-economic strata (Chimere-Dan, 1994). In terms of this argument African fertility is higher than that of the other three regimes because Africans, in a collective sense, are enduring the deepest poverty. Mostert (1998), a leading demographer in South Africa's previous era, maintains that explanations for fertility decline throughout the world have been changing; it can no longer be suggested with certainty that the development processes (as maintained by demographic transition theory) influence fertility though "it can be stated that economic improvement coincides with fertility decline"(Mostert, 1998:117). Mostert (1998: 136) also states:

> In discussions of demographic trends in South Africa, particularly among Africans, it is easy to stress the political factor (apartheid) to the extent that other factors - especially those more difficult to measure - are ignored or underestimated. For instance, some academics disregard evidence that fertility declined by one-third under apartheid. Others contend that apartheid and its socio-economic consequences resulted in a delay in the rate of fertility decline among Africans. Yet others assert that Africans developed socio-economically despite apartheid and that their socio-economic development contributed to the fertility decline among them.

Mostert (1998:124) offers estimates of changing total fertility rates (TFRs) for Africans during the apartheid era. In the 1945-1950 period TFR stood at 6.8. This dropped to 5.8 and then to 4.0 in the 1975-1980 and 1990-1995 period respectively. Could it be that fertility declined because "Africans developed socio-economically despite apartheid"? Since the 1990s there has been much interest in the changing distribution of incomes in South Africa. Charles Simkins's (Whiteford & McGrath, 1994:1) study reporting that per capita income of the African population rose by 6% in the period 1985-1990 whilst white incomes dropped by 5% has led to popular views, cited in other studies, that wealth differentials have been narrowing and that the economic circumstances of African people have been improving. In their study of the distribution of income in South Africa Whiteford and McGrath show that whilst the richest 20%

of African households have indeed enjoyed significant growth in income - much higher than other sectors of the population - the poorest 80% of African households have suffered a decrease in mean income. With respect to the poorest 40% of households, they claim:

> The bottom 40% of African households have fared extremely badly with the mean income of this group declining by almost 40% since 1975. Households in this group would no doubt have been living in poverty in 1975 and the worsening of their situation would indicate a deepening of poverty in South Africa over the past two decades (Whiteford & McGrath, 1994:43).

The years in which fertility is said to have fallen significantly, according to Mostert, are the years in which Whiteford and McGrath claim a large proportion of households have experienced deepening poverty. In 2003, with total fertility rate estimated at 2 according to the last SADHS (2003), a very high proportion of South Africa's population was enduring chronic poverty (Aliber, 2003). My purpose in making these points on the prevalence of different levels of poverty at the macro-level is to emphasise the dangers that might be involved in making linear associations between general indications of fertility decline, general indications of economic improvement and arguments on how socio-economic factors "act upon" people to determine fertility outcomes. Significant fertility decline in African contexts, notwithstanding comparatively stronger economies, might be attributable to a wide range of intersecting factors including experiences of hardship and deprivation.

At the micro-level, fieldwork in Merafeng, Winterveld, has indicated the ways in which experiences of poverty, unemployment and insecurity undermine the formation of families and women's willingness to bear children. But just how poor is Winterveld? Map 1 in **Appendix 2** is a GIS map produced by the Human Sciences Research Council (HSRC) using a 1996 poverty database. It shows the proportion of the population experiencing poverty there to be anything between 14% - 45%. The Minimum Living Level (MLL), an absolute poverty level, was used to determine poverty (mean income less than R800) of "averaged sized households" (Whiteford & McGrath, 1994:59-60) in magisterial districts. This calculation which shows poverty in Winterveld as being equivalent to that experienced in the wealthiest districts of Gauteng conflicts with both my fieldwork observation and other studies over the years (Yawitch, 1981; de Clerq, 1992; Simone, 1998) which suggest that a majority, over 50%, of people living in Winterveld are experiencing poverty. These studies also suggest that the Winterveld population is becoming progressively poorer and marginal as employed people leave and a concentration of more destitute people come to occupy space within the area. Although calculations of absolute poverty are the norm for descriptions of poverty in developing countries, relative definitions are also applicable here. As Simone states:

> While objective measures of poverty make Winterveld no poorer than many other South African communities, the fact that it is so linked to the urban economies of greater Pretoria escalates the cost of living, diminishes the viability and value of practising a more rural livelihood and intensifies the experience of poverty (Simone, 1998: 273).

Winterveld displays all the ambiguities and conflicting livelihood experiences of an area described simultaneously as urban and rural and lodged between the third poorest province, the North West Province, and the wealthiest province, Gauteng, (May et al. 1998) in South Africa. It is constantly referred to by the people who live within it as being caught between two provinces and unwanted by both.

It is not easy to capture the true degree of poverty in areas in which households and household earnings are constantly changing and in which people appear to "move in and out of poverty" (May et al. 1998). Problems also arise in macro-assessments of "poor households" because a close scrutiny of households as individual units often shows gender inequalities and poverty differentials within them. In other words, the earnings of individual household members are not always pooled for the common good and well-being of all its members, making some of them, in particular women and young children, suffer greater degrees of deprivation. Inequalities in male and female access to resources, the lower earnings of women, and their greater child-rearing responsibilities tend to make women more vulnerable to risks of poverty (Posel, 1997:51). All these issues combine to make Lesthaeghe's hypothesis of a crisis-led or hardship-driven fertility transition have particular relevance for the Merafeng case study. At its most basic level it relies on "frustrated aspirations" because of expectations of changes in economic circumstances but continuing experience of "rising costs of childrearing, reduced prospective utility of educated children, and declining opportunities for adults in general" (Lesthaeghe, 1989:477-478). Women in Winterveld, who have lived with uncertainties and insecurities in the past, continue to live with disappointments and unmet expectations of social and economic change in the present. Inability to find independent work leads to attempts to elicit support from familial and other social networks. Lesthaeghe (1989:478) argues that "it is not at all clear whether the added strain leads to tighter solidarity and mutual sacrifice or to harder bargaining". Mutual sacrifice and harder bargaining co-exist in Winterveld. Increasingly, though, the space for bargaining is declining as families and networks resist child-rearing responsibilities, especially when compensation is not forthcoming. "Greater dependency of children on female incomes", which Lesthaeghe (1989:478) cites as an important factor intensifying a sense of crisis, is becoming the norm in Winterveld. Thus in a context where jobs are scarce and where child-rearing support is dwindling, the incentives for child-bearing are not high. Easy access to contraception appears to provide the means to implement control of fertility. It is not being argued that fertility decline in South Africa is largely a consequence of struggle against poverty and hardship. Different factors (some associated with "economic improvement") might be operating at different levels to shape the general picture of lowered fertility. However, Lesthaeghe's argument that fertility could decline, in a sustained manner, owing to the effects of a series of hardships does have relevance for this particular case study. Arguably, it will become all the more significant as the AIDS pandemic begins to affect more significantly familial and intimate bonds, sexual behaviour and levels of mortality. Many more case studies are needed to build more in-depth understandings of why and in which contexts fertility is declining and the structure of family life is transforming.

Can the particular experiences of women in Merafeng, Winterveld, offer general understandings of changing social and reproductive behaviour?

Reproductive regimes in Africa are commonly depicted as high fertility regimes exhibiting patterns of universal marriage, long periods of breast-feeding, customary post-partum sexual abstinence and strong intentions on the part of men and women to produce many children in their life-times. The culture and dynamics of African societies, notwithstanding much diversity within the continent, has conventionally been seen to entrench women in subordinate and dependent roles with their social position analysed as being primarily contingent on their roles as agricultural producers and procreators within corporate kinship groups (see Baylies & Bujra, 2000; Gruenbaum, 1999; Lesthaeghe, 1989). While African fertility in the 1990s remained relatively high, and women's roles largely unchanged, there have been indications that the institution of marriage and meanings associated with having children are undergoing considerable change. In *Nuptiality in Sub-Saharan Africa,* Bledsoe and Pison (1994) bring together a collection of papers that discuss adapted and emerging patterns of marriage and family life in West and East African countries. These papers argue that patterns are changing in certain parts of Africa because of e.g. (1) delayed marriages due to economic changes, recession and exorbitant bridewealth, (2) multiple unions and "outside wives" as a substitute for polygyny, (3)"polyandrous motherhood" as a strategy for eliciting financial support from many different men, and (4) the increasing fluidity of unions and tenuousness of family bonds. Despite the fact that these discussions refer to trends in other parts of Africa, many of these cases suggest that parallels to experiences in Winterveld can be drawn particularly with respect to the transformation of familial structures and conjugal unions.

The case studies in Bledsoe and Pison (1994) show various and changing patterns but the authors are cautious about suggesting that these are leading to fertility decline. There are as many uncertainties about how these changing arrangements might affect fertility in the long run as there have been about the effects of the migrant labour system on fertility in southern Africa. It is now generally conceded, though, that labour circulation played a significant part in lowering fertility levels in the southern African context (Timaeus & Graham, 1989; Mostert, 1998). Labour circulation from the rural areas and Bantustans to places of employment in the industrial centres, whether daily or long-term, has been a feature of life in South Africa. The cumulative effects of spousal separation, "stretched households", fragmentation of kin structures, domestic violence, unemployment and poverty, seen to be shaping family life and reproduction in Winterveld, are not unique. Thus it is very likely that many other areas, within South Africa and surrounding it, which have experienced similar kinds of tensions and economic constraints in the past, might be enduring quite similar insecurities and consequently fluid reproductive decisions as one would find in Winterveld. The instability of union structure, household boundary and reproductive decision-making processes will probably feature as more critical points of discussion in future comparative studies of areas because of the common challenges and tensions which the spread of HIV/AIDS is beginning to introduce.

Central to this study's objectives has been an attempt to look at the resourcefulness of women in contending with the difficulties of their life circumstances and in devising strategies to survive economic hardship and lone parenthood. In the different chapters I have drawn on the voices of women who have sometimes defined themselves as powerless in the face of domineering partners or as victims of sexual abuse or as women whose life chances have been determined by the history and poverty of the places of their birth. At the same time their stories over the past decade have made their efforts at gaining more power in the socio-economic and personal arenas increasingly apparent: these include attempts to wrestle with male power and authority within households, and the manipulation of contraceptive use to control reproductive processes and the timing of births.

Although there is little agreement on the precise meaning of 'women's empowerment' it is generally acknowledged that it implies the acquisition or efforts on the part of women to gain more power, in different spheres and at all levels, to transform their positions of subordination. In Longwe's definition and gender framework (March et al., 1999) women's empowerment is measured in terms of the extent to which women find themselves equal to men on a range of different levels (welfare, access, conscientisation, participation and control). Equating empowerment fundamentally to equality with men has also led to policy changes in the areas of health and reproductive rights. Since the 1990s policies advocating population control have been replaced by those emphasising reproductive choices and joint male and female responsibilities in reproduction. Interventionist programmes aimed at building what are regarded as more nurturing relationships within families (amongst men, women and their children) have been advocated and programmes targeting fathers are particularly popular in the 2000s (Cohen, 1997:5; Morrell & Richter, 2004). In Winterveld, the Planned Parenthood Association has been instrumental in initiating men's groups and in stressing male responsibility in reproductive decision-making. Although an emphasis on the rebuilding and improving of gender relationships in sites such as Merafeng are critical steps in addressing gender inequalities, many women there might not view all aspects of such interventions as desirable. The process of sensitising men to women's issues might require that women disclose to their partners the various methods they have used and the intentions with which they have used them in the past. Attempts to break down gender inequalities and encourage joint reproductive responsibilities in a predominantly poor and patriarchal social environment, without simultaneously addressing the structural roots of poverty, might serve to disempower women who have over the years developed the means to control little else except their own reproductive capacities.

But, to what extent could it be argued that men and women share different expectations and interests with respect to reproduction and family life? Some of the life histories indicate that men and their families have higher demands for children than do women and that there are frequent attempts to control women and subject them to abuse. Nonetheless, whilst there is much evidence of disputes over money and accusations of infidelity I have not found violent confrontations in households as a result of disagreements about the number of children to bear. The rules and norms of African marriage which shape power relationships within prevailing partnerships have long determined that men, with infertile and unwilling wives, who wish to have more children, can legitimately take on other "wives" for this purpose. If the reproductive desires of a woman were lower than that of her partner she might want to prevent the breakdown of her relationship by silently succumbing to his demands. If his support was infrequent and the relationship was burdensome she might welcome his departure because it offers her space to pursue a different and more beneficial relationship. "Attempts at empowerment", maintains Kabeer (1994:228), "have to take note of the trade-offs that women make in order to cope with the ramifications of oppressive relationships in their lives." Men, however, do not commonly desert women to seek other child-bearing partners. On the contrary, a young (unmarried) man often deserts his partner on discovering that she is pregnant. An older man with a wife and children might also desert his family when he finds himself incapable of offering adequate support. The pressures of poverty have reshaped past cultural patterns of high fertility. Although women might experience resistance from men, the reluctance of men to assume new financial burdens often means that women in partnerships can sometimes find opportunities to negotiate family size. For women outside of stable partnerships, power is a fluid concept contingent on the nature of their relationships with men and reassessed and reasserted in each context.

Conceptual approaches in African gender analyses or demographic studies are not usually accessible to notions of women's agency or how women's actions might influence relationships or circumstances through different, sometimes unseen "back door" decisions (Abwunza, 1997). As in many other semi-developed South African areas with lingerings of tribal authority and patriarchal institutions, most women in Merafeng without employment and access to regular sources of money (and sometimes land) find themselves in potentially vulnerable and dependent situations. Their actions and words appear to reflect paradoxes that might be common to women living in other poor environments. These include (1) many references to dependence on male earners for support while at the same time describing life experiences in terms of phases in which economic assistance was derived from multiple sources (and not simply from male partners), (2) expressed desires to be "well married" but recognition at the same time of the precariousness of "marital" bonds and (3) collaboration in perpetuating culturally assigned gender roles and responsibilities while at the same time engaging in actions to subvert and contest them (e.g. these might include struggles over "marital roles", child-bearing tasks and household responsibilities).

In the more recent literature women in developing countries have been analysed as finding opportunites to negotiate, mediate and reassess gender roles (e.g. in Abwunza, 1997, Blanc et al. 1996; Hodgson & McCurdy, 2001; Kabeer, 1994; Mama, 2007) than simply succumbing in passive ways to prevailing constraints and inequalities. As changing family structure, unstable economic conditions and AIDS-related deaths (Bledsoe & Pison, 1994) become recognised as central factors intensifying experiences of poverty, it will become increasingly crucial to develop new understandings of how women analyse and respond to their own crises. The kinds of experiences they have narrated are arguably not unique either to my fieldwork site or Winterveld as a whole but connect with experiences in other parts of South Africa as well. It is therefore probable that in contexts where contraceptive services are strong, and where much poverty and conjugal insecurity is experienced, women might be in the process of strategically contemplating the avoidance of unwanted pregnancy and striving towards greater control over reproduction and relationships than has been the case in the past.

Notes

[1]   The 1998 DHS shows that the mean ideal number of children for all South African women is 2.9, but for currently married women it is 3.3. Ideal number of children for both the Gauteng and Northwest Provinces (in which Winterveld is located) is 2.7 (lower than the South African mean).

Chapter 7

METHODOLOGICAL NOTES: REFLECTIONS ON
FIELDWORK IN A DEMOGRAPHIC PROJECT

Surveys: General Limitations and Concerns

Demographers studying reproductive behaviour and fertility transition have, over the years, depended almost entirely on data gathered from sample surveys, censuses and registration systems. Surveys maintain a central role in demographic research and make an important contribution towards the construction of reliable, scientific and large-scale national and regional understandings of populations. In the past few decades survey programmes, such as the World Fertility Survey (WFS) and Demographic and Health Survey (DHS), have gathered increasing quantities of data on aspects of reproductive behaviour and on fertility levels and trends in most developing countries. Prior to these interventions a paucity of data had existed. With greater efficiency in organisation and with better-trained staff the organisers of the WFS and DHS programmes have begun to facilitate not just the collection of data for individual countries, but the comparison of trends across countries and continents (UN, 1995). Follow-up DHSs in individual developing countries and regions have been designed and undertaken to assess changes in the proximate determinants of fertility and to answer questions on whether or not these countries are undergoing a process of fertility decline.

Alongside the growth in fertility data and some praise for the achievements of the survey programmes has been increasing questioning of the quality, purpose and meaningfulness of the data gathered through surveys. There are many reasons why surveys are frequently criticised. Some of these reasons include: (1) problems associated with the standardisation of questions asked irrespective of global region and limited inclusion of new 'locally relevant' questions to probe various phenomena and (2) the inability of surveys to illuminate dynamic processes, but rather snapshots of demographic trends (Caldwell, 1985); (3) the great dependence on hired interviewers who are entrusted with the huge responsibility (in the case of DHSs) of extracting from women (whom they do not know) intimate details of their marital, sexual and reproductive lives within a short space of time. In addition, (4) fertility survey programmes such as the WFS and DHS have also been questioned because, despite claims of political neutrality, they serve the particular political agendas of governments who seek to influence reproductive trends (Brown, 1987). In this regard, gender activists have raised concerns about the targeting of individual women as objects to be controlled and manipulated (Kabeer, 1994: 187).

The inherent limitations of surveys have since the 1980s been a subject of much discussion and debate and have led to experimentation with alternative methodologies. The pioneering efforts of John and Pat Caldwell in making use of ethnographic methods in demography raised initial arguments on the need to go beyond snap-shot surveys and to develop instead, through extended periods of fieldwork, more in-depth analyses of the socio-cultural contexts and processes shaping kinship relations and reproduction. Although John Caldwell wrote his critique of fertility surveys in 1985 it was only perhaps since the early 1990s that discussion of the integration and use of qualitative techniques and research designs became a lot more vigorous and comprehensive. Perhaps three noteworthy concerns have arisen in recent symposiums and forums focusing on methodology and demographic research. These are concerns about:

The reconciliation of quantitative and qualitative methods: Although the quantitative versus qualitative debate is an old one in sociology it is kept alive by adherence to one of two positions. The first position tends to argue that different epistemologies govern data-gathering to the extent that talk of reconciling quantitative and qualitative approaches becomes illogical. A second position tends to emphasise not only that reconciliation is possible but that, in practice at least, the distinction between quantitative and qualitative methods is blurred. A simple quantitative-qualitative dichotomy tends to ignore a variety of strategies, techniques and hybrid techniques which cannot be clearly linked to either side of the divide. The dichotomy also does not take into account the ways in which researchers combine approaches and methods in practice, e.g. qualitative insights tend to be used by quantitative researchers in the operationalisation of variables, and qualitative analyses particularly in recent years (with the availability of new software and statistical packages) incorporate much counting and categorisation (Obermeyer, 1997; Marshall, 1994: 432).

Constraints and spaces for collaboration posed by multi-disciplinary research: In the international academic arena the increase in the number of researchers doing 'qualitative demography' is being reviewed increasingly in terms of a confrontation between anthropology and demography. Greenhalgh's (1995) and Kertzer and Fricke's (1997) texts have served as powerful critiques of objectivist, quantitative demography at the same time as seeming to present anthropology as the field best placed to inject qualitative and theoretical strength into demographic analysis. Knodel (1997: 847) suggests that this tendency might be due partly to the recent role of international funding organisations and their grant-awarding interventions to influence closer links between anthropology departments and population centres. The suggestion that anthropological methods represent the qualitative methods that are much needed to facilitate a "re-working of the fundamentals" ignores the basic fact, Knodel maintained, that most social science disciplines, including sociology, also make fair use of qualitative methods. In forging cross-disciplinary exchanges there has to be more dialogue about the contrasting histories and cultures of different disciplines and the implications they hold for methods (Greenhalgh, 1997: 823). Qualitative methods used in the different disciplines to further the study of population processes might mean different things and will serve different purposes. Conventional demographers might use qualitative methods to improve "the measurement of variables, discovering new causal factors, and deepening the understanding of survey results" (Greenhalgh, 1997: 821). This might be different from anthropologists whose interests in demography might be precisely to criticise family planning initiatives and governments themselves.

The transformation of conventional demography into a critical science: The inclusion of qualitative data in demographic analysis, some argue, could complement statistics and thus ease "constraints on the demographic imagination" (Greenhalgh, cited by Obermeyer, 1997: 815). Ethnographic research could contribute to the restructuring of economic models of human agency that take account of "incentives, motivations and power relations" (Rao, 1997: 833-838) or rituals that shape reproductive behaviour in differing socio-cultural contexts (Heady, 2007: 555-558). Knodel (1997: 847-853) suggests a modest accommodation of qualitative methods in demographic research. He argues that demographers have "neither the abilities, training, time, nor inclination to become competent anthropologists" (Knodel, 1997: 848) and that methods not requiring extensive fieldwork would be most appealing. Kertzer (1997: 839-845) discusses the central role of qualitative methods for historical demography and the gains to be made through collaborative initiatives between statistically sophisticated demographers, historians and social anthropologists. Fricke (1997: 825-832) and Bernardi and Hutter (2007) emphasise the greater openness to methodological experiment that has created opportunities for multi-disciplinary collaborations (mainly, though not exclusively, between anthropologists and demographers). Transformation, however, would entail not just a creative integration of different types of methods but a reappraisal of the central assumptions of the "conventional" demographic paradigm and the infusion of critical discourses and analysis so that the discipline reshapes itself within a more reflexive and meaningful framework. Whilst conventional demography, as Horton (1999) suggests, is apolitical in orientation, a critical demography will be concerned with going beyond empiricism and seeking theoretical and political explanations for changing demographic situations; it probes power inequalities, questions state decisions and examines the intricacies of social contexts as well as the politics and subjectivities of demographers. These are three concerns that hold great importance in a transforming South Africa.

Historical Legacies and Particular Difficulties with Survey Data in South Africa

The politics of the early demographic fraternity in South Africa stands in direct contrast to the values espoused by a "critical demography". Rather than a critical and engaging discipline demography found itself aligned to the conservative policy-making agenda of the South African state through the articulation of growing concerns about rapidly increasing population numbers and about the political and economic implications of high fertility amongst the black sector of the population. Alarmist neo-Malthusian projections of an impending population explosion were developed which fed into fears that black population numbers were going to increase at an uncontrollable rate (Swartz, 2003; Brown, 1987). Thus, family planning which had mainly catered for an urbanised, English-speaking sector of the white population became a project for black women by the 1970s. Brown (1987: 264) maintains that: "once the government decided to launch a programme to control women's fertility, it spared no expense" (see Chapter 2 for more detail). Between the 1970s and 1980s a strong family planning programme was put in place, which, despite the adverse socio-political and economic conditions, gained popularity amongst black women.

With transition to a post-apartheid society and with the discourses changing from the need to influence fertility reduction to the need to enhance women's empowerment and improved health a new generation of fertility specialists find themselves with new challenges (Anderson, 2003). Whilst it is common to hear strong criticism of the research of past eras and read arguments that the contextual and dynamic realities influencing fertility behaviour should be interrogated more rigorously, in practice demographic methodologies remain largely unchanged with the key priorities of demographers remaining to monitor changes in fertility, reproductive practices and reproductive health and to serve as informants of a changed (albeit a democratic) government's policy-making institutions. Sample surveys remain the primary method for gathering data, and questions relating to "methodological mixes" are virtually absent in contemporary discussions on fertility research. Policy-makers intent on developing reliable facts have prioritised the search for improved macro-level indications of changing fertility to help the policy processes.

Caldwell's introductory comments in The South African Fertility Decline summarise, to some extent, academic opinion on the state of fertility data in South Africa prior to the mid-1990s. He suggested that for a variety of reasons data on the black population had been generally "too deficient to be useable" (Caldwell & Caldwell, 1993: 225) but that more satisfactory data became available after the results of the 1987-1989 DHS-type survey were published. Although he notes that there were many unanswered questions on this survey's methodology, a volume of important fertility data became available. More data has become available through the 1998 and 2003 demographic and health surveys. The 1998 DHS was launched under the auspices of the Department of Health, South Africa's national state health institution, and has been to date a widely used resource in analysis of fertility change in the current era. This DHS, which has had as a key objective the need to "improve demographic data in South Africa", benefited from very wide consultation with a spectrum of interest groups and international specialists. It has been heralded as South Africa's first true demographic and health survey and has been based on the standard international DHS format. It has integrated a wider range of questions, to address specific South African policy needs in health and welfare, than commonly seen in demographic and health surveys. There were questions on the chronic health problems of women and knowledge and awareness of HIV/AIDS (Xiphu, 1998). The broader objective of the survey was to draw on existing expertise and to "build research capacity of the organisations involved, e.g. provincial departments of health ... in planning and implementing a survey ..." (Klugman, 1996: 5). This capacity was further enhanced in preparation for the 2003 survey. Against the background of the drive for more sophisticated data analysis, ultimately for the use of transformative state interventions in the health and welfare field, qualitative data seem to emerge as poorer and second best. In the South African context, surveys are, nonetheless, far from problem-free. Some difficulties with the measurement of socio-economic differentials (ethnicity, rural-urban divides, work and education) in demographic and health surveys are highlighted below.

The problems associated with using quantitative data are most evident when attempting to aggregate and average socio-economic differentials. The first crudity is one which Klugman (1996: 3) suggests is a "positive decision"—that is, to continue to disaggregate data in terms of "the old "population groups", since they have served as proxies for socio-economic status". She adds that it is essential to retain these "so that changes in key indicators of quality of life can be measured." Whilst there was some justification for doing so in the mid-1990s, they are not so apparent in the late 2000s. Race appears to have become reified in survey research and distanced from historical studies and debates on the problematics and politics of simple racial categorisation. With regard to the association between ethnic categories and reproduction, James and Kaufman (1997:1) maintain:

"we argue that this association derives meaning from the process of ethnic identification and the cultural and historical construction of that identity." ...

"Given a strong association between ethnicity and reproduction beyond, or informed by, social and economic status, demographic analysis must address those sets of behaviours, attitude, or contextual factors accompanying ethnic identification that might give rise to particular reproductive patterns".

For example, the 2003 demographic and health survey shows (for the first time) that the total fertility rate for "coloureds"[1] (2.3) is now higher than that of "Africans" (2.1) without any explanation for what contextual, behavioural or related factors has given rise to this recent transition. The higher "coloured" TFR is intriguing and unanticipated given that, as a group, "coloureds" are financially better-off, more urbanised and have access to better health services, than the African sector of the population. Another key differentiating feature in demographic surveys is urban-rural residence.

Although there is recognition of the overlapping between "rural" and "urban" and the various categories that fall in between, the new surveys continue to place emphasis on contrasting "urban" and "rural" (or non-urban) behaviour. In analysing models using rural-urban concepts, Harriss and Moore (1984: 24) suggest, "the rural-urban dichotomy has been asked to bear a heavy burden. In terms of economic activities there is often more overlap between and differentiation within the two sectors than the theorists' models would imply". This burden is particularly problematic in the South African case. There has been, over the years, considerable movement from rural to urban areas due to dispossession of land, the migrant labour system and the search for employment. The consequence of displaced urbanisation (Murray, 1987), movement between rural villages and urban centres, and the growth of peri-urban areas and squatter settlements on the fringes of towns is that a sustained linkage between "rural" and "urban" exists. With the linkage emphasised, is it sensible to talk in terms of discrete urban and rural influences on, for instance, fertility behaviour? South African survey results have tended to emphasise that urban and rural differences are real: differences can be discerned in contraceptive use and desired fertility. Sometimes tensions are unsurprisingly apparent. For example, in analysing some results of the 1987-1989 DHS, Mostert (1990, p.66) offers general points about the projecting of urban-like influences (with respect to contraceptive use) on to the people "within its vicinity". The analysis, however, becomes difficult when he reveals that the Pretoria-Witwatersrand-Vereeniging (PWV) district displayed some of the lowest levels of contraceptive use. He explains this by acknowledging a mixing of influences: he noted that the PWV, as an urban area, has "an influx of people, probably mainly from the rural areas" (Mostert, 1990: 66). The data are also beginning to show less evidence of difference between rural and urban. The 1987-1989 DHS (Du Plessis, 1996) and the 1993-1994 DHS (Nkau, 1999: 4) show no significant differences in desired fertility among younger women living in areas categorised as rural or urban. The 2003 SADHS shows that the TFR in both rural (2.1) and urban (2.0) areas are about the same. In the highly mobile peri-urban spreads or interfaces around the country, most people would not be easily placed in "rural" or "urban" categories.

Similarly, the deep insecurities surrounding women's work and changeability of occupational role undermines neat associations between work and fertility. Survey evidence shows that although working women give birth to and desire fewer children than unemployed women, the differences are minimal. The need to know (through access to better-quality data) about "whether specific kinds of employment make differential impacts" (Klugman, 1996: 5) demands a lot from micro-level quantitative data. Perhaps it would be more reasonable to begin to answer such questions through qualitative interventions in messier social realities—realities in which not just the specific kinds of work can be assessed in order to learn about differential impacts, but also the complexity of work experiences in shaping women's lives. It may not be just the kinds of work that women do which are important to examine, but also fears of job losses, the wages earned, the distribution of household income from which women may or may not benefit, and the various ways in which women might sustain livelihoods. All these have implications for reproductive decision-making and well-being. The 1998 DHS shows that high proportions of South African women are "unemployed" but does not interrogate domestic work, partner's work or informal sector work as factors influencing fertility.

Surveys have been a lot more successful in measuring associations between educational levels and reduced desires for fertility. The positive implications of increased investment in schooling have been emphasised quite strongly over the years. Both the 1987-1989 and 1998 SADHS show that high school education plays an important role in discouraging high fertility over the reproductive life span. The post-apartheid South African state has sought to address gender inequalities in access to schooling and to improve the quality of girls' education. It is anticipated that the long-term effects of continuous exposure to formal education will act to empower and enhance the position of women generally. Schoolgirl dropout rates however are relatively high and the "problem" is often treated (by state officials) as one that can be studied, explained and remedied through improved research and interventions in the school and the family. Redressing the problem, however, requires more than "reliable" statistics on how many teenage girls dropped out of school because of an unplanned pregnancy. It will require textured analyses of teenage experiences. High levels of teenage pregnancy indicate many things surveys are unable to reveal. There are various motivations for early sexual activity. Many of these motivations are not easily established and a careful and deliberate attempt to understand the issues around teenage pregnancy could reveal masses of "data" on the contexts in which reproduction occurs, and what interventions are possible.

The foregoing has been important to set the scene for a personalised account of an experiment with survey work in Merafeng, Winterveld. As already described, in 1998 I set myself the challenging task of conducting a micro-survey modelled on the DHS format to probe the proximate determinants of fertility in Merafeng and was constantly confronted with the question of how one could make the survey work or be sure of what was being measured. The proximate determinants of fertility (viz. entry into marriage, contraceptive use, abortion and breastfeeding) are useful starting points for critical reflection. The socio-economic variables, referred to earlier, are regarded as non-proximate variables and are seen to work through a set of (direct) proximate determinants to influence fertility (Bongaarts, 1978). Marriage has an important place in the Bongaarts model as an indicator of exposure to sexual intercourse and risk of pregnancy. Thus, measuring the proportion married, the ages when first married and sexually active, allows for estimates of children being born and children likely to be born in the future. Data on contraceptive use, induced abortion, breast-feeding (as post-partum sterility) and fecundity (as influenced by STDs) reveal important information on fertility regimes and factors controlling, inhibiting and determining fertility outcomes.

Marriage, partnerships and multiple unions

The confidence of demographers seeking to estimate marriage rates, or to measure the married sector, has waned over time. Whilst close to 50% of women aged 30-34 years old had their first child before 20 years (according to the 1998 DHS) most of these births were outside of marriage. Mostert (1990: 67) in recognising the early pattern of births outside marriage claimed that, notwithstanding this situation, by the age of 50 virtually all (93.1%) will be married. Mostert (1990: 68) concedes, though, that "[m]arriage dissolution through divorce is however high in all age categories—averaging about 15% in every category. The divorce rate has been at a high level for the past three decades." All South African DHSs, including the latest 2003 DHS, asked questions in an attempt to establish whether women are in "marital" or "living-together" unions, whether they are in polygynous unions, or whether women have been married more than once. Increasingly, though, South African researchers have become aware of the small difference marital status makes as evidenced by data on the lifetime fertility of women (between ages 45-49) who are married (4.34) and those who are not married (4.03) (Ntsaluba, 1998: 39).

In asking questions on marriage in my Winterveld survey it became clear that women might sometimes identify themselves as "married" when they were not in a conventionally defined "marital union". Instead, they might have been in a precarious union in which they saw their partner(s) infrequently. In such cases, a woman who was "never-married" might have the same frequency of contact with a male partner and would be likely to have similar needs for contraception as would a "married" woman. In addition, through the course of qualitative work, it also became evident that a large number of women were involved, simultaneously in numerous unions. Whether pursued for reasons of poverty or not, an involvement in multiple unions raises questions on contraceptive use, and on motivations for the timing of and desire for children. Surveys do not adequately capture the ways in which women contend with numerous and unstable unions. If surveys were to refine questionnaire items and include questions to establish the number of partnerships women might have and frequency of sexual relations (which some surveys, including the DHS, have attempted to capture), I do not believe that a one-off survey in which an interviewer attempts to speedily extract data from a respondent would be very revealing. In the 2003 DHS the following question is asked: "Have you been married or lived with a man only once or more than once?" Apart from the confusion that could stem from attempts to interpret women's responses to such questions, what does a woman achieve by telling an unknown researcher intimate and personal details? A question was asked in the 1998 DHS: "In the last 12 months, with how many different men have you had sexual intercourse?" Unsurprisingly, an insignificant number of women responded in the affirmative. Clearly, it is only after a long period of involvement in the lives of women that such information can be shared and clarified.

Modern, traditional and cultural methods

When compared with levels of contraceptive use in other African countries, contraceptive use of African women in South Africa is regarded as being very high. The 2003 DHS suggests that 65% of sexually active women use contraception. This is not very different from initial admissions in my fieldwork site where approximately 70% of women of reproductive age claimed to be using contraception. Whilst previous programmes targeted women only, the spread of HIV has led to the establishment of health and reproductive programmes that require the active involvement of men. Health surveys have only recently begun to ask probing questions about men's use of condoms and about knowledge of AIDS. In the era of AIDS the 1990s became a challenging one for those involved in the construction of health surveys and their specific items.

They were required to display sufficient understanding of cultural constructions of disease, health and ways in which and purposes for which contraception was used. In surveys in the 1990s questions concerning knowledge of AIDS and whether men were using or would be happy to use condoms, were asked without addressing related complications such as whether men would use condoms when they were with their wives or only when they were with other women? There are a number of questions that need to be asked about survey findings on contraceptive use. For example: do women who admit to using contraception also admit that they often use it inconsistently? Why is it that the 2003 data suggest that "there has been a decline in the level of knowledge of contraceptive methods since 1998"? (Department of Health, 2003: 10). Why are women in the field less concerned than researchers about "unmet needs?" Is it partly because of some reliance on "folk methods" which researchers are unable to capture in survey data? Only 13% of women ever used folk methods according to the 1998 SADHS with even fewer women referring to them in 2003 (8.9%). In Winterveld numerous folk methods referred to as "cultural" methods are in use. The most common is burying bottled menstruation (mixed with herbs) outside your home. The bottle is only retrieved and opened when a pregnancy is desired. Despite claims that it is declining in importance, it has become increasingly important to understand the role played by traditional medicine in reproductive health. I learnt, through conducting my own survey, that in a snap-shot survey women tend to feel embarrassed to talk about using "cultural methods" as contraception particularly when interrogated by "well educated interviewers". Thus the tendency is to inflate the significance of modern methods in relation to others.

In the course of fieldwork I have found that women are also shy to talk about their knowledge and use of traditional methods unless they are made to feel comfortable in doing so. Numerous demographers term folk methods (such as abstinence, withdrawal and rhythm) as "inefficient methods" (Mostert, 1990; Du Plessis, 1996). Clearly, they are less effective in preventing pregnancy than the pill or injection. But when the pill or injection are used inconsistently or are given up in favour of traditional methods, then these modern methods also become inefficient. Surveys have not adequately captured the extent to which traditional methods are used solely and in combination with modern methods. This is partly because, when being interviewed about contraception, women prefer to reveal use of more modern forms of "prevention". They might, for example, not consider abstinence as a "method" and therefore not disclose it; interviewers are also unlikely to take time to probe periods of deliberately practised sexual abstinence. Withdrawal is even more difficult to learn about. It is a method dependent on the co-operation of men; women might be reluctant to mention it as a method that they use. I have found it to be widely practised in Merafeng particularly in the post-partum period when sexual relations are often taboo. Withdrawal is also practised when men and women engage in infidelities.

Abortion

It is of course difficult to learn about abortion in any setting. If it is difficult to construct a picture of how prevalent the practice is through long-term ethnographic work, it will be impossible to ascertain anything insightful through surveys. The 1987-1989 SADHS did not ask any questions about it because abortion was previously illegal. Illegality has rarely prevented women, in particular schoolgirls, from resorting to an abortion if the need for it arose. Arguably, it is not the fact that it was previously illegal that makes women hesitate to want to talk about abortion; secrecy is usually maintained because of the fear of negative cultural sanctions. At the same time, although abortions are frowned upon, virtually everyone I interviewed (in my more in-depth interviews) reported that they knew that these were being frequently performed. In the survey not many women disclosed whether they had had an abortion or whether they would resort to one if faced with an unwanted pregnancy. For the same reasons, the 1998 SADHS did not probe or ask women whether or not they had had an abortion. The survey was able to test knowledge: slightly more than 50% of all women were aware that the law had changed and that it was legally permissible to get an abortion. It is important for fertility analysts to establish just how many women continue to end pregnancies, both in clinics and in backstreet operations, rather than give birth to unwanted children. Surveys, however, are not useful instruments for eliciting such information in the South African context.

Breastfeeding

South African surveys are beginning to gather useful data on breast-feeding and post-partum sexual abstinence. Questions however are not being directed towards ascertaining women's knowledge of the role of breast-feeding in lengthening birth intervals. No questions have been asked to date on amenorrhoea and its association with "full" or limited breast-feeding. The 1987-1989 DHS relied on establishing "for how many months did you breast-feed (the last child)?". There are obvious problems with memory. The 1998 and 2003 DHSs ask the same question but attempt to remedy limitations here by looking at supplementation of breast-feeding with other kinds of feeding, such as bottle-feeding, but do not probe whether mothers use breast-feeding to extend birth intervals.

In the course of fieldwork in Merafeng that questions on duration of breast-feeding asked on different occasions provided different answers. I was often surprised by the unhesitant way in which women of all ages would initially offer precise answers to the question of how long they had breast-fed their last child. When probed, women often revealed that they had relied on other indicators, e.g. they remembered that when the child in question had started to walk, talk or celebrate a birthday they had either just stopped breast-feeding or were about to stop breast-feeding. These indicators can hardly result in precise estimations. All the surveys show breast-feeding durations to be fairly short in South Africa when compared with that in other African countries. In Merafeng I found that women tend to present breast-feeding duration as being shorter than it was in practice in cases where the post-partum period of sexual abstinence had been reduced. In other words, it is embarrassing to disclose that you have continued to breast-feed whilst engaging in sexual relations. In Winterveld, at least, there remains a belief amongst a fair number of women about the harm that is caused to children if breast-feeding is not accompanied by sexual abstinence. Whilst all women do not subscribe to this belief, most would be reluctant to admit that they have been breaking cultural rules. Hence it is possible that the length of breast-feeding revealed by surveys is deliberately underestimated given cultural beliefs and social expectations.

This chapter's purpose has been to draw attention to some of the difficulties surveys regularly face in attempting to build "accurate" representations of what influences and determines fertility behaviour in South Africa. In some countries, e.g. Uganda (Blanc et al., 1996), attempts have been made to overcome some of the difficulties of surveys by sensitising questionnaires to cultural and gender dynamics and to link them to focus groups to allow for probing of how reproductive decisions are made and how they change. In a period in which South African policy-makers are mobilising greater expertise to gather more useable data, not many questions are being asked about the inherent difficulties of surveys as research instruments. Greater care in questionnaire construction and in the conducting of fieldwork can play an important part in withstanding some of the problems posed by a complex and fluid South African social context (see Madhavan et al., 2007). Despite calls for a greater multi-disciplinary involvement in demography (Du Plessis, 1995) to reshape its tools and underlying philosophy, fertility research remains primarily quantitative. Anthropologists, historians and sociologists using qualitative methods have established an extensive literature on South African family life and kinship over the years. The extent to which these contributions can invite collaborations and methodological experiments requires greater investigation. There are three possibilities for experiments that I refer to below.

Discussion: Considering Different Methodological Experiments

The international literature is now abundant with case studies using qualitative methods for demographic research. I cite three exceptional case studies, which, although initiated in the 1990s, offer useful lessons for application both in the contemporary Winterveld and a broader South African context. All three are studies that have been conducted in poorer, developing social environments making them especially relevant to the current study.

Case study 1: Axinn, Fricke and Thornton's (1991) micro-demographic community study approach

In Axinn et al.'s study of social change, family process and fertility among the Tamang in Nepal the attempt was to simultaneously apply survey and ethnographic methods within two sites. A sample survey was not conducted. Every person over the age of eleven (a total of 1,415 people) in two small communities was interviewed. The researchers who initiated the study called themselves the investigators. It was the task of the investigators to become familiar with the cultural context and to get to know the language, the histories and social activities of the local people. It was only after this initial process that the research instruments could be meaningfully structured. These included the household census, family genealogy schedules and an individual questionnaire. For the purpose of administering these formal instruments interviewers from the local community were recruited and trained. Survey work was undertaken immediately after investigators had visited the individual household as part of the introductory and rapport-building process. Investigators and interviewers lived together in common quarters. Each evening survey interviews would be cross-checked against ethnographic work for errors and omissions. In addition to reducing non-sampling errors, this integrated approach was useful to the investigators because it raised awareness about issues and events that were not considered prior to the survey being constructed. It thus allowed for the adaptation of the questionnaire in the field. New categories on clan membership, marriage, and expected behaviour in families were included. Axinn et al. (1991: 212) maintain, thus, that "[q]ualitative data-gathering techniques designed as a simple supplement to surveys, which focus on the topics covered in the survey, are not likely to provide the means of attaining ... additional goals."

In combining rigour in the application of survey methods with fieldwork efforts to become sensitised to the historical and social context within which the Tamang people live and interact, Axinn et al.'s work has gained much credibility. My survey in Merafeng preceded a qualitative investigation of women's lives and would have benefited from a more coherent connectedness between the micro-survey and the fieldwork. My purpose in conducting the survey was partly to develop a sense of what patterns existed with respect to particular aspects of fertility behaviour and partly to assess how the patterns in this area differed from those evident in large-scale national surveys. Some important differences were discerned such as the larger number of women living in informal unions, higher levels of contraceptive use and less evidence of the role of education in shaping fertility preferences. The experience of conducting the survey, however, became more useful for raising problems associated with the asking of sensitive questions in a brisk manner. An application of Axinn et al.'s (1991) methodology could make surveys a lot more workable in Merafeng. In saying this, however, there are limitations to using this approach in Winterveld or similar kinds of South African environments. Axinn et al. (1991) depict the Tamang communities as though they are both stable and "captive audiences". There is relative uniformity in custom and social practice, enabling a problem-free data-gathering process. Investigators and interviewers will find that they are less capable of such rigour in many South African areas. Identities, practices and family formations are diverse. Instability is a feature of everyday life to the extent that an entire "community" will not be easily "contained" as an object of study by an outside group. A large consignment of researchers who root themselves in the area for a comparatively short space of time is bound to be resisted, manipulated and tested for, amongst other things, financial benefits by those being researched. I am also doubtful whether reliance on insider-interviewers to elicit detail on intimate subjects such as sexual behaviour and reproductive practices will gain the most insightful results.

Case study 2: Bledsoe, Banja and Hill's (1998) open-ended survey and investigative fieldwork approach[2]

In 1992 as the first phase of a study on fertility in rural Gambia, Bledsoe et al. undertook a survey of 2,980 women in forty villages. In the course of the survey open-ended questions led to the gathering of extensive fieldnotes on certain questions, particularly with respect to contraceptive use and child-spacing. The findings revealed low levels of modern contraceptive use (mostly Depo-Provera) and low levels of traditional methods. It was an area in which high fertility was said to be valued. Here women sought to "gain a competitive edge over present and future co-wives and sisters-in-law by bearing a number of children" (Bledsoe et al., 1998: 22). Birth intervals were found to be regular (children were spaced about 2.5 years apart); the spacing of births had been analysed previously as being governed largely by natural fertility patterns. A closer and more qualitative look at the survey results, however, revealed other things not easy to explain. Among them was the need to explain why, out of the 150 women using modern contraception, 27 (18%) were using contraception after a miscarriage or still-birth (a "reproductive mishap"). Bledsoe et al. stated that "[a]n outsider's first reaction might be to attribute these reported actions to data error or statistical aberration". The inconsistency as they saw it was threefold:

- The women were using modern contraception when it was generally suggested that contraception had little place in rural Gambia.

- The motive for the 18% of contraceptive users could not be said to be child-spacing ("there was no child to space").

- Contraception was being used by women who ultimately desired children and whose marriages and futures depended on their ability to produce children.

They then attempted to further investigate why women who had experienced recent reproductive mishaps, might want to use contraception and delay future births rather than attempt another pregnancy soon. In the course of their investigation an alternative view of reproduction and ageing was developed—one in which intentions to use contraception were linked with "health reasons" or the need to find "recuperative space" rather than for the reasons of birth-spacing or the cessation of child-bearing. In focusing on the meanings attached to miscarriages and still-births, Bledsoe et al. (1998: 49) raise criticisms of contemporary demographic approaches which treat "live births as the only reproductive currency".

My purpose here is not to detail the findings of Bledsoe et al. but merely to emphasise that an examination of issues which do not appear to "make quantitative sense" and that might seem contradictory to general patterns, can lead to important insights and alternative ways of looking at motives influencing reproduction. Bledsoe et al. sought to explore anomalies presented by the quantitative data and to unmask complex motivations by studying responses to open-ended questions. There is surely sufficient evidence of anomalies in South African data to warrant a qualitative probing. Numbers offered by different datasets could be questioned with more critical insights drawn from investigative qualitative work. Perhaps an emphasis on small-scale studies to address gaps in existing data could be of greater value to the policy-making process than an onslaught of surveys and aggregate level statistics.

The Merafeng case study has drawn some parallels in that it has also revealed varying motivations for contraceptive use which appear to be out of place but which are ultimately guided by a wide set of responses to experiences of still-births, disease and violence. It is not just survey work that reveals inconsistencies. Different kinds of qualitative work often reveal experiences that appear to be aberrant. With a mingling of people originating from all parts of the country and with the arrival of increasing numbers of Mozambicans and Zimbabweans in Winterveld, uncovering how fertility trends are being determined there will become an increasingly challenging task. Qualitative work could play an important role in examining seemingly contradictory factors and forces influencing fertility change.

Case study 3: Nancy Scheper-Hoghes's (1997) critical interpretive demographic approach

Scheper-Hoghes's methodology contrasts quite strongly with that of Axinn et al.'s and Bledsoe et al.'s. Her starting-point is that objectivist and interpretive frameworks offer opposing convictions about the nature of reality and that these convictions shape conceptions of what are seen as "useful data" and what form research should take. She rejects conventional objectivist, quantitative research in demography and suggests that whilst such research efforts

"can strive to be culturally sensitive and can illuminate, for example, the cultural logic and alternative shapes of rationality that may govern the fertility and reproductive decision-making of Third World women ... there is often a striking lack of awareness of the ways in which the culture of their science structures the questions asked and overdetermines the findings" (Scheper-Hughes, 1997, p.203).

She presents her critical interpretive approach as a much more radical undertaking. Her approach is a simple but intense one: it involves years of immersion within a fieldwork site in which the researcher is not a neutral recorder of facts but an active campaigner in the lives of people. Rather than being merely an observer the researcher is central to social interventions in the area. Scheper-Hughes speaks with the experience of having remained within a particular fieldwork site (albeit intermittently) for 25 years. Her fieldwork in the Brazilian shantytown of Alto do Cruzeiro entailed a careful studying of the causes, meanings and effects of child mortality in a largely poverty-stricken area. In addition to drawing out reproductive histories, details about women's lives, their marriages, and their attitudes towards the deaths of their children, Scheper-Hughes wrestles with moral dilemmas and with her status as an academic researcher.

With the current emphasis of research institutes on short-term research for speedy results, few academics can afford 25 years for fieldwork. The advantage though of sustaining links with a particular small setting is that it allows for the deeper exploration of that which is hidden from public records and scrutiny. Scheper-Hughes uncovered and spent much time exploring considerable underreporting of infant deaths. In Winterveld where secrecy has marked the nature of living over the years, infant births and deaths, HIV-deaths, marriages, separations and ways in which people earn a living are often hidden from official records. In my tenth year of fieldwork I am still uncovering new strategies of a changing population in which many people continue to live without birth certificates, identity documents and licences and where there is little interest in being accurate about numbers or about reporting births and deaths.

My attempt was to engage a small group of "marginal" women in Merafeng, to hear their stories and, in a sense, to make their experiences more visible. Involvement in their lives, a practice unanticipated at the beginning of fieldwork, became imperative in time. It has not, as yet, become anything close to "a radical undertaking". Winterveld, as most other areas in South Africa, has not been short of activist campaigners over the years. Many of these campaigners are now part of the policy-making machinery of the post-apartheid democratic government. Rather than become a political campaigner, I aligned myself with achievable goals by linking some income-generation activities with fieldwork. Such involvement amidst the poverty in Merafeng did much to build relationships with women. It has also, for me, reinforced much faith in the value of long-term, "engaged" qualitative work (in particular, ethnographic work) for developing deeper insights into how poverty destabilises and keeps marital relations, fertility, family and "community life" in a state of flux. As general points, some qualitative work entails simply the analysis of open-ended questions asked in the surveys. Some may involve a small number of individual or group interviews detailing aspects of women's life experiences and reproductive histories. The strength of the analysis will depend on the opportunity taken by the researcher(s) to learn about the women being interviewed, and to become familiar with their social environment and experiences. A temporal perspective is thus crucial to the quality of a qualitative design.

With respect to collaborative kinds of involvements, Scheper-Hughes (1997, p.219) argues that "there is no need for more collaborations between qualitatively-trained anthropologists or demographers in which the realm of the social is reduced to a set of reified and lifeless variables." She calls for a "praxis-oriented, critically applied and politically engaged anthropology to illuminate the complex and multifaceted ... dilemmas of vulnerable populations ..." (Scheper-Hughes,1997, p.219).

South African policy-makers are not averse to revising policy and making strategic decisions on the basis of approaches that are essentially qualitative, for example, opinions of community leaders, consultants or academics. For arguments to be regarded as credible, however, it is usually expected that they be backed by "hard" data. In Scheper-Hughes's view, advocates of an "engaged" qualitative methodology, tend not to be mere servants of the policy-making processes. They are "free agents" in pursuit of a deeper understanding of the complex issues influencing women's lives and their reproductive histories. We live in an era where researchers often have neither the time nor the patience to delve into deeper matters, and where quantitative data is being reclaimed for the grim tales that they could tell about the conditions of women's lives and the struggles they encounter (Oakley, 2000). These statistics will be highly contested, however, as the questions researchers ask and the claims they make are interrogated more rigorously.

Conclusion

The purpose of this final chapter has been to review some of the contemporary literature on the problems posed by surveys and the possibilities raised by different kinds of qualitative approaches for doing fertility research. My concern here has been to draw attention to the specific difficulties of the South African, and in particular Winterveld terrain for measuring and eliciting detail on social practices and experiences. The case studies were intended to show the different ways in which qualitative work can be pursued: (1) as linked to survey research in a micro-demographic study, (2) as investigative work arising from prior survey work or (3) as a critical and engaged attempt to explore familial and reproductive issues over an extended period of time. Although I am of the view that a fully-fledged qualitative approach has a lot to offer to contemporary South African demography, I do not anticipate that many demographers would actively seek to become qualitative specialists. South African demography has not been sufficiently unsettled by debate on choice of methods. It remains a discipline with staunch adherence to survey methods and macro-level statistical analyses. It is possible, though, that the frustration of policy-makers will increase as the meaningfulness of quantitative data and their usefulness in informing social interventions become more frequently questioned. It will be in a context of questioning and rethinking paradigms and politics that the debate on "micro-macro mixes" and "engaged" qualitative methodologies will become more relevant.

Notes

[1]   Despite changed politics, reference to apartheid created racial classifications is still common practice in contemporary South African social science research. In the previous era, South Africans were registered from birth as members of one of the four following racial groups: whites, coloureds (i.e. those of 'mixed' largely white-black heritage), Indians and Africans (the black majority indigenous population).

2   Bledsoe et al. do not give their approach a particular name. I use this name merely because it appears to my mind to best summarise what it entailed.

BIBLIOGRAPHY

Aliber, M. 2003. 'Chronic Poverty in South Africa: Incidence, Causes and Policies'. *World Development*, 31 (3): 473-490.

Anarfi, J.K. 2003. 'The impact of HIV/AIDS on Africa.' *New Agenda. South African Journal of Social and Economic Policy*, 9: 33-45.

Abwunza, J.M. 1997. *Women's voices, women's power. Dialogues of resistance from East Africa*. Ontario: Broadview.

Amin, S. and Okediji, F.O. 1971. 'Land use, agriculture and food supply, and industrialization.' In Cantrelle, P et al. (eds.) Population in African development. Vol.1: 409-423.

Amoateng, A.Y. 1997. 'The structure of urban black households: new survey evidence from a Coloured and an African community on the Cape Flats in the Western Cape of South Africa.' African Sociological Review. 1 (2): 22-40.

Amoateng, A.Y. and Richter, L. 2003. 'The state of families in South Africa'. In State of the Nation. South Africa 2003-2004. Pretoria: HSRC. Chapter 11: Pages 242-267.

Anderson, B.A.2003. Fertility, poverty and gender. In Department of Social Development (Ed.), Fertility. Current South African Issues of Poverty, HIV/AIDS and Youth. Seminar Proceedings (pp.27-56). Pretoria: HSRC.

Angrosino, M.V. 1989. Documents of interaction: Biography, autobiography, and life history in social science perspective. Gainesville: University of Florida Press.

Axinn, W. G., Fricke, T.E. and Thornton, A. 1991. 'The micro-demo-graphic community-study approach. Improving survey data by integrating the ethnographic method.' Sociological Methods and Social Research. 20 (2): 187-217 (November 1991).

Ayida, A.A. and Chikelu, G.P.O. 1975. 'Demographic aspects of development planning'. Population Debate. New York: UN.

Bassey, M. 1999. Case study research in educational settings. Buckingham: Open University Press.

Baylies, C. 1999. 'Welfare considerations influencing family size preferences in the context of high HIV prevalence in Zambia.' Paper presented at workshop on fertility in Southern Africa, Centre for African Studies, University of London (22-24 September 1999).

Baylies, C. and Bujra, J. 2000. *AIDS, Sexuality and Gender in Africa. Collective strategies and struggles in Tanzania and Zambia.* London: Routledge.

Bernardi, L. and Hutter, I. 2007. 'The anthropological demography of Europe'. *Demographic Research.* 17 (18): 541-566.

Bertrand, J.T, Banni, E.K, Lesthaeghe, R.J, Montgomery, M.R, Tambache, O. and Waiver, M.J. 1993. *Factors affecting contraceptive use in Sub-Saharan Africa.* Washington: National Academy Press.

Bhalla, A.S. & Lapeyre, F. 2004. *Poverty and exclusion in a global world* (2nd ed.). London: Macmillan.

Blanc, A.K., Wolff, B., Gage, A.J.,Ezeh, A.C., Neema, S. and Ssekamatte-Ssebuliba, J. 1996. *Negotiating Reproductive Outcomes in Uganda.* Maryland: Macro International.

Bledsoe, C. and Isiugo-Abanihe, U. 1989. 'Strategies of child-fosterage among Mende Grannies in Sierra Leone.' In Lesthaeghe, R.J. *Reproduction and social organisation in Sub-Saharan Africa.* Berkeley: University of California.

Bledsoe, C. and Pison, G. 1994. *Nuptiality in Sub-Saharan Africa.* Oxford: Clarendon.

Bledsoe, C., Banja, F. and Hill, A. 1998. 'Reproductive Mishaps and Western Contraception: An African Challenge to Fertility Theory.' *Population and Development Review* 24 (1): 15-57.

Bongaarts, J. 1978. 'A framework for analyzing the proximate determinants of fertility.' *Population and Development Review* 4 (1): 105-132.

Bongaarts, J. and Potter, R.G. 1983. *Fertility, biology and behaviour. An analysis of the proximate determinants.* London: Academic Press.

Bozzoli, B. 1991. 'The meaning of informal work: some women's stories.' In Preston-Whyte, E and Rogerson, C. *South Africa's informal economy.* Cape Town: Oxford University Press.

Bradley, C.1995. 'Women's empowerment and fertility decline in western Kenya.' In Greenhalgh, S. (ed.) *Situating fertility: Anthropology and demographic inquiry.* Cambridge: Cambridge University Press

Brown, B. 1987. Facing the "black peril": The politics of population control in South Africa. Journal of Southern African Studies, 13(2), 256-273.

Burgard S. 2004. Factors associated with contraceptive use in late and post-apartheid South Africa. *Studies in family planning* 35(2) 91-104.

Cain, M. 1982. 'Perspectives on family and fertility in developing countries.'*Population Studies* 36 (2): 159-175.

Caldwell, J.C. 1982. *Theory of fertility decline*. London: Academic Press.

Caldwell, J.C. 1985. 'Strengths and limitations of the survey approach for measuring and understanding fertility change: alternative possibilities." In Cleland, J. and Hobcraft, J. (eds.) *Reproductive Change In Developing Countries. Insights from the World Fertility Survey.* Oxford: Oxford University Press.

Caldwell, J.C., Orubuloye, I.O. and Caldwell, P. 1992. 'Fertility decline in Africa: A new type of transition?' *Population and development review* 18 (2):211-239.

Caldwell, J.C. and Caldwell, P. 1993. 'The South African fertility decline.' *Population and Development Review* 19 (2): 225-261

Calitz, J.M.1996. *Population of South Africa: updated estimates, scenarios and projections 1990 - 2020*, Midrand: DBSA.

Camlin. C.S., Garenne, M. and Moultrie, T.A. 2004. 'Fertility Trend and Pattern in a Rural Area of South Africa in the Context of HIV/AIDS'. *African Journal of Reproductive Health,* 8(2): 38-54.

Campbell, C., Mzaidume, Y. and Williams, B. 1998. 'Gender as an obstacle to condom use. HIV prevention amongst sex workers in a mining community.' *Agenda* 39: 50-57.

Central Archives Depot, Pretoria: Archives of the Native Affairs Department, NTS 3707: 1765/308: Winterveld.

Chimere-Dan, O. 1994. 'Determinants of racial fertility differentials in some urban areas of South Africa.' *Journal of Bio-Social Science* 26: 55-63.

Chipkin, I. and Ngqulunga, B. 2008. 'Friends and Family: Social Cohesion in South Africa'. *Journal of Southern African Studies* 34 (1): 61-76.

Cleland, J. 1985. 'Marital fertility decline in developing countries: theories and the evidence." In Cleland, J. and Hobcraft, J. (eds.) *Reproductive Change In Developing Countries. Insights from the World Fertility Survey.* Oxford: Oxford University Press.

Cohen, P. 1997. 'A population policy for the twenty-first century.' *Africa Today* 3 (4):5-7.

Cooper, D., Harries, J., Myer, L., Orner, P. and Bracken, H. 2007. "Life is still going on": Reproductive intentions among HIV-positive women and men in South Africa. *Social Science & Medicine*, 65 (2): 274-283.

Creel L. C. and Perry R.J. 2003. *Improving the quality of reproductive health care for young people.* Population Reference Bureau, Washington DC.

Cross, C., Gelderblom, D., Roux, N. and Mafukidze, J. (eds.) 2006. *Views on migration in Sub-Saharan Africa: proceedings of an African migration alliance workshop.* Cape Town: HSRC Press.

de Clercq, F. 1994. 'Putting community participation into development work: The difficult case of Winterveld.' *Development Southern Africa* 11 (3):379-393.

Denzin, N.K. and Lincoln, Y.S. (eds.) 1998. *Strategies of qualitative enquiry.* London: Sage.

de Jong, R.C. 1995. *A short history of the settlements around Tswaing.* Unpublished report for the National Cultural History Museum, Pretoria.

Department of Health. 2004. South African Demographic and Health Survey 2003, Preliminary Report. Pretoria: Department of Health.

Development Bank of South Africa (DBSA). 1987. *Winterveld Agency Programme. Special Report.* Midrand: DBSA.

Dickson, K. 2002. 'Youth and fertility'. In *Fertility – Current South African Issues: Poverty, Youth and HIV/AIDS.* Seminar Papers. Pretoria: HSRC and DSD.

Du Plessis, G. 1995. 'The development of demography in South Africa: A relevant social science or a tool for counting subgroups?' *Southern African Journal of Demography* 5 (1):52-59.

Du Plessis, G. 1996. 'Reproductive choice and motivation in South Africa, 1987-1989.' *Southern African Journal of Demography* 6 (1): 33-47.

Du Plessis, G. 2002. 'HIV and Fertility in South Africa: Some Theoretical and Methodological Considerations'. Seminar Proceedings. Fertility - Current South African Issues: Poverty, Youth and HIV/AIDS. Pretoria: HSRC and DSD.

Du Toit, A. 2005. *Chronic and structural poverty in South Africa: challenges for action and research. CPRC Working Paper 56.* Cape Town: PLAAS.

Easterlin, R.A and Crimmins, E.M. 1985. *The fertility revolution. A supply-demand analysis.* Chicago: University of Chicago Press.

Elder, G.S. 2003. *Hostels, Sexuality, and the Apartheid Legacy: Malevolent Geographics.* Ohio: Ohio University Press.

Erasmus, J. 1995. *South Africa's nine provinces: A human development profile.* Midrand: DBSA.

Erasmus, J. 1999. *Coping strategies of the unemployed. Labour market analysis.* Pretoria: HSRC.

Findlay, A. and Findlay, A. 1987. *Population and development in the third world.* London: Methuen & Co.

Fleish, B., Nkacha, T. and de Clercq, F. 1993. 'Squatter Education - Where "private" schooling means poverty.' *Matlhasedi* December: 3-6.

Forgey H, Dimant T, Corrigan T, Mophuthing T, Spratt J, Pienaar D & Peter N (2001) *South Africa Survey 2000/01,* Johannesburg: SAIRR.

Fricke, T. 1997. 'The uses of culture in demographic research: a continuing place for community studies.' *Population and Development Review* 23 (4): 825-832 (December 1997).

Gaisie, S.K. 1998. 'Fertility transition in Botswana.' *Journal of Contemporary African Studies* 16 (2): 277-296.

Garenne, M. and Halifax, J. 1999. 'Pattern of premarital fertility in Southern Africa, and its correlates.' Paper presented at workshop on fertility in Southern Africa, Centre for African Studies, University of London (22-24 September 1999).

Goldman, N. and Pebley, A. 1989. 'The demography of polygyny in Sub-Saharan Africa.' In Lesthaeghe, R.J. 1989. *Reproduction and social organization in Sub-Saharan Africa.* Berkeley: University of California.

Gould, W.T.S. and Brown, M. 1996. 'A fertility transition in Sub-Saharan Africa.' *International Journal of Population Geography* 2: 1-22.

Greenhalgh, S.1990. 'Toward a political economy of fertility: anthropological contributions.' *Population and Development Review* 16(1): 85-106.

Greenhalgh, S.1995. 'Anthropology theorizes reproduction: integrating practice, political economic, and feminist perspectives'. In Greenhalgh, S. (ed.) *Situating Fertility: Anthropology and Demographic Inquiry.* Cambridge: Cambridge University Press.

Greenhalgh, S. 1997. 'Methods and meanings: reflections on disciplinary difference.' *Population and Development Review* 23 (4): 819-824 (December 1997).

Gruenbaum, E. 2001. *The Female Circumcision controversy: An anthropological perspective.* Philadelphia: University of Pennsylvania.

Hall, J. 2003. *Tackling poverty: South Africa's biggest challenge,* In Hindson, V. 2003. Newsletter 23 of 2003. Available online www.hologram.org.za (accessed 12 February 2005).

Handwerker, W.P. 1991. 'Women's power and fertility transition: the cases of Africa and the West Indies.' *Population and Environment: A Journal of Interdisciplinary Studies* 13 (1): 55-77.

Handwerker, W.P. 1993. 'Empowerment and fertility transition on Antigua, WI: Education, employment, and the moral economy of childbearing'. *Human Organization* 52 (1): 41-52.

Harrison, A and Montgomery, E. 2001. 'Life Histories, Reproductive Histories: Rural South African Women's Narratives of Fertility, Reproductive Health and Illness'. *Journal of Southern African Studies* Vol 27 (2): 311-328.

Harriss, J. and Moore, M. 1984. *Development and the rural-urban divide.* London: Frank Cass.

Heady, P. 2007. 'What can anthropological methods contribute to demography – and how?' *Demographic Research* 16 (18): 555-558.

Hill, A.G. 1991. 'African demographic regimes, past and present.' In Rimmer, D. (ed.) *Africa 30 years on.* London: James Currey.

Himmelstrand, U., Kinyanjui, K. and Mburugu, E. 1994. *African Perspectives on Development.* London: James Currey.

Hirschowitz, R. and Orkin, M. 1995. *A national household survey of health inequalities in South Africa. Overview Report.* Johannesburg: CASE.

Hodgson, D and McCurdy, S.A (eds.). 2001. *"Wicked" Women and the Reconfiguration of Gender in Africa.* Portsmouth: Heinemann

Honey, P. 2000. 'A-Tishoo! We all fall down.' *Financial Mail* (14 January 2000).

Horton, Hayward D. (1999). Critical demography: The paradigm of the future? Sociological Forum, 14(3), 363-367.

Human Sciences Research Council (HSRC), 2004. 'Fact Sheet. Poverty in South Africa'. Fact Sheet 1. 26/07/2004. Pretoria: HSRC.

Hunter, M. 2002. 'The materiality of everyday sex: thinking beyond prostitution' *African Studies* 61 (1): 99-119.

Hunter, M. 2007. 'The changing political economy of sex in South Africa: The significance of unemployment and inequalities to the scale of the AIDS pandemic'. *Social Science & Medicine*, 64 (3): 689-700.

Indongo, N. 2007. Contraceptive Use Among Young Women In Namibia: Determinants and Policy Implications. *Pretoria: University of Pretoria, South Africa. (Unpublished PhD thesis).*

Isiugo-Abanihe, U.C. 1994. 'Demographic transition in the context of Africa's development.' In Himmelstrand, U., Kinyanjui, K. and Mburugu, E. *African Perspectives on Development.* London: James Currey.

James, D. and Kaufman, C. 1997. The reproductive consequences of shifting ethnic identity in South Africa. Paper presented at the International Union for the Scientific Study of Population seminar on Cultural Perspectives on Reproductive Health, Johannesburg, South Africa, 16-19 June 1997.

Johnson-Hanks, J. 2007. 'What kind of theory for anthropological demography?' *Demographic Research* 16 (1): 1-26.

Johannson, S.R. 1997. 'Fertility and family history: using the past to explain the present.' *Population and Development Review* 23 (3): 627-637.

Kabeer, N. 1994. *Reversed realities. Gender hierarchies in development thought.* London: Verso.

Kaufman, C.E. 1998. 'Contraceptive use in South Africa under apartheid.' *Demography* 35 (4):421-434.

Kertzer, D.I. 1995. 'Political-economic and cultural explanations of demographic behaviour.' In Greenhalgh, S. (ed.) *Situating fertility: Anthropology and demographic inquiry.* Cambridge: Cambridge University Press.

Kertzer, D.I. 1997. 'Quantitative and Qualitative Approaches to Historical Demography.' *Population and Development Review* 23 (4): 839-846 (December 1997).

Kertzer, D.I. and Fricke, T. (eds.). 1997. *Anthropological Demography. Toward a new synthesis.* Chicago: University of Chicago Press.

Kistner, U. 2003. Sovereign power and bare life with HIV/AIDS: bio-politics South African style. (Accessed from http://wiserweb.wits. ac.za/PDF%20Files/biopolitics%20-%20kistner.PDF)

Klugman, B. 1996. 'Demographics and Population Policy.' Chapter 1. In *The South African Health Review*. Durban: Health Systems Trust.

Knodel, J. 1997. 'A Case for Nonanthropological Qualitative Methods for Demographers.' *Population and Development Review* 23 (4): 847-853 (December 1997).

Koen, C. 1998. 'The structure of urban black households: New survey evidence from a coloured and an African community on the Cape Flats in the Western Cape of South Africa: A comment on Amoateng's methods and findings.' *African Sociological Review* 2(1): 165-173.

Kotze, J.C. 1992. Children and the family in a rural settlement in Gazankulu. *African Studies* 51(1):143-166.

Kotze, J.C. and Van der Waal, C.S. 1995. *Violent social relationships and family life in two Transvaal lowveld settlements*. Pretoria: HSRC.

Landman, J.P. 2003. *Breaking the grip of poverty and inequality in South Africa 2004-2014: current trends, issues and future policy options. Executive summary*. Stellenbosch: EFSA.

Lesthaeghe, R.J. 1989. 'Social organization, economic crises, and the future of fertility control in Africa'. In Lesthaeghe, R.J. *Reproduction and social organization in Sub-Saharan Africa*. Berkeley: University of California.

Lesthaeghe, R.J. 1989. *Reproduction and social organization in Sub-Saharan Africa*. Berkeley: University of California.

Levin, C. and Dubler, N.N. 1990. HIV and childbearing. Uncertain risks and bitter realities: The reproductive choices of HIV-infected women. *The Milbank Quarterly*, 68 (3): 321-351.

Lotter, J.M. 1990. 'Historical trends in fertility', in Mostert, W.P and Lotter, J.M. *South Africa's demographic future*. Pretoria: HSRC.

Madhavan, S., Collinson, M., Townsend, N., Kahn, K. and Tollman, S.M. 2007. 'The implications of long term community involvement for the production and circulation of population knowledge'*Demographic Research* 17 (13): 369-388.

Makiwane, M. and Udjo, E. 2007. No proof of 'child farming' in awarding of child support grants. *HSRC Review*. 5 (1): 6-7.

Mama, A. 2007. 'Gender and Challenges of Intellectual Development in Africa'. *New Agenda. South African Journal of Social and Economic Policy,* 27 (3rd Quarter): 52-58.

Manona, C.W.1991. 'Relying on kin. Ex-farm Workers' Adaptation to Life in Grahamstown.' In Spiegel, A.D. and McAllister, P.A. *Tradition and Transition in Southern Africa.* Johannesburg: Witwatersrand University Press.

March, C., Smyth, I. and Mukhopadhyay, M. 1999. *A guide to gender-analysis frameworks.* Oxford: Oxfam.

Marshall, G. 1994. *Oxford concise dictionary of Sociology.* Oxford: Oxford University Press.

Masanjala, W. 2007. 'The poverty-HIV/AIDS nexus in Africa: A livelihood approach'. *Social Science & Medicine,* 64 (5): 1032-1041

Mason, K.O. 1996. *Women's empowerment and demographic change: what do we know?* Hawaii: Program on Population East-West Center.

May, J, and Norton, A. 1997. '"A difficult life": The perceptions and experience of poverty in South Africa.' *Social Indicators Research* 41: 95-118.

May, J. (ed.) 1998. *Poverty and Inequality in South Africa.* Report prepared for the office of the executive deputy president and the interministerial committee on poverty and inequality. Pretoria: Government Press.

Mburugu, E.K. 1994. 'The persistence of high fertility in Africa and prospects for fertility decline.' In Himmelstrand, U., Kinyanjui, K. and Mburugu, E. 1994. *African Perspectives on Development.* London: James Currey.

McNicoll, G. 1994. 'Institutional analysis of fertility.' In Lindahl-Kiessling, K. and Landberg, H. *Population, Economic Development, and the Environment.* Oxford: Oxford University Press.

Meekers, D. 1994. 'Sexual initiation and premarital childbearing in Sub-Saharan Africa.' *Population Studies* 48: 47-64.

Mfono Z. (1998). Teenage contraceptive needs in urban South Africa: A case study. *International family planning perspectives* 24 (4):180-183.

Mies, M. 1993. 'Feminist Research: Science, Violence and Responsibility.' In Mies, M and Shiva, V. *Ecofeminism.* London: Zed Books.

Morrell, R. and Richter, L. 2004. 'The Fatherhood Project: confronting issues of masculinity and sexuality'. *Agenda*, 62: 36-44.

Mostert, W.P. and Hofmeyr, B.E. 1988. 'Socio-economic factors affecting fertility in developing countries and of the developing population groups in South Africa. *Southern African Journal of Demography* 2:1.

Mostert, W.P. 1990. 'Recent trends in fertility in South Africa.' In Mosert, W.P. and Lotter, J.M. (eds.) *South Africa's demographic future*. Pretoria: HSRC.

Mostert, W.P. and Hofmeyr, B.E. 1997. *Fertility and related indicators in South Africa, 1991-1994*. HSRC (unpublished).

Mostert, W.P., Hofmeyr, B.E., Oosthuizen, J.S. and Van Zyl, J.A. 1998. *Demography. Textbook for the South African student*. Pretoria: HSRC.

Moultrie, Tom A. & Timaeus, Ian M. (2001). Fertility and living arrangements in South Africa. Journal of Southern African Studies, 27(2), 207-223.

Murray, C. 1977. High bridewealth, migrant labour and the position of women in Lesotho. *Journal of African Law* 21: 1: 79-96.

Murray, C. 1981. *Families Divided*. Johannesburg: Ravan Press.

Murray, C. 1987. 'Displaced urbanisation'. In Lonsdale, J. (ed.) 1988. *South Africa in question*. Cambridge: University of Cambridge.

Naidoo, K. 2002. 'Reproductive dynamics in the context of economic insecurity and domestic violence: a South African case study', *Journal of Asian and African Studies*, 37(3-5), 376-400.

Naidoo, K., Matebeni, Z and Pietersen-Snyman, M. 2004. 'Complexities and Challenges: Men's responses to HIV and AIDS in Winterveld, South Africa'. *Commonwealth Youth and Development*, Vol 2 (No.2): 45-62.

Naidoo, K. 2005. 'The 'politics of poverty' in a post-apartheid South African metropolis'. *African Sociological Review*, Vol 9 (No. 2): 55-78.

Naidoo, K. 2007. 'Researching Reproduction: Reflections on Qualitative Methodology in a Transforming Society'. *Forum Qualitative Sozialforschung / Forum: Qualitative Social Research*, 9(1), Art. 12, http://www.qualitative-research.net/fqs-texte/1-08/08-1-12-e.htm.

Naidoo, K. and Misra, K. 2008. 'Poverty and Intimacy: Reflections on Sexual Exchange, Reproduction and AIDS in South Africa'. *South African Review of Sociology*, 39: 1-17.

National Building Research Institute. 1993. *Winterveld. Report on educational facilities.* Johannesburg: NBRI.

Ndegwa, D.G. 1996. 'International thinking on population policies and programmes from Rome to Cairo: Has South Africa kept pace?' *Southern African Journal of Demography* 6 (1): 49-56.

Nkau, P. 1999. *Fertility trends in South Africa.* Unpublished report. Pretoria: HSRC.

Nkosi, B. and Daniels, P. 2007. 'Family Strengths: South Africa'. *Marriage and Family Review*, 41 (1): 11-26.

Ntsaluba, A. 1998. *South Africa demographic and health survey.* Preliminary report. Pretoria: Department of Health.

Oakley, Ann (2000). Experiments in knowing: Gender and method in the social sciences. New York: The New Press.

Obermeyer, C.A.1997. 'Qualitative Methods: A Key to a Better Understanding of Demographic Behaviour?' *Population and Development Review* 23 (4): 813-818 (December 1997).

Oyen, E., Miller, S.M. and Samad, S.A. 1996. *Poverty: A global review. Handbook on international poverty research.* Oslo: Scandinavian University Press.

Page, H. 1989. 'Childrearing versus childbearing: coresidence of mother and child in Sub-Saharan Africa'. In Lesthaeghe, R.J. *Reproduction and social organisation in Sub-Saharan Africa.* Berkeley: University of California.

Pebley, A. and Mbugua, W. 1989. 'Polygyny and fertility in Sub-Saharan Africa.' In Lesthaeghe, R.J. 1989. *Reproduction and social organization in Sub-Saharan Africa.* Berkeley: University of California.

Phillips, A. (ed.) 1953. *Survey of African marriage and family life.* London: Oxford University Press.

Posel, D. 1997. 'Counting the poor: who gets what in which households.' *Agenda.* 33: 49-60.

Potts, D. and Marks, S. 2001. 'Fertility in Southern Africa: the Quiet Revolution'. *Journal of Southern African Studies,* 27 (2): 189-205.

Preston-Whyte, E.M. 1990. 'Qualitative perspectives on fertility trends among African teenagers' in Mostert, W.P and Lotter, J.M. *South Africa's demographic future.* Pretoria: HSRC.

Pretoria News. 'SA Population growth rate "set to fall by 71%"' (January 17 2000).

Rao, V. 1997. 'Can Economics Mediate the Relationship Between Anthropology and Demography?' *Population and Development Review* 23 (4): 833-838 (December 1997).

Ratsaka, M., Jewkes, R., Levin, J., Khunou, L. and Kabi, B. 1998. *How parents communicate with their sons and daughters in Winterveldt.* Report to the Planned Parenthood Association.

Reinharz, S. 1992. *Feminist methods in social research.* Oxford: Oxford University Press.

Robinson, W.C.1992. 'Kenya enters the fertility transition.'*Population studies* 46:445-457.

Russell, M. 1998. 'Black urban households in South Africa.' *African Sociological Review* 2 (1): 174-180.

Schatz, E. and Ogunmefun, C. 2007. Caring and contributing: The role of older women in rural South African multi-generational households in the HIV/AIDS Era. *World Development,* 35 (8): 1390-1403.

Scheper-Hughes, N. 1997. 'Demography without numbers'. In Kertzer, D.I and Fricke, T. (eds.) *Anthropological Demography. Toward a new synthesis.* Chicago: University of Chicago Press.

Schlemmer, L. 2005. Advancement of blacks: hype outstrips the reality. *Pretoria News.* 23 August: 3.

Seekings, J. & Nattrass, N. 2004. *Class, race and inequality in South Africa.* New Haven, Connecticut: Yale University Press.

Segal, A. 1993. 'Africa's population and family planning dynamics.' *Africa Today.* Oxford: Oxford University Press.

Segel, T. and Labe, D. 1990. 'Family violence: wife abuse.' In McKendrick, B. and Hoffmann, W. (eds.) *People and violence in South Africa.* Cape Town: Oxford University Press.

Simone, A. 1998. 'Winterveld.' In *Case studies on local economic development and poverty.* Pretoria: Isandla Institute for the Department of Constitutional Development.

Skade, T. 2008. 'We have options out of poverty – Ndungane'. http://www.iol.co.za/general/news/newsprint.php?art_id

Smith, D.M. 1992 (ed.) *The apartheid city and beyond. Urbanization and social change in South Africa.* London: Routledge.

South African Demographic and Health Survey, 1998. *Full Report.* Pretoria: MRC and Department of Health.

South African Demographic and Health Survey, 2003. *Preliminary Report.* Pretoria: Department of Health.

Spiegel, A. D.1991. 'Polygyny as myth. Toward understanding extramarital relations in Lesotho.' In Spiegel, A.D. and McAllister, P.A. 1991. *Tradition and Transition in Southern Africa.* Johannesburg: Witwatersrand University Press.

Spiegel, A.D. and McAllister, P.A. 1991. *Tradition and Transition in Southern Africa.* Johannesburg: Witwatersrand University Press.

Spiegel, A.D., Watson, V. and Wilkinson, P. 1996. 'Domestic diversity and fluidity among some African households in Greater Cape Town.' *Social Dynamics.* 22 (1): 7-30.

Spiegel, A.D. and Mehloana, A.M. 1997. *Family as social network: kinship and sporadic migrancy in the Western Cape's Khayelitsha.* Pretoria: HSRC.

Surplus People Project (SPP) Reports. 1983. 'Winterveld.' Vol 5. The Transvaal. *Forced Removals in South Africa.* Cape Town: SPP.

Swartz, L. 2003. Fertility transition in South Africa and its impact on the four major racial groups. In Department of Social Development (Ed.), Fertility. Current South African issues of poverty, HIV/AIDS and youth. Seminar Proceedings (pp.7-26). Pretoria: HSRC.

Taitz, L. 1999. 'One in three teens gets pregnant.' *Sunday Times.* (September 12 1999).

Thornton, R. 2003. Flows of 'sexual substance' and representation of the body in South Africa. http://wiserweb.wits.ac.za/events%20-%20body.htm

Thorpe, M. 2002. Masculinity in an HIV intervention. *Agenda,* 53: 61-68.

Timaeus, I. and Graham, W. 1989. 'Labor circulation, marriage and fertility in South Africa'. In Lesthaeghe, R.J. *Reproduction and social organisation in Sub-Saharan Africa.* Berkeley: University of California.

Tladi, L.S. 2006. 'Poverty and HIV/AIDS in South Africa: an empirical contribution'. *Journal of Social Aspects of HIV/AIDS* 3 (1): 369-381.

Townsend, N.1997. 'Reproduction in anthropology and demography.' In Kertzer, D.I. and Fricke, T.(eds.) *Anthropological demography. Toward a new synthesis.* Chicago: University of Chicago.

Ulicki, T and Crush, J. 2000. 'Gender, Farmwork, and Women's Migration from Lesotho to the New South Africa. *Canadian Journal of African Studies* 34 (1): 64-79.

United Nations. 1995. *Women's education and fertility behaviour. Recent evidence from the Demographic and Health Surveys*. Population Division. ST/ESA/SER.R/137.

United Nations. 1991. *The World's Women 1970-1990: Trends and statistics.* SalesNo. E. 90. XVII.3

United Nations. 2005. *Population, Development and HIV/AIDS with particular emphasis on Poverty. The Concise Report.* Department of Economic and Social Affairs. New York: United Nations.

United Nations Family Planning Association (UNFPA). 1994. *Population and development strategies*. New York: UNFPA.

Van de Kaa, D.J. 1996. 'Anchored Narratives: The story and findings of half a century of research into the determinants of fertility.' *Population studies* 50: 389-432.

Van de Walle, E. 1992. 'Fertility transition, conscious choice and numeracy.' *Demography* 29(4): 487-502.

Van Onselen, C. 1993. 'The reconstruction of a rural life from oral testimony: critical notes on the methodology employed in the study of a black South African sharecropper.' *The Journal of Peasant Studies* 20 (3): 494-514.

Walker C (ed) (1990) *Women and gender in Southern Africa to 1945*, Cape Town: David Philip.

Whiteford, A. and McGrath, M. 1994. *Distribution of income in South Africa.* Pretoria: HSRC.

Whitaker D.J., Miller K.S., May D.C. and Levin M.L. (1999). Teenage partners' communication about sexual risk and condom use: The importance of parent-teenage discussions. *Family planning perspectives* 31(3):117-121.

Wilson, F. 1996. 'Drawing together some regional perspectives on poverty.' In Oyen, E., Miller, S.M. and Samad, S.A. 1996. *Poverty: A global review. Handbook on international poverty research.* Oslo: Scandinavian University Press.

Wojcicki, J.M. 2005. 'Socio-economic status as a risk factor for HIV infection in women in east, central and southern Africa: a systematic review'. *Journal of Biosocial Science*, 37: 1-36.

Wood, K. and Jewkes, R. 1997. 'Violence, rape and sexual coercion: Everyday love in a South African township." *Gender and Development* 5 (2): 41-46.

Xiphu, T. 1998. *NHISSA. Newsletter of the NHISSA* Committee. Pretoria: Department of Health.

Yawitch, J. 1981. 'Women and squatting: a Winterveld case study'. In Bonner, P. (ed.) *Working Papers in Southern African Studies*. Vol 2:199-227. Braamfontein: Ravan Press.

Ziel, S.C. 1997. 'Family Law, Family Ideology and Multiculturalism in South Africa.' *African Sociological Review* 1 (2): 41-59.

APPENDIX 1

SUMMARIES OF FAMILY (MOTHER - DAUGHTER) LIFE HISTORIES

The vignettes that have been integrated in the different chapters have been taken from detailed family or mother-daughter life histories. Summarised versions of these stories are presented here to offer some background and to situate the comments of the individual women.

FAMILY LIFE HISTORIES [# 1]
LEBO, SOPHY AND SINAH MAKWELA

Lebo was born in 1952 in the township of Alexandra, bordering Johannesburg. She did not live long in Alexandra because her parents moved from place to place in their attempts to find employment. In 1958 they finally settled in Winterveld. Lebo attended school in Winterveld but her schooling was interrupted by an unplanned pregnancy. She was able initially to draw on the support of her extended family for childcare. She thus left her baby to be cared for by other family members while she sought work in Pretoria. She earned poorly in her first job (in a laundry) and gave up the work when she learnt that she had fallen pregnant. The second pregnancy was a consequence of a casual relationship and she did not see the man again. In 1973 her daughter, Sophy, was born. In 1976, another family (the Makwelas) moved into Winterveld. The Makwelas originated from Belfast in Mpumalanga and had come to Winterveld to live as tenants and work in the nearby towns. Lebo and one of the Makwela sons (Simon) began having a relationship. She had two children with Simon Makwela before they married in 1980. Shortly after she formally married, Lebo's natal family support base disintegrated as most family members, except two of her brothers, left the area.

In the 1980s Lebo and her children experienced increasing poverty as Simon's contribution to the household coffers dwindled, as he changed jobs, and as he spent more of his earnings in the local taverns and on his own needs. The situation worsened after he, in terms of the levirate custom, took over his brother's wife as his second wife. With her husband often absent, Lebo grew dependent on an extra-marital relationship for financial support. To add to her distress, two of her young daughters, Sophy and Sinah (Lebo's third child), fell pregnant and added their children as responsibilities of their mother's household. These were particularly difficult years: money was needed to feed infants and put older children through school. Lebo's main strategy for gaining money was to apply pressure simultaneously on her husband, partner and daughters. She did not attempt to use her brothers as resources for fear that this would lead them to question her husband about his financial responsibilities thereby increasing the potential for domestic conflict.

In 1996 Sophy found short-term domestic work and in 1997 Lebo worked as a labourer digging trenches and laying water pipes. Since 1997 the Rand Water Board (referred to locally as "RDP Water") has sought local labour to lay the foundations for Winterveld's development. When Sophy's work as a domestic worker came to an abrupt end Lebo found both Sophy and Sinah jobs as labourers at RDP Water. Lebo had hoped that she would gain sub-contraction work to oversee the labour of others but her application was unsuccessful. In any case, the attempt to use local labour to complete the reticulation and water-supply processes was stalled in 1998 by the political resistance of plot-owners.

Sophy and Sinah, who were both in their twenties, had few opportunities outside unskilled jobs. Both had dropped out of school at the junior secondary level and had not acquired any other training. Sophy had a short spell as a domestic labourer and suffered rape in 1998. Shortly thereafter she left Winterveld to find work in Johannesburg. She failed to find 'decent work' there but was introduced, instead, to the financial benefits of prostitution. Of all the *ad hoc* work Lebo and her daughters had previously done, Sophy's turn to prostitution brought home the most income. Although Sinah developed a few relationships with working men and managed to elicit some measure of support, for Lebo, it was Sophy's line of work that brought in the most income and had rescued the household from sinking into deepening poverty. In 1999, Lebo and her daughters were facing the prospect that they could be HIV-positive. Sophy died of AIDS in 2001 after giving birth to a son. Sinah remained in Merafeng in 2008, bringing up one child.

Issues illustrated: These life histories reveal often unseen strategies adopted by de facto female-headed households such as the collaboration of mothers and daughters to earn a living through manipulating men and sustaining multiple unions. Outside of these household relations, bonds between kin appear to be fluid. Child-bearing was not taking place within the context of stable family life. The younger women, Sophy and Sinah, had two and one child respectively. Both talked about avoiding pregnancy but would possibly have contemplated additional children if it was practically and financially possible.

FAMILY LIFE HISTORIES [#2]
THOKO SKOSANA AND MARTHA SIBIYA

Thoko was born in 1930 in the Free State. Her father was a labour tenant who moved frequently between farms in search of work. When her father worked in the fields her mother often assisted him but her general responsibility was usually to perform domestic chores in the main house. Thoko's parents had never attended school and they did not attach any value to educating their children. Thoko married when she was about thirteen years old. The *magadi* (bridewealth) of ten cattle was paid and shortly after the marriage celebrations she moved into her in-laws' homestead. In 1944 her daughter, Martha, was born.

In the early stages of her marriage Thoko spent most of her time in child-rearing activities. She began to see less of her husband, Mhlezi Skosana, because he found work in town and often lived away from home. Her difficulties, as she described them, arose at the time Mhlezi enrolled at a night-school to learn basic literacy skills. Night-school brought Mhlezi into contact with another woman whom he brought home as a second wife. Thoko's relationship with Mhlezi subsequently deteriorated. However, their relationship improved a while later because Mhlezi made numerous attempts to reconcile with her. Mhlezi's second wife, who bore no children whilst married to him, passed away after an illness. When reflecting on her life, Thoko described herself as someone experiencing much poverty and little power in her relationships.

The Skosanas moved into Winterveld when they grew tired of farm life and when they sought cheap accommodation in close proximity to Pretoria. Not long after settling in Winterveld, and at the age of eighty years, Mhlezi passed away. Since then Thoko has lived a relatively independent existence. She has relied on her pension and none of her children, except perhaps Martha, have been of any real support to her in her old age.

Unlike her mother, Martha did not spend a considerable amount of time in her in-laws' home. Not long after marrying and bearing a child, when she was about twenty years old, Martha was widowed. She left her in-laws' home after the death of her husband but returned with another child borne in a later relationship. She left her children to be reared by her late husband's family and went to work as a domestic labourer. Her working experiences were insecure and she talked about having spent much time evading the police who, in the 1970s and 1980s, harassed workers for their permits to be in the towns. Just after giving birth to her second child Martha had herself sterilised. She did not contemplate remarriage and saw this action as essential to avoid the burden of bearing additional children in casual relationships. Since her husband's death she had maintained relationships with men whom she claimed were either violent or who were trying to exploit her for her money. She said: "If my husband was alive I would accept what I got." She saw no purpose in being "accepting" in these non-formal relationships.

Issues illustrated: Thoko and Martha's life histories illustrate contrasting issues with respect to power and reproductive decision-making. While Martha's relationship with her in-laws suggests some degree of accommodation and negotiation, Thoko has experienced confinement and duty over which she has exercised few choices. For Martha, who had been released from her in-laws' homestead, sterilisation represented a decisive way in which she sought to guard herself against unwanted fertility. Since marriage was undesired, and Martha was not dependent on male support, further child-bearing was regarded as burdensome.

FAMILY LIFE HISTORIES [#3]
NOZIZWE AND FLORA RADEBE

Nozizwe Radebe was born in the Free State in 1933. When she was six years old her parents arrived as one of the first land-owners in Winterveld. Her parents were instrumental in setting up many projects, including a school and a church. They had come to Winterveld, like most other families that came to live there, to begin farming. Nozizwe performed well in primary school but dropped out before completing high school because she became pregnant. She stayed home and began training to become a dressmaker. Later she married the father of her child, Zama Radebe, and went to live with his family.

Initially, after marrying, Nozizwe spent most of her time in her in-laws' home in the Johannesburg area, serving them and bringing up her children. After a few years Nozizwe and her husband opened a medicine shop in Thokoza. They later converted it to a grocery store and experimented with the selling of all kinds of goods and the offering of a range of services, including dressmaking. Their joint business venturing came to an abrupt end in 1971. Their relationship deteriorated and they finally divorced. Nozizwe said: "At first we were aiming high and we wanted to build a good home, have a business, have children. Something changed along the way. When you think you're on the right track your husband finds other women." Between the 1970s and the 1990s Nozizwe tried her hand at numerous small business ventures. Most of these were failures because, as she claimed, "people would take advantage of me" because she was "too soft" and because she "was a woman". As chairperson of the *Office* group Nozizwe at first displayed tremendous business acumen in winning outside support and funding for her group. These efforts, however, were later undermined by in-fighting and petty conflicts and Nozizwe finally left the group.

Nozizwe bore five children, some of whom spent years being brought up by her parents and other relatives, as she struggled to apply herself to the tasks associated with running her businesses. Her daughter, Flora, who was born in 1960, claimed that she was brought up by her grandparents and not by her mother. Flora also claimed that she hardly got to know her brothers and sisters because they lived apart and she seldom visited them.

In 1969 Flora left Thokoza for Winterveld and lived there with her grandmother. She was in high school in 1979 when she learnt that she was pregnant. She had been using contraception since she was about seventeen years and was thus surprised at finding herself pregnant. Her boyfriend abandoned her; she then married another man (whilst pregnant) who convinced her that he would treat her child as if it were his own. They married through customary rites and lived together in his family home for three years before they separated. The relationship broke down partly through interference from other family members but mainly because her husband chose to marry someone else. Flora was not legally married so when her husband pursued a new marriage partner she left her in-laws' home and returned to Winterveld. Her grandmother had by then passed away and this time she lived with her mother and child. Without child support and being in need of full-time work, Flora sent her child to be brought up by her brother and his wife.

Flora claimed that she enjoyed few good relationships and few good employment opportunities from the mid-1980s onwards. For many years she aspired towards a middle class lifestyle but earned poor (on the breadline) wages. Throughout these years the prospect of bearing additional children or getting married were furthest from her mind. In 1999 Flora passed examinations enabling her to set up a travel agency business. She also developed a new, but visiting, partnership. It was at this stage that she contemplated the possibility of an additional child. By 2003, however, this relationship ended and her reproductive life effectively ended.

Issues illustrated: These stories of women who are comparatively better off seem to show their ability to mobilise resources and take advantage of business opportunities, but their family lives appear to be fairly similar to those of women living in poorer circumstances. Insecurity was a factor preventing Flora from pursuing a permanent relationship or bearing additional children. Child-bearing was thus being re-assessed and contingent on the ability to find rewarding employment and a stable partnership.

Khanyi was born in 1921 in Zebediela in the Northern Province. Zebediela was a rural area in which her family had lived and worked as fruit farmers for generations. Khanyi's parents were cousins who had been brought together through an arranged marriage. They had only two children, Khanyi and Rosina. In 1928, when she was almost seven years old, Khanyi's parents left Zebediela for Eastwood in Pretoria. In 1931 Khanyi attended school for the first time and went as far as Std. 4 (sixth school level). Her parents could have afforded to have kept her in school for longer but her father took her out of school at that stage arguing that girls should not become "too clever". Shortly after leaving school Khanyi married a man whom she had met in Eastwood. She gave birth to her first child in 1941 and a second child shortly thereafter. Her marriage, however, developed problems and her husband eventually deserted her. Ten years later Khanyi met and married Philemon Mabetwa. In the late 1950s, after they were forcibly removed from Eastwood, Khanyi and Philemon moved to Winterveld.

Philemon bought four plots and built four shops in Winterveld. Over the years, Khanyi often helped in the running of the shops but her main preoccupation was with rearing her ten children. It was a common sight for people to see her working in the shops with a baby on her back. In Winterveld Khanyi enjoyed a fairly stable household and marriage. Despite their good relationship the fact that Mabetwa was a well-off man meant that he had many "special woman friends". Khanyi claimed that she did not mind Philemon's other relationships because she was still his only wife and he was a responsible father. When Philemon died in 1969 Khanyi became very religious. She joined the Methodist Church and then converted to the St. John's Apostelic Church of Prophecy. Remarriage was never a serious consideration.

In the aftermath of Philemon's death most of Khanyi's free time was spent overseeing the running of the shops, seeing to her children's needs, attending church and running a creche. Between 1973 and 1997 she ran a creche in a big rented house but this project gradually came to an end as attendances dropped. The profitability of her shops also dwindled as people left the area or appeared to have less money to spend. In the 1990s she leased two of her shops to Mozambican traders who had come to live in Winterveld. Since then she has lived a relatively solitary existence with occasional help from her children and grandchildren. Khanyi and her daughter, Louisa, have never had a particularly good relationship. This is despite the fact that Khanyi took over Louisa's first two children and brought them up for many years.

When Louisa's schooling was interrupted by a pregnancy in 1969 she was quite distraught. Her boyfriend left her and she had to rely on her parents for support. She said that her father was quite happy because he saw her as being old enough. Her mother, however, was at first very unsupportive. In September 1969 when Miriam (Louisa's daughter) was three months old, Khanyi agreed to look after her thus giving Louisa an opportunity to find work. Louisa found a number of short-term jobs including a part-time teaching post at a primary school. Some years later Louisa bore two more children in an effort to secure a marriage to a man with whom she had developed a serious relationship. It was whilst pregnant for the third time that her partner, Philip, paid the *magadi* (bridewealth) and they were married. Her marriage to Philip was a turbulent one and she endured extreme physical abuse and mental torment. They divorced in 1994 but she received no maintenance for the support of her children from him. During the years in which her marriage was faltering, Louisa was rejected by members of her family, including Khanyi, who believed that she should withstand the abuse to keep her marriage intact. She then resorted to all kinds of work (including some illicit) to make money to keep her children fed and in good schools. Her main work activity since 1994 had been to sell vegetables at Mabopane Station. In 1997 she resumed a new, but equally troublesome, relationship – which sustained itself until 2005. In 2005 as well, Khanyi passed away at the age of 84.

Issues illustrated: Mother and daughter told different stories and shared diverse experiences of hardship and family life. Although Khanyi had endured tough times in her early life and talked about being deprived in her old age, she had borne most of her children in a secure marriage and whilst enjoying economic stability. Louisa's large number of children, on the other hand, can be seen partly as an attempt to win security and supporting different intimate unions. It is a familiar strategy of struggling women whose fertility over the life course can sometimes be understood as a product of early child-bearing, unplanned pregnancies and survivalist efforts to nurture economic security.

FAMILY LIFE HISTORIES [#5]
BONGI AND MARY MSIMANG

Bongi was born in Hammanskraal in 1956. Her mother was a domestic worker and her father was a traditional healer. Her parents had a difficult relationship and they separated when she was quite young. She had two brothers and two sisters. Both her brothers died as children. When her father remarried, Bongi and her sisters remained with him and his new family. They did not have a good relationship with their stepmother and they were often severely disciplined. Bongi had to give up school in Std. 8 (tenth school level) because she fell pregnant. On discovering that she was pregnant her father ordered her out of the house after which she went to live temporarily with her mother. Her mother found the cost of maintaining Bongi and her child to be too high and suggested that she find work and live elsewhere. Bongi's first job was in a furniture company before she became a waitress at a Greek Clubhouse in Pretoria. For a short while she earned well and was able to maintain a reasonable standard of living for herself and her child. In 1983 she met Msimang, a driver for a food company, and bore a child. In 1986 Bongi left her job in Pretoria to live with Msimang in Winterveld.

Shortly after Bongi arrived in Winterveld Msimang was jailed, allegedly for failing to pay his ex-wife child maintenance. In Winterveld Bongi spent time getting involved in informal sector activities: selling beer and vegetables. Her memories of selling during the 1980s included incidents in which she, together with other vendors, were often confronted by the police who would kick down stalls and confiscate their goods. She continued with selling activities for many years, even after her husband was released from jail. After his release, he was unemployed for a long while during which time he drank heavily and subjected her to much beating and abuse. Social workers based at one of the clinics intervened regularly to rescue Bongi from his abuse. Since being married Bongi has used contraception to avoid further pregnancies. Her unwillingness to have further children became, for a short while, a source of much conflict between herself and her husband. Notwithstanding her husband's disapproval, Bongi took the decision in 1999 to have herself sterilised. Bongi complained that her husband often did not come home, that he was a poor provider and that she would have too many children to maintain.

Mary, Bongi's first child, was about ten years old when her mother married and moved into Winterveld. She was about twelve years old when her father was imprisoned. She suffered depression and failed school that year. Except for that setback her school days were relatively problem-free. During the school boycotts in the early 1990s Mary would leave the school premises or stay at home to avoid participating in activities. At the age of twenty years she managed to complete her high school education and begin a university degree through correspondence. Whilst studying for her degree she began having a relationship with a man who worked as a security guard. When she fell pregnant the man denied paternity and his family intervened to prevent any claims of money: Mary argued that "his mother and sister were talking for him" and that the family reacted in the manner that they did because they "did not want him to give me any money." Mary found it very difficult to cope with her boyfriend's betrayal and her lone task of bringing up her child. Since the child's birth in 1997 she has been grateful for her mother's frequent support. During my last interview with her she told me that she was struggling to find work and that she desired only one further child, but only when she could afford to - and later in life.

Issues illustrated: These life histories reiterate that collaboration between kin, in more recent years, with respect to child-rearing support is primarily between mother and daughter. Here mother and daughter attempt to curb hard times by resisting the possibility of bearing children they cannot afford and by delaying marriage until economic and personal circumstances appear to be more favourable. This case also illustrates the defensive tendencies of poor households: whilst the burdens young girls impose on their households are absorbed with some reluctance, the households of young men react to prevent any new financial responsibilities.

FAMILY LIFE HISTORIES [#6]
FREDA AND SANKIE MOTJIENG

Freda Motjieng was born in Lady Selborne in 1955. She was very young when her family lived there and remembers only that it was densely populated. Freda was the youngest of four children. Her father was a lorry-driver and her mother was a domestic worker. Shortly after her mother gave up work to look after the children her father became unemployed. Her brothers were then forced to give up school and find short-term menial jobs. Freda was sent to live with her grandparents who worked as sugarcane farmers in Tzaneen. Freda attended a farm school in Tzaneen and completed Std 2 (fourth school level) there. She was twelve years old at the time. When her father gained new employment her family requested that she be sent back home. The Motjiengs had now moved to Winterveld. Freda then attended primary school in Winterveld; she claimed that the classes there were much bigger and the teachers much harsher than in Tzaneen.

In 1969, when she was in Std 4 (sixth school level) and aged fourteen years, Freda became very ill and failed her examinations. She had been suffering with allergies. In 1970, when Freda was fifteen years and repeating Std 4 she met Jacob, a 23-year-old working man. At fifteen, she knew nothing about contraception, neither was it talked about, nor was it freely available. In fact, she did not know that she was pregnant until the late stages of her pregnancy. Jacob Sebola's parents paid a sum of money as bridewealth (*magadi*). Freda's father had asked for a small amount of money because he did not want to delay the marriage by asking for cattle. Freda and Jacob married only after the second child was born. After the second child was born Freda began to endure much violent abuse. There were many occasions during which she was forced to run away from home, but she always returned shortly thereafter. She fell pregnant twice when returning home (after running away). At both times she had forgotten to take her pills. "When you are being chased away by your husband you cannot stop and say "can I take my pills?" She would return home unprotected. When Jacob lost his job their domestic situation worsened as he would constantly accuse her of having relationships with other men. Their relationship finally ended after he attacked and killed a neighbour in the belief that Freda was having a relationship with him. Jacob was then imprisoned for a long while, and she never saw him again.

Shortly after her third child died of measles in the mid-1980s, Freda began working full-time as a domestic worker. Those were difficult days in which people lived with daily harassment and fear of being caught without their relevant work permits. Freda's parents died in 1988 and her younger daughter, Sankie, took over the role of watching over her two siblings in her absence. Shortly after her parents died, Sankie's brothers broke the house down and sold everything of value such as window frames, doors and the kitchen sink. Freda had to then invest money in hiring help to build another mud house close to the original home for herself and her children.

In 1993 Freda had herself sterilised after beginning a relationship with a married man. Through this relationship Freda gained money to put her children through school. In 1999 she reflected unhappily on the fact that whilst all her daughters completed their high school studies, none had found decent jobs. When Freda's eldest daughter, Sankie, completed high school she wanted to be a social worker but could not find the money to enrol for a degree. A year later she fell pregnant after being inconsistent in taking the pill. Although her boyfriend lived apart from her she described him as being fairly helpful in offering some financial support and in taking care of the child when needed. After her daughter was born Sankie went on the contraceptive injection. She was still using contraception in 2002 and had made no attempt to have another child. She also argued that the loss of her job and her inability to find further secure employment was a factor preventing her from having more children. She had hoped to have had a second child by the time she turned thirty after which she wanted to sterilise herself. Sankie believed that she would marry at some later point when financial circumstances had improved.

Issues illustrated: The Motjieng life histories illustrate the way in which insecurity brought on by factors such as violence, unemployment or economic struggle inhibits women from desiring large numbers of children. Both mother and daughter have considered sterilisation as a method to bring reproduction to an end. Although child-bearing, for Sankie, had not taken place within the context of marriage, she was not abandoned and was capable of drawing on the support of her partner's family. Nonetheless the pattern of visiting union, which has established itself in Winterveld, is still regarded as a tenuous and financially insecure alternative to a stable partnership.

FAMILY LIFE HISTORY [#7]
ELSIE AND ZENELE MASHININI

Elsie was born on a farm in 1918 in the Free State. Her father was a farm labourer and her mother was a domestic worker. They had met and married in KwaZulu Natal but had moved later to the Free State to find work. Elsie was the eldest of ten children. Her parents sent her to school when she was ten years old. In 1934 she passed Std. 5 (seventh school level) which was a major achievement for a farm girl in the 1930s. After giving up school Elsie became a domestic worker. She married Joseph Mashinini, a farm worker from Heidelburg, in 1940 shortly after having her first child. Elsie gave birth to seven children in total. She gave birth to her third child, Zenele, in 1944 when they lived on a farm in Greylingstad. Zenele has vivid memories of being cared for by different members of an extended family whilst her parents were working away from the house. The family had access to a piece of land on which they could grow their own vegetables. Zenele and her siblings would also assist by planting and treating the soil.

Elsie's life was not an easy one on the farm in Greylingstad. The house was crowded with members of her husband's family and there were many arguments. One of Elsie's older sisters-in-law asked her to take her children "and go back to where you belong". It was during a period when her husband was not frequently at home and when it appeared that he was being influenced by his kin to hold a negative view of her. During this time Elsie and her children would get less food, and "pap without milk". During winter they would use sacks as blankets after their blankets were confiscated by their relatives. They began to feel extremely discriminated against and increasingly impoverished. Elsie then left the farm and found accommodation for herself and her children on another farm. She saw her husband again and was reconciled with him after about four years. Years later, in 1974, they left for Winterveld.

Zenele attended school in Greylingstad. The school operated in terms of three month cycles. They would attend classes for three months, then be released to do farm-work for the next three months after which they would return to school for the next three months of study. Because of the problems in her home environment at the time, Zenele gave up school in Std. 4 (sixth school level) thus leaving before attaining anything more than just basic reading and writing skills. She then worked as a domestic worker on the farms and in town. Zenele gave birth to her first child in

1960 when she was sixteen years old. She had become the second wife of a much older man who worked as a farm labourer on a farm elsewhere in Greylingstad. She felt oppressed in his home and was always being given orders, mainly by her mother-in-law. She was unhappy about the fact that her husband would hand over his earnings to his mother and also because his mother would permit him to have other girlfriends. When she would challenge him about money matters or about his other relationships he would beat her up. She did not send her children to school because it had become too expensive to do so, and because her mother-in-law did not allow her to have any money. Zenele gave birth to seven children, but four of them died whilst babies or young children. Zenele eventually decided to leave her in-laws' home and go back to live with her mother. She left her children with her mother and then looked for work in Pretoria.

In Pretoria, she worked for numerous employers, and her experiences were mixed. Some of her jobs were sleep-in jobs that kept her away from her family for long periods but most, particularly during more recent years, were piece-jobs. Since 1982 she had been in a visiting relationship with a man from Winterveld. In 1989 Zenele was deeply affected by the murder of one of her sons in Winterveld. In 1999 she gave up work and went to live with her mother and her youngest son and his family. With all of them being unemployed at the time there was some reliance on Elsie, who received a pension, for support. Zenele passed away in 2005 from tuberculosis. Elsie was devastated at Zenele's sudden and untimely death, and became ill herself. Bedridden, she grew to rely on her older son, who most often appropriated her pension remittance leaving her with just the basic necessities – sugar, mealie meal and milk. Elsie passed away in 2008.

Issues illustrated: These life histories offer insights into the nexus of familial relationships which women often contend with and the role they sometimes play in debilitating conjugal bonds. Whilst there are indications that extended family structures offer child-rearing support, women generally experience oppression and subordination within them. The intergenerational stories showed little interference by husband's kin in reproductive decisions and few claims on children when their mothers left the homesteads.

FAMILY LIFE HISTORIES [#8]
THANDI AND PINKY RAMASHALA; CLARA AND DIMAKATSO MOLEFE

Thandi was born in 1962 in the Northern Province. She was brought up by her father, and only got to know her biological mother in 1988. When she was a young girl her parents divorced, and her father gained custody of herself and her brother. Her father then enlisted the support of his sisters, Clara and Dimakatso Molefe, who played an important role in raising Thandi. Clara and Dimakatso allowed Thandi's mother to take her brother away because he was a baby at the time and needed his mother's nurturing. Clara and Dimakatso had not attended formal school and were both illiterate. Clara was born in approximately 1934 and Dimakatso in 1944. They grew up on the farms around Pietersburg looking after cattle, cleaning and doing other domestic chores.

Clara left home as a young woman to find work in the towns. She spent many years working as a domestic servant in Johannesburg and Pretoria. Later she earned money through sewing clothes and making aprons. In her early life she had numerous relationships with men, a fact leading to her contraction of STDs. She married as a young woman and bore two children before her relationship broke down. Years later she bore an additional two children in an attempt to encourage a man, who had had a family elsewhere, to remain with her in Winterveld. The man left, however, and in time Clara encouraged her children to find their own means of support and to desist from relying on her. In 1999 all her children lived apart from her (including one who was at the time serving a prison sentence for theft).

Dimakatso, the youngest of twelve children, was born after her mother had been diagnosed as infertile. Her birth was therefore referred to, for many years thereafter, as a miracle. Dimakso, however, saw herself as having been born into a miserable life. Her mother's sister arranged a marriage for her when she was a very young girl. She was unhappy in this marriage and suffered the death of a child and a still-birth. She was disliked by her husband's family and she believed that her inability to keep her children alive was a result of them bewitching and "poisoning" these births. When her marriage deteriorated as a result of her childless status she went back to her natal home. She then worked as a domestic worker until 1990 when Nelson Mandela was released. She gave up her job in Pretoria and went back to Winterveld in the belief that "Mandela was going to give money." Since then she has done odd-jobs such as embroidery and cooking.

In 1999 Thandi and her children, Pinky, Anna and Gift, lived in Winterveld with Clara and Dimakatso. Thandi had not lived continuously with her aunts since childhood. When her father married for the second time, he moved into Mamelodi in Pretoria. Thandi, who was thirteen years old at the time, went to live with her father and stepmother. Thandi and her stepmother did not have a good relationship. Her stepmother saw her as being favoured by her father over her own children. Thandi then left her father's home and lived with other relatives until she turned sixteen years old. She was in Std. 7 (ninth school level) at the time. Her grandmother encouraged her to marry an older cousin. She gave birth to a daughter, Pinky, in 1980. Her marriage, however, deteriorated in the course of her experiencing excessive physical abuse. In 1982 she married Petros Ramashala. Their marriage was turbulent from the start and Petros had many other relationships whilst married to Thandi. They often fought over money. Thandi had worked earlier in her life as a domestic worker. Later she joined the embroidery project at the Sisters of Mercy and became a highly skilled trainer. Although this assured her of some income the income was irregular because the selling of embroidery was dependent on seasonal markets.

The crisis in Thandi's marriage deepened when she discovered that Petros had been abusing her daughter, Pinky, whom he later impregnated. Thandi had not told Pinky that Petros was not her biological father for fear, she claimed, that she might not respect him. Pinky was sent away from her home, and when the baby was born Thandi took her to the clinic to be put on contraception. Pinky went back to school and completed her high school studies. Thandi's marriage came to an end and Petros left the area. In 2002 Thandi passed away and Pinky, who was 22 at the time, became the guardian of her two younger siblings.

Issues illustrated: These life histories illustrate experiences of violence which the women of the three generations experienced (albeit different in form) and the ways in which such experiences intervene to shape reproductive histories and personal lives. The older women had experienced rejection and isolation in their marriages by bearing too few or no children. The younger woman had sterilised herself after bearing few children and put her daughter on contraception as a strategy to guard against the possibility of abuse.

FAMILY LIFE HISTORIES [#9]
PATIENCE AND TEBOGO KHUTSOANE

Patience was born in 1951 in the Vereeniging district. Her parents had previously lived in the Free State where they worked as labour tenants. In 1964 Patience's father, under threat of eviction, left the farm on which he worked to live and work in Meyerton. In 1966 Patience's family was forcibly removed and relocated in the township of Sebokeng. In Sebokeng her father did piece-jobs and her mother sold mealies and made home-made beer. In 1970 Patience gave up school after discovering that she was pregnant. She then married Isaac Khutsoane, the father of her child. Unlike Patience's natal family, the Khutsoanes were wealthy land-owners who had arrived in Sebokeng from Lesotho to pursue business interests there. They had initially strongly disapproved of Patience who was seen to have come from much poorer family circumstances.

Isaac Khutsoane's business interests were varied; he invested money in property and opened up a series of shops in which Patience also worked. His political interests were conservative and these interests led him to become a councillor in Sebokeng. In 1984, with the rise of the mass democratic movement, the Khutsoane's home was attacked by activists. Patience and Isaac then left for Winterveld where Isaac's family had bought land. Isaac built homes to lease on his land and re-established shops in and around Winterveld. By 1989 Patience had had eight children and spent most of her time in child-rearing activities with occasional involvement in the shops. In 1990 Isaac Khutsoane died suddenly and unexpectedly of a heart attack. In the aftermath of her husband's death Patience faced three dilemmas. First, the tenants on her plot aligned themselves with a movement to boycott rents, second, she was being pursued by many other men in the area because she was believed to be a wealthy widow, and third, she was uncertain about her ability to adequately support and maintain her many children.

Patience's eldest daughter, Tebogo, had run away from home when she was a teenager because she had fallen pregnant. After Isaac's death Tebogo returned home with her child. Patience's second daughter also fell pregnant and had a child in 1995. One of Patience's sons added to the expanding household by unexpectedly bringing home a "wife" in 1997. While Patience's main day-to-day preoccupation turned to dressmaking to earn a living, Tebogo went back to school and completed her secondary education. She married her school-teacher and bore her second child. After her second child was born Tebogo sterilised herself. Her husband approved of the sterilisation because he had already had two children from a previous marriage. Tebogo then managed to find funding, enrolled at a full-time university and completed a Nursing Science degree. The five years of study took a toll on her marriage and she returned to Winterveld in 1999 and has since lived there with her mother.

Issues illustrated: The Khutsoane stories illustrate the difficulties of women land-owners, who appear to be better-off, but who face constraints in managing resources in a broader context of poverty. In this case there was much reliance on decreasing savings and disparate income-generating activities to maintain a large and demanding household. Whilst the mother's story suggests that high child-bearing was encouraged because it was both affordable and wanted by the husband, the insecurities in her daughter's relationship and her attempt to follow an independent career, led to few children being desired.

FAMILY LIFE HISTORY [#10]
DUDU MABUNDA AND KEBONE THOBEJANE

Dudu was born in 1932 in Ventersdorp in the Transvaal. She was the second of eight children. Her mother was a so-called coloured woman originating from Cape Town. Her father was a Zulu-speaking miner who contracted a lung disease which led to his early death in 1945. On his death bed Dudu's mother asked her to pray for her father. Since then Dudu saw herself as having had a calling to attend to sick people and offer them prayers in their last hours. When her father died Dudu and her family began to experience much poverty. Her mother had to take on many jobs to support herself and her children. Dudu and her older brother were also encouraged to work for money; thus they looked for work and delayed going to school. Dudu worked first on a farm and assisted in gathering potatoes and mealies during harvest-time. The initial poverty they experienced was a factor prompting her mother to set up an early marriage for Dudu. She gave her consent to a marriage between Dudu and a school-teacher from a relatively well-off family, Solomon Mabunda. Dudu agreed to the marriage, and then gave up school and moved with her husband to Winterveld. Mabunda's family had bought land in Winterveld after their land in Leeuwspruit was expropriated after the passing of the 1936 Land Act.

Dudu taught for a short while as an unqualified school-teacher and then upgraded her qualifications and gained a teaching certificate. Her teaching career was interrupted by numerous breaks which she took to bear and raise her seven children. Dudu said that she had hoped to have had only two to three children but Mabunda's family had been disappointed with the fact that no sons were born. After Dudu bore seven daughters she stopped "trying for a son" and began to use contraception. She placed a strong emphasis on the education of her daughters and all, except one daughter, completed university studies. She took measures to ensure that her daughters did not fall pregnant whilst at school and also attempted to exercise some degree of control over when (and who) they married. Over the years Dudu had been an active campaigner for social welfare benefits and better services for the elderly. She was central to setting up fourteen clubs in Winterveld, and throughout the 1990s she worked tirelessly in conducting funeral services and counselling the bereaved.

Of all her daughters Dudu has always been most concerned about her eldest daughter, Kebone. Kebone was born in 1954. In 1959 she enrolled at a primary school in Winterveld. In 1966, during a school music lesson, she was hit her on the head with a cane. She suffered concussion. Shortly after that she was diagnosed an epileptic, a condition that affected the quality of her life ever-since. Kebone's schooling was interrupted by a few periods of hospitalisation and treatment for epilepsy and depression. She failed her final matriculation examination and then went on to do short-term work at a supermarket. She also did typing, cooking and dressmaking. Because Dudu was of the view that Kebone needed special care she was particularly keen to ensure that Kebone did not find an unsuitable partner. Kebone was using contraception since she was nineteen and only married in her thirties. Dudu and Solomon had turned down numerous marriage proposals over the years for Kebone. She finally married Thebe Thobejane whose family had originated from Botswana but who was living in Winterveld and working as a security officer in Ga-rankuwa. It was a good marriage initially but it began to develop problems when Kebone failed to fall pregnant and Thebe started to drink heavily. Kebone was unhappy about being stigmatised as an infertile woman. Medical examinations showed no reason why Kebone could not bear children. She suspected that the problem laid with her husband but was unable to persuade him to seek medical advice. In 1999 Kebone still taked about the prospect of having a child, despite the fact that she was now in her forties. Her marriage however broke down in 2003 and after her father, Solomon, passed away in 2005, she came back to live with her mother. Dudu was now more active in AIDS work and the burial of young people.

Issues illustrated: These life histories reveal different experiences of mother and daughter. Whilst Dudu was married off at a young age to ease her mother's economic burden she took time in influencing the selection of suitable partners for her daughters and ensured that they first received an education. These stories illustrate the strategies which families might sometimes adopt, in environments where relationships dissolve frequently and where poverty is rife, in efforts to secure "good marriages" for their daughters. In Kebone's case it led to early use of contraception, a considerably delayed marriage and the possibility of bearing no children in the long run.

FAMILY LIFE HISTORIES [#11]
LUCY AND PHUMZILE DLALI

Lucy Dlali was born in Lady Selborne in 1938. Her family was originally from a place called Devil's Kloof, near Tzaneen. Her mother, Betfina, was a traditional healer and her father, Lucas, worked as a handyman. Her early childhood memories were of a busy household as people came from all over the Transvaal to consult her mother and seek advice and medicine. Her parents had nine children, two of whom died in childhood and three of whom died in separate tragic events in early adulthood. Lucy attended school in Lady Selborne but dropped out before completing her Std. 8 (tenth school level) examinations. She was nineteen years old at the time. She gave up school and left without her parent's permission to join a singing group based in Johannesburg, *The Duck City Sisters*. After a short while Lucy's parents, fearing for their daughter's saftety in the big city of Johannesburg, sent family members to bring her back to Lady Selborne. In 1958 Lucy married Simon Mailula, a man whom she met in Johannesburg. Simon, Lucy and the Dlali family lived in Lady Seborne for only a few more years after that because in 1962 they were forcibly removed. They moved first to Atteridgeville and then to Winterveld.

Simon worked as a railway policeman and Lucy worked as a domestic worker in Mountain View in Pretoria. They had four children between 1958 and 1967. Their marriage, however, was a difficult one and they divorced in 1969. Lucy had suffered considerable violence at the hands of her husband. She said: "He would hit me with forks, sticks and even with his boots." Her family had intervened to try and control him until they agreed that separation was the best solution for Lucy. Bringing up her children on her own was quite difficult, particularly since Simon had stopped his child maintenance payments six months after their divorce. Her youngest daughter, Phumzile, was sent to her childless older sister to be reared. Her toughest challenge was when her remaining three children developed a "sleeping sickness" and she was unable to help them recover quickly because she had no money for medicine. In the mid-1970s Lucy developed a new relationship and bore a fifth child in 1976. Her partner, who was from Botswana, lived in Winterveld and worked in the Rustenberg mines. In 1995 he returned to Botswana to join his wife and children there. Lucy retired from domestic labour work when she turned sixty and was then able to rely on a pension. In 1995 Phumzile arrived in Winterveld to live with her mother.

Phumzile grew up with her aunt in Atteridgeville in Pretoria. She attended the primary school there and was seventeen years old when she gave up middle school to have a baby. She had had little interest in school and was often outside of school during school hours. Her aunt was particularly strict with her and gave her little money for her own personal needs. Phumzile's first relationship was with an employed older man whom she met whilst truanting school. She would meet with him frequently and he would offer her gifts. When she fell pregnant, however, he denied paternity and abandoned her. Her aunt rejected her and she lived thereafter with an older sister who supported her. She worked part-time doing mainly the washing of clothes for different families. She earned very little money. In 1987 she gave birth to a second child in a relationship in which she had become dependent for money. The man abandoned her but members of his family arrived later and took the child away from Phumzile. Phumzile was living in poverty then and offered little resistance. In 1991 she fell pregnant for the third time. She had been using contraception and the pregnancy was a mistake. The man argued that the baby could not be his. He also beat Phumzile up severely leaving her with fractured joints. He assaulted her because he learnt that she had been using his money for gambling and was participating in stokvels (rotating credit associations). In 1998 Phumzile found work in a shop in Lebotlwane but gave it up after a while because she did not find sufficient time, she claimed, to look after her children and because she did not earn much. She had decided to look for work closer to her home. In 2008, she continued with ad-hoc piece jobs and remained in Winterveld with her mother, bringing up her children.

Issues illustrated: These life histories illustrate some of the factors which contribute to the persistence of unstable and fragile partnerships: violence in marital unions, relationships with workers who have families elsewhere and bearing children in serial unions in an attempt to secure financial support. Whilst displaying many failing strategies of women who struggle to overcome hardship, the life histories also indicate women's resilience in seeking work and finding ways to support their children.

FAMILY LIFE HISTORIES [#12]
NANI, NOMASONTO AND NOMPUMELELO NKOMO

Nani Nkomo was born in 1942 in Lady Selborne. Her father worked at a glass factory and her mother was a domestic worker. Despite their poor incomes her parents managed to set aside money to buy a small plot in Winterveld after which a large part of their extended family moved to live there. Her father started farming immediately: he planted mealies, sorghum and water melons. These initial farming activities were relatively successful since they drew on the labour of many family members.

Nani was the third of eight children. She left school after Std. 3 (fifth school level) because it was believed that she had a calling to be a sangoma (traditional healer): she had been experiencing dizzy spells and had recurring dreams about herself "dancing the sangoma dances". She was fourteen years old at the time and her parents were pleased that she was to give up school and train to become a sangoma. Her trainer was a well-known sangoma, Johanna Nkomo, who was respected as both a skilled trainer and healer. Nani met Johanna's son, Elijah, whom Johanna was in the process of training at the same time. In 1964 Nani married Elijah Nkomo and moved to his family plot in Winterveld.

They set up a traditional medicine shop and at first conducted fairly good business. Nani bore eight children. She explained that they desired a large number of children; they never discussed the number of children they ought to have and they did not believe in family planning. She also claimed, however, that she strove towards a large number of children to encourage Elijah to remain with her. He married other women over the years and had other children in these relationships. Elijah's other relationships became a source of stress for Nani, particularly since their business was making progressively less profits, and his ability to support many wives was being curbed. Elijah shared his time among different wives and was often not at home.

Nani's eldest son was of some support to her during times of financial need, but her daughters, she claimed, brought new burdens. Two of her older daughters found themselves in unhappy situations by marrying at early ages and by remaining within abusive relationships. When one of her daughters, Nomasonto, fell pregnant at the age of thirteen years Elijah chased her away from home. He chased Nani away as well accusing her of being a bad mother. Nomasonto later married a colleague of Elijah's, and had a second child seven years later. Like her father her husband, Jacob, was a polygynist with other wives and children to support. Two of Jacob's wives left him over the years because, she maintained, "he was too strict". Jacob often beat Nomasonto after accusing her of being unfaithful to him. In 1998 Nomasonto gave birth to her third child. She began to use "cultural methods" to prevent further pregnancies. Shortly after Nomasonto gave birth to her third child, Jacob brought home a teenage wife. At the time that her marriage was breaking down, her father, Elijah, was arrested for his role in a set of political activities in Winterveld. Nomasonto went back to live with her mother during this time. She spent many hours during the day gambling in an effort to win money.

In 1999 Nomasonto's younger sister, Nompumelelo, was also looking after a baby and living with her mother, Nani. Nompumelelo had dropped out of school at the age of 22 after finding herself pregnant. She had had a boyfriend for four years and had been on contraception. The pregnancy was thus a mistake. She did not regret it though and still maintained a visiting relationship with her boyfriend who offered her financial assistance from time to time. She maintained that he was not in a position to marry her or live with her because he supported his family as well. Nompumelelo was only going to seek work when her child was older. Both sisters spent less time with their children and parents in the 2000s, seeking to pursue lives outside of Winterveld.

Issues illustrated: The life histories of mother and daughter illuminate the insecurity which entrenches itself within polygynous and visiting unions. With respect to polygyny, contact with partners is infrequent and relationships between co-wives are constantly strained. Whilst Nani had coped with the difficulties of a polygynous marriage, her daughter Nomasonto had not been as tolerant, particularly about living with a new wife and reduced economic means. Nompumelelo's visiting relationship was more respectable, in this sense, because competition from other wives was not evident.

FAMILY LIFE HISTORIES [#13]
DORA, MINGE AND MARGARET MKIZE

Dora Mkize was born in 1953 in Soweto, Johannesburg. Her father, Isaac, was a policeman originally from the Free State and her mother was a nurse at Baragwanath Hospital in Soweto. Her parents did not have a good relationship and her father frequently beat up her mother. She was about seven years old when her mother deserted the family, leaving Dora and her four siblings to be brought up by their father. It was very difficult for her father to bring them up alone. It became more problematic when he brought home other girlfriends. Dora claimed that one of his girlfriends tried to have them killed. She said: "This girlfriend of my father's wanted to kill us. She tried to poison us. Then she put crushed bottle into the milk and pap. My sister's tongue was cut. Then we started to get scared." Dora went to school for only one year and then stopped going to school altogether. The children were by then showing severe signs of neglect and Dora's aunt (her mother's sister) took them away to be brought up by their maternal grandmother. She said: "My grandmother used to work very hard in the home. She had many boyfriends because she was still young. It was not nice to stay with her. She did not have money. She was not working and was being maintained." Their aunt then took them away from their grandmother and left them with their mother.

Dora's mother was living on a farm with a lorry-driver who used to transport vegetables to the market. When they arrived their mother explained that she had deserted them because their father had been assaulting her. The mother's new relationship, however, appeared to be equally troublesome. Although she was not being assaulted, her partner used to take away all her earnings and did not allow her to send the children back to school. When Dora's aunt brought them to their mother their mother's partner decided to fetch his two children from a previous marriage to live on the farm as well. Dora's mother gave up her nursing job, and worked on the farm growing vegetables and looking after the seven children. Dora and her siblings grew up as farm labourers doing domestic chores and packing fruit in boxes. Their mother's partner eventually deserted them and took away his two children. Shortly after that their mother became ill and died of tuberculosis. The farm owner persuaded them to remain on the farm and continue with their mother's job. However, the children, who were teenagers then, decided to leave after the farmer attempted what she referred to as "funny things" with Dora's older sister. They left for Boekenhoutfontein and joined the masses of people gathering there (on Winterveld's doorstep) and built a shack there. Dora lived with her older sister while her other siblings left for other places.

They encountered varied and grim experiences on the peri-urban fringes of Pretoria: poor paid domestic labour jobs, lack of food, rape and harassment. Dora met her husband when she was twenty years old. Having being sexually abused before, she was not at first keen on marriage. She bore five children over a period of eighteen years. She claimed that the last two of them were mistakes because she had been using contraception to prevent both these births. Her husband, Mkize, worked as a cleaner for a bank and came home on weekends. In the 1990s Dora spent many hours, during these weekends, arguing over money matters with her husband. She said: "He is fisting me because I tell him he does not give enough money. He buys small packets."

Dora's two teenage daughers, Minge and Margaret, had been of tremendous help to their mother particularly since 1998. Margaret had helped in doing chores and assisting with the younger children and Minge had brought home money from modelling and beauty contests in which she had been participating since she was sixteen. Both sisters were being encouraged to use contraception to prevent pregnancy. Dora was unhappy about Minge's refusal to use contraception in the belief that it would spoil her figure. Margaret and Minge had both attended "private schools" in Winterveld and thus lost a few years when they re-enrolled in public schools later on. Both girls told stories of living with financial hardship; they displayed much knowledge of contraception and expressed wishes to marry much later and bear few children. They were keen to complete their high school education and find good jobs. In reality, though, both girls did not complete high school, and bore one child each out of wedlock. In 2006, Minge passed away, allegedly from AIDS.

Issues illustrated: The mother's life history shows her strength in the face of much hardship experienced since her childhood. She continues to experience problems in her marriage and has admitted to having borne more children than desired. The stories of the mother and daughters, however, raise important issues about the ways in which mothers might attempt to manipulate their daughters and harness their talents for financial purposes. Encouragement to use contraception is thus one way of ensuring that daughters remain 'safe' whilst placing themselves in vulnerable situations. In the case of Minge, however, 'safety' became subverted and she succumbed to illness in 2006.

FAMILY LIFE HISTORIES [#14]
MANTO MOSELE AND SARAH GAMEDE

Manto was born in 1940 in Makapanstad, on the other side of Hammanskraal, in the North West Province. It was a rural area under the authority of a chief. Manto grew up in the chief's *kraal* (dwelling) in one of the villages which made up Makapanstad. Her father had lived originally in Warmbaths but moved as a young man into Makapanstad to help with the building of homes. The chief exonerated him from ploughing and allowed him to concentrate mainly on building, carpentry and religious duties. He reared many animals and accumulated a large herd of cattle. Manto's father bought two ten-morgen plots in Winterveld for cattle-grazing and farming. Manto's parents and her two siblings lived on one plot while she lived initially with her grandparents on the other plot. Manto claimed that she learnt the value of hard work through being compelled to do hard labour jobs as a child. She would be involved in ploughing as well as domestic duties. In 1955, at the age of fifteen, Manto fell pregnant and gave up school. Manto maintained a relationship with her boyfriend, a boy in her school, and bore a second child in 1959. Her parents were furious at her "fall", particularly since the father of her child gave little support and eventually left for Johannesburg without marrying her. In the four years that Manto spent at home she managed to complete her high school studies through correspondence. In the years between 1961 and 1964 Manto had done some part-time teaching and decided to follow a teaching career. It was quite demanding to be a teacher in Winterveld. Teachers not only taught regular classes but had to involve themselves in building additional classrooms (out of corrugated iron), teach morning and afternoon sessions (sometimes in the open) and they often had to intervene in families to persuade parents to give their children time to do homework.

Manto waited for five years for her boyfriend to return from Johannesburg. When he did not, she married a fellow teacher, Mosele, and had, over the years, four additional children with him. Mosele did not accept Manto's two older children. He often punished them severely and sent them to live with relatives. Manto's eldest child died when he was fourteen years old and her daughter, Sarah, still carries the emotional scars of those early years. Manto spoke with much sadness of the treatment of her two oldest children. She also said: "Since 1969 divorce was on my mind. It was like someone was sitting on my neck and I could feel his weight." Mosele had desired many children but they decided finally that they could not have more than four children. Manto and her husband were told by doctors that Manto had a health condition which would have made it dangerous for her if she were to experience too many conceptions. In 1999 Manto had just retired as a school-teacher and was becoming active in community activities.

Despite her unhappy childhood, Sarah made good progress through primary and middle school. When she was in high school Manto encouraged her to use contraception to avoid disrupting her schooling as she had done before. Notwithstanding this, Sarah fell pregnant at the age of sixteen. She went back to school when she was twenty years old, and later enrolled at a teacher training college. In 1983 she started teaching in Winterveld. In 1991 she was a highly-respected senior teacher in a Winterveld secondary school. In 1992 she married a fellow school-teacher, Peter Gamede. In 1999 she said: "God has given me a nice guy - so far. It has been a good relationship." Sarah and Peter discussed issues of child-bearing and child-rearing whilst they were courting. She said: "The things we said before marriage still apply. Sometimes when we forget we remind ourselves." They decided to have only one child after which Sarah sterilised herself. Peter, a Zimbabwean, came from a very poor family and had no intentions of re-living the poverty he had experienced there. Bringing up children was thought to be costly and he had no desires for many children. Both of them have expended their energies on developing their careers and educating their two children. Sarah's older daughter was in high school in 1999. Sarah was thus taking special care to counsel her and to advise her to "show restraint" until she "was ready" for a relationship. In the 2000s, Sarah continued to have a good relationship with her husband and both shared domestic and child-rearing responsibilities.

Issues illustrated: Manto and Sarah's life histories illustrate the patterns of early child-bearing, the difficulties posed by stepparenthood and the different factors, including fears of poverty, which influence "reproductive decisions". Whilst Manto experienced her marriage as oppressive, partly because of the poor treatment of the children from her first relationship, Kebone had managed to discuss these issues prior to and during the course of her marriage. She wields more power in her relationship than her mother did; the space to negotiate family size also existed because of mutual preferences, and concerns about poverty, for a small family.

FAMILY LIFE HISTORIES [#15]
JOSINA AND LINDI DLAMINI

Josina Dlamini was born in Mozambique in 1956. She claimed to have lived in South Africa since the 1970s (albeit for short periods) but considered herself to be living permanently in Winterveld since the late 1980s. Some members of her family were killed during the struggle against Portuguese rule in the 1970s and many more were killed by Renamo in the 1980s and 1990s. Josina had never attended school and grew up aquiring skills associated mainly with farming and craft work. Her family lived on a farm in Magude in Mozambique which she suggested resembled Winterveld, except that it was under the authority of a chief. Her close association with Winterveld over the years was due to her perception of the pleasantness of life in its more rural-like parts and because income-earning opportunities there offered a route out of poverty in Mozambique. In 1997 some member's of Josina's family were apprehended (as aliens) and sent back to Mozambique during large-scale government attempts at repatriation.

When she was a teenager, Josina married a Mozambican mine-worker who worked on the Rustenberg mines in South Africa. She would receive remittances from him once a year when he visited her in Mozambique. In 1977, during a period in which she sought to earn money in South Africa doing piece-jobs, Josina gave birth to her first child, Lindi. Lindi was born in Winterveld - a fact which made it easier for her to apply for South African citizenship. After much movement to and from Mozambique, Josina returned with intentions to live in South Africa more permanently in 1989 after receiving news that her husband had been made redundant. He remained in South Africa and attempted to find all kinds of alternative work including selling recycled tins and containers.

In 1999 Josina suggested that in most months she received about R30 to R50 from her husband, but on few occasions she received a lot more. Most of Josina's free time was spent gardening, alongside about a hundred other Mozambican women, on a five-morgen plot adjacent to St. Michael's church. The women bought seeds from the church and planted carrots, lettuce, beetroot and chinese spinach. They made little money from gardening; they mainly grew just enough to fulfil daily feeding purposes.

In 1990, and after having had four children, Josina had herself sterilised. She was fearful of being left with the responsibilities of bringing up too many children. In 1994, however, her husband brought home a second wife and two additional children. The women did not share a good relationship and after much discord the second wife ran away leaving her two children behind. In that year, Lindi, who was in high school, fell pregnant. Her boyfriend denied paternity and abandoned her. Lindi claimed that she had maintained a sexual relationship both for love and money. Her boyfriend gave her money each time they met. The pregnancy, however, resulted in her having to spend all the money she could access to support her child. Josina sent Lindi back to school to complete her schooling but only after making sure that she had been put on contraception. When Lindi went back to school in 1999 Josina found herself supporting seven children. Among the women on Selinah's plot, common Mozambican origins, kin and friendship bonds, have, throughout the years, nurtured a loosely integrated support structure. In the absence of the men, the sharing of food and resources have served as a buffer against the experience of economic hardship. In 1999 Josina complained, though, that this reciprocation and support was declining and the bonds between women had been weakening as some households improved their circumstances in comparison to others. Since most Mozambican women lived in very poor economic circumstances it was not surprising to hear of them resorting to numerous liaisons with local men to gain money. Josina, however, did not adopt this strategy. In 2008, Lindi lived with just one child.

Issues illustrated: The life histories of mother and daughter emphasise different strategies in the struggle against poverty. The strategies to withstand poverty include: sterilisation, contraceptive use, savings, maintaining relationships for money and reliance on a partner's earnings from disparate activities. The adoption of these strategies, however, introduced risks that could intensify the experience of hardship such as unplanned pregnancies, HIV/AIDS and economic burdens associated with husband's new relationship and children.

APPENDIX 2

MAPS

Map 1: Winterveld in relation to Pretoria

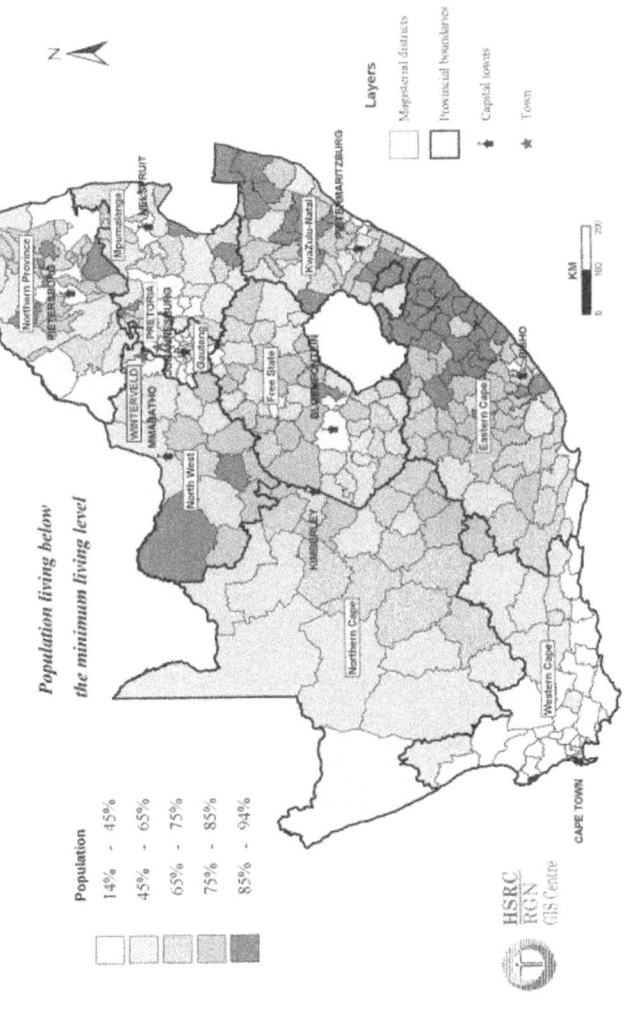

Source: Poverty database WEFA 1996; Produced by the HSRC, GIS Centre

Map 2: Winterveld and the surrounding areas

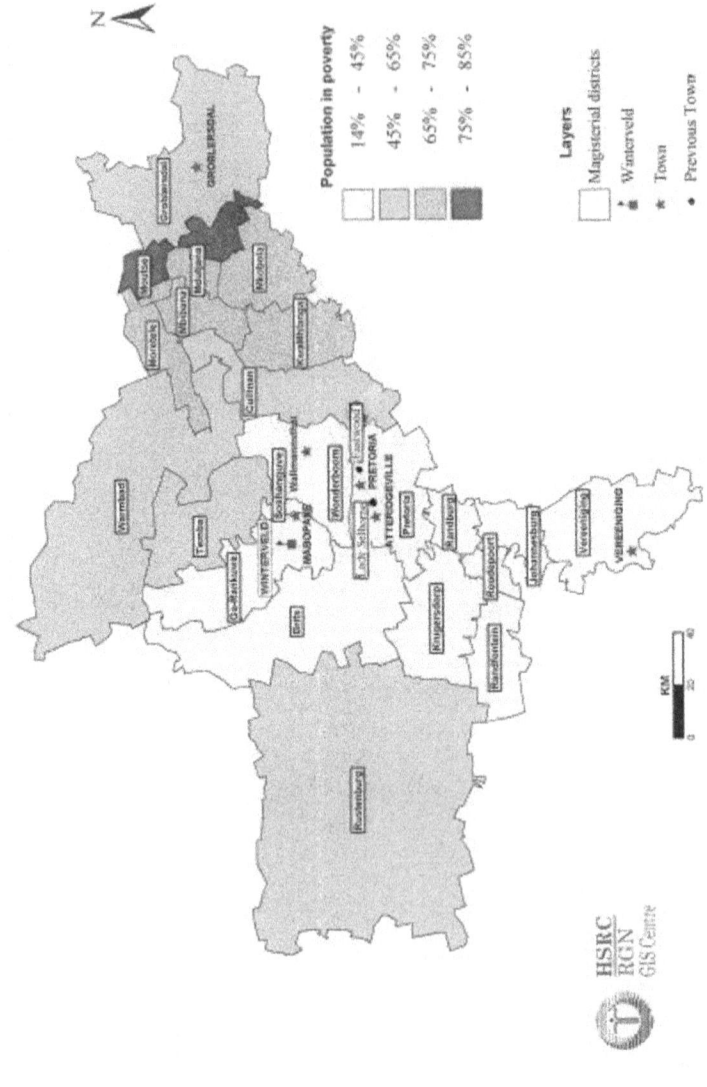

Source: Poverty database WEFA 1996; Produced by the HSRC, GIS Centre

Map 3: Population density Winterveld

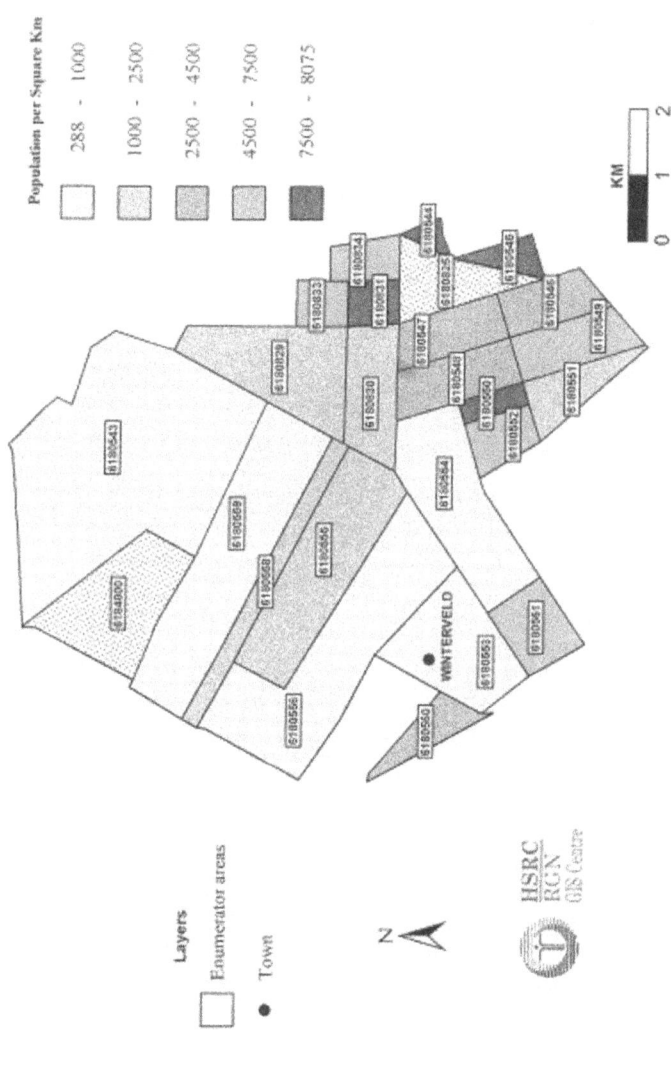

Source: Statistics S.A. Census 1996; Produced by GIS Centre: HSRC

APPENDIX 3

NEWSPAPER CLIPPINGS

Newspaper clipping 1: *Pretoria News* **28/08/1996**

Members of the Winterveldt Plot-owners Association toyi-toyi on the grounds of the Union Buildings demanding the government intervene to move squatters from their land. PICTURE: KENDRIDGE MATHABATHE

Plot-owners demand action

Johnny Masilela
STAFF REPORTER

Plot-owners from Winterveld near Soshanguve have marched on the Union Buildings to ask the government to resolve weeks of confrontation between them and the 250 000 squatters on their land.

Following recent clashes in which at least three homes in the sprawling settlement were burnt down, the Winterveldt Plot-owners Association (WPA) spearheaded the protest march yesterday to demand the personal intervention of Deputy President Thabo Mbeki.

The plot-owners demanded he remove the squatters from their properties.

The squatters are engaged in a biting rent boycott which has resulted in hundreds of thousands of rands in lost income for the bulk of the plot-owners.

Speaking at the end of the march yesterday, WPA chairman Khehla Nyamakazi said Winterveld had become the "dumping ground" of criminal elements.

In the memorandum, the WPA and its supporters bemoaned the fact that the government had chosen to sideline their organisation and instead recognised the Transitional Representative Council, which the plot-owners claim is made up of squatters who have no title to the land.

Receiving the memorandum, Deputy President departmental director Lucille Meyer said Mr Mbeki was in Cape Town and that the document would be brought to his attention "within a few days".

Newspaper clipping 2: *The Star* 29/06/1999

The Star 29/6/99

NEGLECTED WINTERVELDT

'I was a gangster, but now I have hope'

By Ross Cromwell

APPENDIX 4

PHOTOGRAPHS

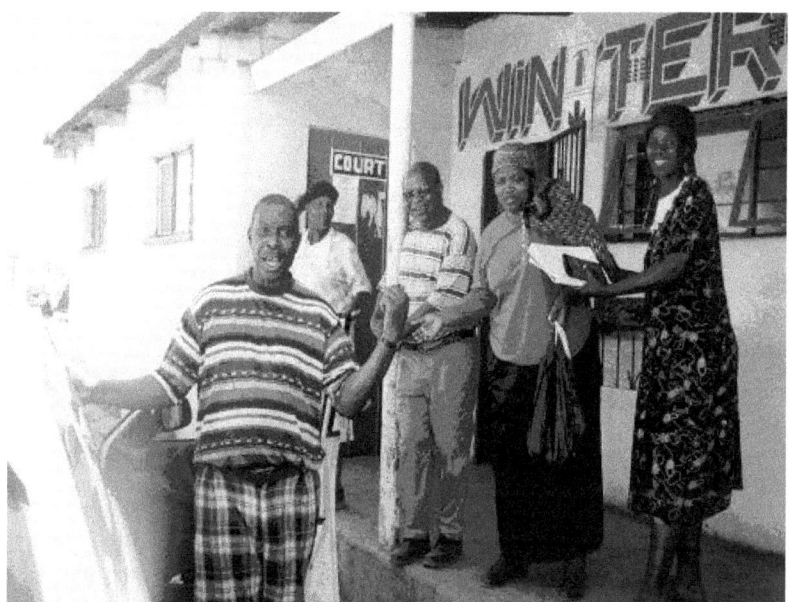

A few plot-owners standing outside the Winterveld Community Authority (WCA) Office. "The office" has been at the centre of much tension and controversy in the area.

A woman tenant who, together with her children, had just completed building her home on someone else's land. The vast majority of Winterveld's residents are tenants who occupy self-built dwellings.

A woman demonstrating the way the water pump works. All landowners have boreholes, such as this one, on which people have relied for their daily water requirements. Selling water to tenants used to assure landowners of some (though not much) money each month. In 2000, public taps and card-operated water pumps were being provided by the Rand Water Board.

Although most people travel by taxi and cars are common, donkeys are still used for transport. In this picture the men are transporting firewood. The area remains without electricity in 2009 and energy resources are generally limited.

Women working collaboratively on an income generating embroidery project.

Women pensioners cutting foam to make cushions to sell locally and elsewhere. (A number of groups, such as these two, have been formed over the years in Winterveld.)

Secondary school children outside a mobile clinic that used to be parked within the school-grounds of the Winterveld Secondary School. Schoolchildren could get condoms and contraceptive advice at the van. They could also have themselves examined for STDs.

Pre-school children and a woman resident in the area.

Pumla Maila, my interpreter, and young school-leavers who participated in focus group discussions.

Kehla Nyamakazi, with hands raised, celebrated his release from imprisonment. Plot-owners were wearing UDM T-shirts and declaring their support for the UDM in this pre-election 1999 period.

INDEX

Lightning Source UK Ltd.
Milton Keynes UK
UKHW02n1527140318
319441UK00003B/119/P